Beyond *Capital*

Beyond *Capital*

Marx's Political Economy of the Working Class
Second Edition

Michael A. Lebowitz
Professor Emeritus of Economics,
Simon Fraser University, Canada

First edition published by Macmillan 1992
Second edition published 2003 by
PALGRAVE MACMILLAN
Houndmills, Basingstoke, Hampshire RG21 6XS and
175 Fifth Avenue, New York, N.Y. 10010
Companies and representatives throughout the world

PALGRAVE MACMILLAN is the global academic imprint of the Palgrave
Macmillan division of St. Martin's Press, LLC and of Palgrave Macmillan Ltd.
Macmillan® is a registered trademark in the United States, United Kingdom
and other countries. Palgrave is a registered trademark in the European
Union and other countries.

ISBN 0–333–96429–2 hardback
ISBN 0–333–96430–6 paperback

This book is printed on paper suitable for recycling and made from fully
managed and sustained forest sources.

A catalogue record for this book is available from the British Library.

Library of Congress Cataloging-in-Publication Data
Lebowitz, Michael A.
    Beyond capital : Marx's political economy of the working class /
Michael A. Lebowitz – 2nd ed.
        p. cm.
    Includes bibliographical references and index.
    ISBN 0–333–96429–2 – ISBN 0–333–96430–6 (pbk.)
        1. Marxian economics. 2. Labor economics. 3. Capital. I. Title.

    HB97.5.L3147 2003
    335.4'12—dc21   2003040523

10   9   8   7   6   5   4   3   2
12   11   10   09   08   07   06   05   04

Printed and bound in Great Britain by
Antony Rowe Ltd, Chippenham and Eastbourne

Contents

List of Figures

Preface to the Second Edition

A reviewer of the first edition of this book wrote that it might be the worst possible time to publish a book about Marx. And it was. Capitalism was triumphant (with little apparent opposition) and its putative alternative, 'Actually Existing Socialism' (AES), appeared to have ended in a miserable fit of the blues.

For those on the Right, that combination was sufficient to prove the error of Marxism. Many wondered – how could you still talk about Marx? Are you *still* teaching Marxist economics? (Of course, in one of those ironies that Marx would have appreciated, it was possible to find conservatives of various hues quoting scriptures and declaring that capitalism's successes and the failures of AES confirmed that Marx was right.) Some on the Left concluded, simply, that capitalist relations of production do not *yet* fetter the development of productive forces. What can you do against History? And so it was that, rather than socialism, for some the only feasible alternative to barbarism became barbarism with a human face.

Others on the Left responded to the absence of the 'revolt of the working class' that Marx projected by concluding that Marx had it all wrong – that his privileging of workers as the subjects of social change constituted the sins of class reductionism and essentialism. For these 'post-Marxists', the multiplicity of modern democratic struggles counts as a critique of Marx's theory; in place of an analysis centred upon capitalist relations of production, they offer the heterogeneity of political and social relations, the equality and autonomy of all struggles, and the market-place of competing discourses.

Beyond Capital should be understood as a challenge to this retreat from Marx. It argues that the only way that they can separate struggles such as those over health and living conditions, air and water quality, women's rights, government social programmes, the costs and conditions of higher education, and democratic struggles in general from workers is by beginning with the theoretical reduction of workers to one-sided opposites of capital. Only by limiting the needs of workers to wages, hours and conditions of work can the 'post-Marxists' theoretically posit new social movements as the basis for a critique of class analysis; rather than considering the worker as a socially developed human being within modern capitalist society, they utilize the narrow stereotype of the Abstract Proletarian.

Yet, the 'post-Marxists' did not invent that stereotype. *Beyond Capital* argues that the concept of the Abstract Proletarian is the product of a one-sided Marxism that has distorted Marx's own conception of workers as subjects. It situates the roots of this one-sided Marxism in the failure to recognize that Marx's *Capital* was never intended as the complete analysis of capitalism but, rather, as an explanation and demystification for workers of the nature of capital.

For one-sided Marxists, *Capital* explains why capitalism will come to an end. Inexorable forces make history. It is a world of things and inhuman forces, of one-sided subjects (if, indeed, there are any subjects) – rather than living, struggling beings attempting to shape their lives. And, in this world, the Abstract Proletariat finally rises to its appointed task and unlocks the productive forces that have outgrown their capitalist shell. If the facts do not appear to support *Capital*, so much the worse for the facts. As Marx commented about disciples (see Chapter 2), the disintegration of a theory begins when the point of departure is 'no longer reality, but the new theoretical form in which the master had sublimated it'.

But this is not the only aspect of the disintegration of Marxist theory. Both in theory and practice, Marxism has attempted to free itself from the constraints imposed by the one-sidedness inherent in the exegesis of the sacred text – and it has done so through eclecticism. In practice, it has attempted to extend beyond narrow economistic appeals to its Abstract Proletariat; and, in theory, it engages in methodological eclecticism to modify the doctrine underlying practice. Both in theory and practice, 'modernization' becomes the rallying-cry and the latest fad. Nothing, of course, is easier than eclecticism.

Yet, the freedom attained through such sophistication is neither absolute nor without a price. For, the text remains, unsullied by its eclectic accretions; and the one-sided reading it permits provides a standing rebuke and never lacks for potential bearers of its position. Thus, not freedom but a vulnerability to fundamentalist criticism; and, not new directions but swings, more or less violent, between the poles of the real subject and the reified text. There is, in short, fertile ground for an endless dispute between fundamentalism and faddism.

Nor is it self-evident what precisely is saved by eclecticism – whether Marxism as a theory 'sufficient unto itself' survives the addition of alien elements, whether the new combinations may still be called Marxism. It has been the basic insight of fundamentalists that eclectic and syncretic combinations threaten the very core of Marxism as an integral conception. In short, neither the purveyors of the Abstract Proletariat of *Capital* nor the eclectic dissidents traverse the gap between the pure theory of *Capital* and the reality of capitalism. Both are forms of one-sided Marxism, different aspects of the disintegration of Marxist theory. They are the result, on the one hand, of the failure of Marx to complete his epistemological project in *Capital* and, on the other hand, of the displacement of the understanding of Marx's method by the exegesis of sacred texts.

Beyond Capital should be understood as a call for the continuation of Marx's project. By stressing the centrality of Marx's method and using it to explore the subject matter of Marx's unfinished work – in particular, his projected book on Wage-Labour, it focuses on the missing side in *Capital* – the side of workers. *Beyond Capital* restores human beings (and class struggle) to the hub of Marxian analysis by tracing out the implications of that missing book. It challenges not only the economic determinism and reductionism of one-sided Marxism but also the accommodations of the 'post-Marxists'. Marx's conception of the political economy of the working class comes to the fore; next to its focus upon the collective producer (which contains implicit within it the vision of an alternative society), the 'post-Marxist' view of human beings as consumers (with, of course, heterogeneous needs) stands revealed as so many empty abstractions.

This is not at all an argument, however, that class struggle is absent from *Capital* or that references to class struggle by workers are missing. But, *Capital* is essentially about capital – its goals and its struggles to achieve those goals. Its theme is not workers (except insofar as capital does something to workers), not workers' goals (except to mention that they differ from those of capital) and not workers' class struggle (except insofar as workers react against capital's offensives). Even where Marx made sporadic comments in *Capital* about workers as subjects, those comments hang in mid-air without anything comparable to the systematic logical development he provides for the side of capital. The result, I argue, is that some quite significant aspects of capitalism are missing and not developed in *Capital* and, indeed, that there are problematic aspects of the latter. Those who think that 'it's all in *Capital*' should explain the continuing reproduction of a one-sided Marxism.

In the Preface to the first edition, I noted that this book took a long time to come together and that it was still in the process of development. This edition, written eleven years later, demonstrates this point well. In fact, in preparing this edition, I came to look upon the first edition as a first draft. Every chapter from the original edition was changed. Some alterations were relatively minor and merely updated and strengthened points made earlier (drawing now, for example, upon the publication of Marx's 1861–3 *Economic Manuscripts*). However, this edition also reflects the further development of my thinking on the questions raised.

One of the most significant changes involves the division of the original concluding chapter ('Beyond Political Economy') into two separate chapters ('From Political Economy to Class Struggle' and 'From Capital to the Collective Worker'). This allowed me to expand in particular upon the concepts of the Workers' State and of the collective worker, respectively – areas I have been exploring in the context of recent papers and a book in progress on the theory of socialist economies. While this elaboration had been intended from the outset of plans for a new edition, two other new chapters emerged in the course of the revision. The new Chapter 6 ('Wages') explicitly considers the effect upon the theory of wages of relaxing Marx's assumption in *Capital* that workers receive a 'definite quantity of the means of subsistence'; in the course of this investigation, the degree of separation among workers (a variable noted in the first edition) takes on significantly more importance.

Finally, there is a completely new opening chapter ('Why Marx? A Story of Capital'). In the course of writing a chapter on Marx recently for a collection on the views of economists on capitalism, it occurred to me that *Beyond **Capital*** was missing an introduction to Marx's analysis of capital. It wasn't there originally because I had conceived of the book as a supplement to *Capital*; however, given the way this new chapter opens up questions to which I subsequently return, it is hard for me to believe now that the chapter wasn't always there.

I am extremely grateful to the many people who have encouraged me in this work since its original publication. Among those I want especially to thank are Gibin Hong, translator of the Korean-language edition, Jesus Garcia Brigos and Ernesto Molina (who told me Che would have liked the book). At this point, though, I am especially appreciative for the critical feedback on new material for this edition that I've received from various readers. Some of this feedback has saved me from serious errors; so, thank you to Greg Albo, Jim Devine, Alfredo Saad-Filho, Sam Gindin, Marta Harnecker, Leo Panitch, Sid Shniad and Tony Smith.

At the time of the writing of this Preface, chronologically the final part of this edition, capitalism's triumph is not as unproblematic as it may have seemed at the time of the first edition. Strong protest movements have emerged in opposition to the forms of capitalist globalization, and the development of new international links in the struggle against global capital proceeds. Further, capital appears to be undergoing one of its characteristic crises, and the contest as to which particular capitals and locations is to bear the burden of excess global capacity as well as the depth of the crisis are yet to be determined.

If there is one important message from this book, however, it is that economic crises do not bring about an end to capitalism. Once we consider the worker as subject, then the conditions within which workers themselves are produced (and produce themselves) emerge as an obvious part of the explanation for the continued existence of capitalism. *Beyond Capital* stresses the manner in which the worker's dependence upon capital, within existing relations, is reproduced under normal circumstances; and, thus, it points to the critical importance not only of that demystification of capital upon which Marx himself laboured but also of the process of struggle by which workers produce themselves as subjects capable of altering their world.

This essential point about the centrality of revolutionary practice for going beyond capital affords me the opportunity to close with the quotation from George Sand with which Marx concluded his *Poverty of Philosophy* (Marx, 1847a: 212). (In the context of capital's demonstrated tendency to destroy both human beings and Nature, the statement has taken on added meaning.) Until 'there are no more classes and class antagonisms…, the last word of social science will always be … Combat or death, bloody struggle or extinction. Thus the question is inexorably put.'

Preface to the First Edition (1992)

I date the beginnings of this book back to 1973 when I first read the English-language translation of Marx's *Grundrisse*. There, a side of Marx which had not been apparent since his early writings surfaced – a focus on human needs. And, I became convinced that this was a side which had been obscured by Marx's failure to write the book that he at that time had planned to write, the book on wage-labour.

My initial thoughts on this question were brought together in a 1975 paper, 'Human Needs, Alienation and Immiseration', presented to the Canadian Economics Association. Subsequently, an abridged version of this paper was published in 1977 as 'Capital and the Production of Needs' (which serves as a foundation for Chapter 2 [now 3]). The idea of a missing book, however, offered more than a link between the Young Marx and the later writings. It also seemed to provide an explanation for the gap that feminist Marxists were at that time pointing out – Marx's silence on household labour. This was a question addressed in an article published in 1976, 'The Political Economy of Housework: a Comment', as well as in an unpublished talk from the same year, 'Immiseration and Household Labour'; elements of both can be found in Chapter 6 [now 8].

How significant, though, was a missing book on wage-labour? It wasn't enough to attempt to glean the *Grundrisse* for quotations that might have found their way into such a book had it been written. The real issue was what such a silence implied about the adequacy of *Capital*. Even to pose this question, however, meant the necessity to develop a standard by which to judge *Capital*.

As it happened, in 1980 I turned my attention to an explicit study of Marx's methodology. The stimulus came from an entirely different source. For several years, Neo-Ricardians (and others influenced by Piero Sraffa) had been criticizing Marx's economics. While I was convinced that they were wrong in their description and criticism of Marx's theory, I was unsatisfied by the lack of coherence in my alternative understanding. I went back, then, to Hegel to develop an argument stressing the distinction in Marx between an analysis conducted at the level of Essence (capital in general) and one at the level of Appearance ('many capitals' or the competition of capitals). My conclusion in an unpublished paper ('Marx's Methodological Project') was that the Neo-Ricardians (and many others) were fixated at the level of Appearance whereas the more central problems to explore in Marx's theory were at the level of Essence.

But, this brought me back to the implications of the missing book on wage-labour. In a paper presented later that year, 'Capital as Finite', I attempted to reconstruct the logic of *Capital* and argued that there was a critical problem of 'one-sidedness' in the theory presented in *Capital* – as judged by Marx's own methodological standards. Some ideas from this paper appear in Chapters 7 and 8 [now Chapters 9 and 11]; the main section, however, was published in 1982 as 'The One-Sidedness of Capital' and is the basis for Chapter 3 [now 4]. This was followed by a subsequent 1982 article, 'Marx after Wage-Labour', elements of which appear in Chapters 2 and 5 [now 3 and 7].

All this became for several years the 'book' that I would someday write – a book on the missing side of wage-labour that I was convinced (and kept assuring my students) provided the answer to many problems in *Capital*. Aside from a focus on the worker as subject and upon the centrality of praxis, however, there was still little in the projected book which related directly to existing struggles or which provided more than an interesting academic interpretation.

The next element of the book fell into place as the result of another one of my digressions. In 'The Theoretical Status of Monopoly Capital', I had returned to the question of Marx's method to explore the relation between the essence of capital and the competition of capitals in the tendency toward centralization (monopoly). It was an attempt to demonstrate exactly how the competition of capitals executed the inner tendencies of capital, a concept that Marx stressed repeatedly in the *Grundrisse*. At a time of increasing international competition, however, the question which presented itself was: what was the relation between competition and the side of wage-labour? Was the competition of workers also the way in which the inner tendencies of wage-labour were realized? It was easy to show that Marx rejected this parallel. But, why was there this asymmetry? The answer to this question was developed in 'The Political Economy of Wage-Labour', published in 1987, which sets out the concept of Marx's alternative political economy; this is the basis for Chapter 4 [now 5].

These, then, are the main elements of a book which began in 1973. Its development has clearly been a process which has continued. Even in the course of what I had anticipated would be a mere consolidation of material, new sides and aspects continually presented themselves. The result is that much of what I now consider to be among the most important contributions is newly developed in the book. There remain, of course, aspects of the argument that call for further elaboration; I think, however, that this is an appropriate point to permit that further development to be a collective process.

Precisely because the process of producing the book has been so long, it is difficult to thank everyone who has helped and encouraged me along the way on this particular project. I can thank those, however, who read and commented on all or part of this manuscript: Nancy Folbre, John Bellamy Foster, David Laibman, Alain Lipietz, Bill Livant, James O'Connor, Leo Panitch, Michael Perelman, Michèle Pujol, Roy Rotheim, Jim Sacouman, Paul Sweezy, Donald Swartz, George Warskett and Rosemary Warskett. Although I haven't followed all of their advice, they have identified gaps and potential sources of embarrassment, and for that I am most grateful.

My greatest debt is to my comrade and severest critic, Sharon Yandle, whose direct involvement in the women's movement and trade union movement over these years has been a constant source of stimulation. This is not the book she has wanted for her members, but it is, I hope, a step in that all-important direction.

MICHAEL A. LEBOWITZ

Acknowledgements

Portions of this work have previously appeared in 'Capital and the Production of Needs', *Science & Society*, Vol. XLI, No. 4; 'The Political Economy of Wage-Labor', *Science & Society*, Vol. 51, No. 3; 'The One-Sidedness of *Capital*', *Review of Radical Political Economics*, Vol. 14, No. 4; and 'Marx After Wage-Labor', *Economic Forum*, Vol. XIII, No. 2. Permission to reprint is gratefully acknowledged.

1
Why Marx? A Story of Capital

> It is the ultimate aim of this work to reveal the economic law of
> motion of modern society...
>
> Karl Marx (1977: 92)

Why bother to talk about Marx or Marxism in the twenty-first century? Marx wrote in the nineteenth century, and a lot has changed since then – not the least of which is capitalism. So, rather than resurrect a long-dead economist who studied nineteenth-century capitalism in Western Europe, why not just look at what modern economists have to say, or, if we don't like that, why not do what Marx himself did – analyse the *modern* economic system?

These are legitimate questions to pose. For now, let me offer two answers. Firstly, Marxism is more than an economic theory. At its core, Marxism rejects any society based upon exploitation and any society that limits the full development of human potential. Thus, determination of fundamental social decisions in accordance with private profits rather than human needs is among the specific reasons that Marxists oppose capitalism. That resources and people can be underutilized and unemployed when they could be used to produce what people need; that our natural environment, the basic condition of human existence, can be rationally destroyed in the pursuit of private interests; that we can speak of justice when ownership of the means of production (our common heritage) permits a portion of society to compel people to work under conditions that violate their humanity; that people will be divided by gender, race, nationality, etc. because of the benefits accruing to capitalists when coalitions among the underlying population are thwarted – all these 'rational' characteristics of capitalism are viewed by a Marxist as inherent in the very nature of capital and count among the reasons to struggle to go beyond capital.

My second answer relates specifically to Marxism as economic theory – there has never been an analysis of capitalism (past and present) as powerful and insightful as that of Marx. Nor is there an analysis of the system that is more important for people living within it *today* to understand. Perhaps the best way to begin to communicate this is to tell a story about capitalism drawn from Marx's *Capital* (supplemented by his notebooks and drafts for that work). My specific concern here is to describe 'the economic law of motion' of capitalism as developed in *Capital*. In my view, *Capital* provides a powerful account of the dynamics of the system; however, as we will see in subsequent chapters, I consider this tale problematical in significant respects and, indeed, to be only *part* of the story.

I Capitalist relations of production

If we want to understand a society, Marx stressed, we need to grasp the character of its relations of production. Accordingly, to understand capitalist society, we must focus upon its distinguishing characteristic, its unique relationship between capitalists and wage-labourers. Capitalism is a market economy but it requires as a historical condition not only the existence of commodities and money but also that the free worker is 'available, on the market, as the seller of his own labour-power' and is, indeed, 'compelled to offer for sale as a commodity that very labour-power which exists only in his living body' (Marx, 1977: 272–4). Further, central to capitalist relations of production is that the purchaser of the worker's ability to perform labour is the capitalist: 'the relations of capital are essentially concerned with controlling production and... therefore the worker constantly appears in the market as a seller and the capitalist as a buyer' (Marx, 1977: 1011).

These historical conditions do not drop from the sky. For them to be satisfied, there are several requirements. Two that Marx identified explicitly in *Capital* are: (1) that the worker is free (i.e., that she has property rights in her own labour-power, is its 'free proprietor'); and (2) that the means of production have been separated from producers and thus the worker is 'free' of all means of production that would permit her to produce and sell anything other than her labour-power (Marx, 1977: 271–2). A third requirement (implicit in *Capital*) is that capitalists are not indifferent as to whether they rent out means of production or purchase labour-power – that is, that capital has *seized possession of production,* thereby compelling producers who are separated from the means of production to sell their labour-power.[1]

Let us consider first the side of capital within this relation. It's no great insight to say that capitalists want profits. What Marx wanted to do, though, was to reveal what profits are and what capital is. Considering all forms of capital – both before and after the development of capitalist relations of production – he proposed that what is common to capitalists is that they enter the sphere of circulation with a certain value of capital in the form of money in order to purchase commodities and then sell commodities for *more* money. Their goal, in short, is to secure additional value, a surplus value: 'The value originally advanced, therefore, not only remains intact while in circulation, but increases its magnitude, adds to it a surplus value, or is valorized...' (Marx, 1977: 252).

This is what Marx described as 'the general formula for capital': *M-C-M'*, that movement of value from money (*M*) to commodity (*C*) to more money (*M'*). While its purest manifestation is the case of the merchant capitalist who buys 'in order to sell dearer', Marx viewed the basic drive for surplus value as common to all forms of capital (1977: 256–7, 266). 'Capital', he commented, 'has one sole driving force, the drive to valorize itself, to create surplus value...' (1977: 342).

Capital's impulse, its 'ought', however, is more than just the search for profit from a single transaction. The simple formula of *M-C-M'* illustrates what is at the core of the concept of capital – *growth.* 'The goal-determining activity of capital', Marx declared, 'can only be that of growing wealthier, i.e. of magnification, of increasing itself.' By its very nature, capital is always searching and striving to expand. Whatever its initial starting point, the initial sum of capital, capital must drive beyond it – there is 'the constant drive to go beyond its quantitative limit: an endless process' (Marx, 1973: 270). The capitalist, he proposed, 'represents the absolute drive for self-enrichment, and any definite limit to his capital is a barrier which must be overcome' (Marx and Engels, 1994: 179). Indeed, every quantitative limit is contrary to the nature, the quality, of capital: 'it is therefore inherent in its nature constantly to drive beyond its own barrier' (Marx, 1973: 270).

As we will see, the *essence* of this story is that capital by its very nature has an impulse to grow which constantly comes up against barriers – both those external to it and those inherent within it – and that capital constantly drives beyond those barriers, positing growth again. Its movement is that of Growth–Barrier–Growth. 'Capital is the endless and limitless drive to go beyond its limiting barrier. Every boundary [*Grenze*] is and has to be a barrier [*Schranke*] for it' (Marx, 1973: 334).

˙ But what is capital? Marx believed that in order to understand capital, we need to understand money. Commenting that bourgeois economists had never even attempted to solve 'the riddle of money' (1977: 139, 187), Marx demonstrated in his opening chapter, 'The Commodity', that the secret of money is that, as the universal equivalent of the labour in all commodities, it represents the social labour of a commodity-producing society.[2] By this logic, then, *M-C-M'* represents a process whereby capitalists, who own the representative of a certain portion of society's labour, are able to obtain a claim on *more* of that labour via exchange.

How? Where does it come from? Marx was clear that, in the case of *pre*-capitalist relations, it came at the expense of the independent producers – for example, 'from the twofold advantage gained, over both the selling and the buying producers, by the merchant who parasitically inserts himself between them' (Marx, 1977: 267). Buying low to sell dearer here means that the merchant captures an additional portion of society's labour through a process of unequal exchange. Exploitation by capital here occurs outside capitalist relations of production.

Consider, however, capitalist relations, where the worker sells her ability to perform labour to the capitalist. Because she lacks the means of production to combine with her labour-power, her labour-power is not a use-value for her; accordingly, she offers her labour-power as a commodity in order to acquire the social equivalent of the labour within it – its value in the form of money. She is able to secure that equivalent because her labour-power is a use-value for someone else, the capitalist. Thus, the worker gets money (which she can use to purchase the articles of consumption she requires), and the capitalist gets to use her labour-power. Finally, for the purpose of analysis, Marx assumes that labour-power, like all other commodities, receives its equivalent; thus, unequal exchange is precluded as the explanation of the existence of surplus value. In these respects, labour-power is like other commodities.

There is something different, however, about the sale and purchase of labour-power. Unlike other commodities, that ability to perform labour is not separable from its seller – labour-power exists, after all, only in the living body of the worker. One effect is that the labour necessary to produce this commodity is the labour necessary to produce the worker herself, the sum of social labour (as represented by money) that enters into the worker's consumption. The other effect is that the worker must be present when the commodity she has parted with is consumed by its purchaser. Thus, rather than a separable commodity, what the worker really has sold is a specific property right, the right to dispose of her ability to perform labour for a specified period.

There is another difference concerning this particular transaction – the purchaser. The reason why the capitalist buys labour-power is not simply to consume it. His interest is not in the performance of labour itself (as in the case of an individual consumer for whom specific services are a use-value). After all, recall the concept of capital: *M-C-M'*. What the capitalist wants is added value, surplus value. 'The only use value, i.e. usefulness,' Marx commented, 'which can stand opposite capital as such is that which increases, multiplies and hence preserves it as capital' (Marx, 1973: 271). Thus, what the capitalist wants from the worker is surplus labour; and because (and only because) he anticipates that he will be able to compel the performance of surplus labour and that this surplus labour will be a source of enrichment, the worker's labour-power is a use-value for him.

How the capitalist gets that surplus value, though, is not in the sphere of exchange (as in the case of pre-capitalist relations). Rather, it occurs outside of the market transaction. Now that this transaction in which there was the exchange of equivalents is over, Marx noted, something has happened to each of the two parties. 'He who was previously the money-owner now strides out in front as a capitalist; the possessor of labour-power follows as his worker' (Marx, 1977: 280). And where are they going? They are entering the sphere of production, the place of work where the capitalist now has the opportunity to *use* that property right which he purchased.

II The sphere of capitalist production

So, what happens in production after labour-power has been purchased as a commodity by the capitalist? 'Firstly, the worker works under the control of the capitalist to whom his labour belongs' (Marx, 1977: 291). The goal of the capitalist determines the nature and purpose of production. And, *why* does the capitalist have this power over workers? Because this is the property right he purchased – the right to dispose of their ability to perform labour.

'Secondly, the product is the property of the capitalist and not that of the worker, its immediate producer' (Marx, 1977: 292). Workers, in short, have no property rights in the product that results from their activity. They have sold to the capitalist the only thing that might have given them a claim, their capacity to perform labour. The capitalist, accordingly, is the residual claimant – he is in the position both to compel the performance of surplus labour and also to reap its reward.

How does this occur? Come back to the question of the value of labour-power, to what the capitalist pays for the labour-power at his disposal. 'The value of labour-power', Marx proposed, 'can be resolved into the value of a definite quantity of the means of subsistence. It therefore varies with the value of the means of subsistence, i.e. with the quantity of labour-time required to produce them' (Marx, 1977: 276). Thus, at any given time, there is a set of commodities that comprises the worker's daily consumption bundle. If we know the general productivity of labour, the output per hour of labour, then we can calculate the hours of labour necessary to produce these requirements (which Marx called *necessary labour*):

$$w = U/q \qquad (1.1),$$

where w, U and q are necessary labour, the worker's consumption bundle and the productivity of labour, respectively. For any given standard of living (U), the higher the level of productivity (q) the lower will be the level of necessary labour (and its value-form, the value of labour-power).

It is simple, then, to identify the condition for capital to satisfy its drive for surplus value. Capital must find a way to compel workers to perform surplus labour, labour over and above necessary labour. We can represent this condition as follows:

$$s = d - w \qquad (1.2),$$

where s and d are hours of surplus labour and the workday (in terms of length and intensity), respectively.[3] If the worker provides more labour to the capitalist than is necessary to reproduce her at the given standard of necessity, then she performs surplus labour, 'unpaid' labour. The ratio of surplus to necessary labour (s/w) measures the degree of exploitation (and underlies the rate of surplus value, its value-form).

So, how does capital compel the performance of surplus labour? The story, of course, begins with that transaction in the sphere of circulation – where the worker has no alternative but to sell her labour-power and the capitalist only purchases labour-power if it can be a source of surplus value. However, the deed is done only in the sphere of capitalist production, where the worker works under the control of the capitalist. By using its power to extend or intensify the workday (d) and by increasing the level of productivity (q), capital can increase surplus labour, the rate of exploitation and the rate of surplus value.[4] The story Marx proceeded to tell about developments in the capitalist sphere of production focused in turn upon these two variables – the workday and the level of productivity.

Capitalist production begins once capital formally subsumes workers by purchasing their labour-power. The capitalist now commands the worker within this 'coercive relation' (Marx, 1977: 424). Since, however, this production initially occurs on the basis of the old, pre-existing mode of production (a labour process characterized, for example, by handicraft), the capitalist is initially limited to using this new relation of domination and subordination (the 'formal subsumption' of labour under capital) to increase the amount of labour performed by the worker:

> The work may become more intensive, its duration may be extended, it may become more continuous or orderly under the eye of the interested capitalist, but in themselves these changes do not affect the character of the actual labour process, the actual mode of working (Marx, 1977: 1021).

The surplus value that results from an increase in the workday, Marx designated as *absolute surplus value* 'because its very increase, its rate of growth, and its every increase is at the same time an absolute increase of *created* value (of produced value)' (Marx and Engels, 1988b: 233).

Given capital's impulse to grow, it follows that capital will attempt to extend the workday without limit; its drive is to 'absorb the greatest possible amount of surplus labour'. Capital, Marx declared, is 'dead labour which, vampire-like, lives only by sucking living labour, and lives the more, the more labour it sucks' (Marx, 1977: 342). He describes how capital's 'werewolf-like hunger for surplus labour' (Marx, 1977: 353), its 'vampire thirst for the living blood of labour' (Marx, 1977: 367), means that it attempts to turn every part of the day into working time, 'to be devoted to the self-valorization of capital' (Marx, 1977: 375).

Yet, there are obvious barriers to capital's attempt to grow in this way. The day is only 24 hours long and can never be extended beyond that. Further, the worker needs time within those 24 hours to rest and to revive and, indeed, 'to feed, wash and clothe himself' (Marx, 1977: 341). Clearly, this checks capital's ability to generate absolute surplus value. Further, Marx notes that there are moral and social obstacles – 'the worker needs time in which to satisfy his intellectual and social requirements' (Marx, 1977: 341). Nevertheless, capital's tendency is to drive beyond all these: 'in its blind and measureless drive, its insatiable appetite for surplus labour, capital oversteps not only the moral but even the merely physical limits of the working day' (Marx, 1977: 375).

Left to itself, capital thus would usurp 'the time for growth, development and healthy maintenance of the body' in order to ensure 'the greatest possible daily expenditure of labour-power, no matter how diseased, compulsory and painful it may be'; accordingly, it 'not only produces a deterioration of human labour-power by robbing it of its normal moral and physical conditions of development and activity, but also produces the premature exhaustion and death of this labour-power itself' (Marx, 1977: 375–6). In short, 'capital therefore takes no account of the health and length of life of the worker, unless society forces it to do so' (Marx, 1977: 381).

And, as Marx recounts about the limits placed upon the workday in nineteenth-century England, 'society' *did* force capital to find another way to grow. He describes the resistance of workers to the extension of the workday, the long period of class struggle in which workers attempted to maintain a 'normal' workday (Marx, 1977: 382, 389, 412) and, finally (with the support of representatives of landed property), the passage of the Ten Hours' Bill, 'an all-powerful social barrier by which they can be prevented from selling themselves and their families into slavery and death by voluntary contract with capital' (Marx, 1977: 416).

Under such circumstances, capital's 'insatiable appetite for surplus labour' compels it to attempt to grow in another way – by reducing necessary labour through increases in the productivity of labour. The growth of surplus value on this basis, one in which the necessary portion of the workday is 'shortened by methods for producing the equivalent of the wages of labour in a shorter time', Marx designated as *relative surplus value*. To generate this, however, capital must transform the mode of production that it has inherited, creating in the process 'a specifically capitalist mode of production'. More than just a social relation of domination and subordination increasingly emerges. Now, the worker is dominated technically by means of production, by fixed capital, in the production process. The formal subsumption of labour under capital is 'replaced by a real subsumption' (Marx, 1977: 645).

Initially, capital altered the mode of production by introducing manufacture – the development of new divisions of labour within the capitalist workplace. As the result of new forms of cooperation and individual specialization within the organism that became the capitalist workshop, productivity of labour advanced substantially. Yet, Marx pointed out that there were inherent limits to the growth of capital upon this basis. In particular, production remained dependent upon skilled craftsmen whose period of training was lengthy and who insisted upon retaining long periods of apprenticeship (Marx, 1977: 489). Manufacture (making by hand) as a method of production restricted the growth of capital because it was based upon the historical presupposition of the 'handicraftsman as the regulating principle of social production'.

With the introduction of machines, however, 'the barriers placed in the way of domination of capital by this same regulating principle' fell (Marx, 1977: 490–1).

Thus, capital's further alteration of the mode of production was based upon machinery and the factory system. Initially, its advance was limited because machine-builders themselves were 'a class of workers who, owing to the semi-artistic nature of their employment, could increase their numbers only gradually, and not by leaps and bounds' (Marx, 1977: 504). With the development of production of machines by machines, however, capital now created for itself 'an adequate technical foundation' (Marx, 1977: 506). Characteristic of the new factory system is its 'tremendous capacity for expanding with sudden immense leaps'; indeed, 'this mode of production acquires an elasticity, a capacity for sudden extension by leaps and bounds' (Marx, 1977: 579–80). This change, clearly, was not a random development – it was the way capital drove beyond a specific barrier; it is 'not an accidental moment of capital, but is rather the historical reshaping of the traditional, inherited means of labour into a form adequate to capital' (Marx, 1973: 694).

Adequate to capital insofar as barriers within production to the development of productivity and the generation of relative surplus value are transcended. Production is transformed into 'a process of the technological application of science' (Marx, 1977: 775). Now, necessary labour can be driven further and further downward (and relative surplus value up) as 'the accumulation of knowledge and of skill, of the general productive forces of the social brain, is thus absorbed into capital'.[5] Thus, Marx proposed that 'capital has posited the mode of production corresponding to it,' once 'the entire production process appears as not subsumed under the direct skilfulness of the worker, but rather as the technological application of science' (Marx, 1973: 694, 699).

This is a mode of production adequate to capital, though, in another sense. In addition to increasing productivity, the machine permits the intensification of the workday, provides capital with 'the most powerful weapon for suppressing strikes, those periodic revolts of the working class against the autocracy of capital' (Marx, 1977: 562), solidifies the despotism of the capitalist workplace with the development of 'a barrack-like discipline' (Marx, 1977: 549), abolishes thinking in the workplace 'in the same proportion as science is incorporated in it as an independent power' (Marx, 1977: 799), and produces 'a surplus working population, which is compelled to submit to capital's dictates' (Marx, 1977: 532).

Thus, the story of capital within the sphere of production is that of its tendency to drive beyond all barriers. Capital's 'ceaseless striving' to grow reveals its universalizing tendency, its historic mission in that it 'strives toward the universal development of the forces of production' (Marx, 1973: 325, 540). What can hold back capital?

III   The capitalist sphere of circulation

One of the mistakes of classical political economy, Marx noted, was that it conceived of 'production as directly identical with the self-realization of capital', a view that fails to grasp that capitalist production is a unity of production and circulation (Marx, 1973: 410, 620). So far, all that we have been considering is the production of surplus value. Yet, as Marx pointed out, this is only 'the first act':

> As soon as the amount of surplus labour it has proved possible to extort has been objectified in commodities, the surplus-value has been produced. But this production of surplus-value is only the first act in the capitalist production process … Now comes the second act in the process (Marx, 1981b: 352).

In that second act, the commodities must be sold. The circuit that capital must pass through may be described as:

$$M\text{-}C \ldots P \ldots C'\text{-}M'.$$

Beginning from its money-form (M), capital has purchased labour-power (C) and put it to work alongside means of production, generating within that production process (P) commodities pregnant with surplus value (C'). But, capital's goal is not C' – those commodities must make the mortal leap from C' to M' if that potential surplus value is to be made real.

Thus, whereas it looked previously as if the only obstacles to the growth of capital were in the sphere of production, it now transpires that capital by its very nature faces additional barriers to its growth – this time in the sphere of circulation. It encounters one 'in the available magnitude of *consumption* – of consumption capacity' (Marx, 1973: 405). If capital is to grow, it must drive beyond this barrier: 'a precondition of production based on capital is therefore the production of a *constantly widening sphere of circulation*' (Marx, 1973: 407). Accordingly, 'just as capital has the tendency on the one side to create ever more surplus labour, so it has the complementary tendency to create more points of exchange'. In short, the drive of capital to expand is present in the sphere of circulation as well as within production: 'the tendency to create the *world market* is directly given in the concept of capital itself'. For capital, 'every limit appears as a barrier to be overcome' (Marx, 1973: 408).

Inherent in this concept of capital, this expanding, growing capital, is that it requires 'the production of new consumption'. And, it pursues this in three ways: (1) 'quantitative expansion of existing consumption', (2) 'creation of new needs by propagating existing ones in a wide circle' and (3) 'production of *new* needs and discovery and creation of new use values' (Marx, 1973: 408). All this is part of capital's 'civilizing' aspect; in its drive to expand, capital treats what were the inherent limits of earlier modes of production as mere barriers to be dissolved:

> Capital drives beyond natural barriers and prejudices as much as beyond nature worship, as well as all traditional, confined, compla-cent, encrusted satisfactions of personal needs, and reproductions of old ways of life. It is destructive towards all of this and constantly rev-olutionizes it, tearing down all the barriers which hem in the devel-opment of the productive forces, the expansion of needs, the all-sided development of production, and the exploitation and exchange of natural and mental forces (Marx, 1973: 409–10, 650).

Yet, the barriers capital faces in the sphere of circulation are not only external – they are also inherent in its own nature. Capital must not only sell its products as commodities (which means that they must be use-values for purchasers who possess their equivalent in the form of money), but it also must return (this time as seller) to a sphere of circu-lation that is marked by capitalist relations of production. Thus, the real-ization of surplus value takes place:

> within a given framework of antagonistic conditions of distribution, which reduce the consumption of the vast majority of society to a minimum level, only capable of varying within more or less narrow limits. It is further restricted by the drive for accumulation, the drive to expand capital and produce surplus-value on a larger scale (Marx, 1981b: 352–3).

Accordingly, Marx (1981b: 365) observed, there is a 'constant tension between the restricted dimensions of consumption on the capitalist basis, and a production that is constantly striving to overcome these immanent barriers'. And, here we see an additional characteristic of cap-italist production. Capital's problem in the sphere of circulation is not simply that it must expand the sphere of circulation but that it tends to expand the production of surplus value *beyond* its ability to realize that surplus value. The result is the tendency towards '*overproduction*, the fundamental contradiction of developed capital' (Marx, 1973: 415).

To describe overproduction as 'the fundamental contradiction' indicates the importance that Marx attributed to it. For Marx, the inherent tendency of capital for overproduction flows directly from capital's successes in the sphere of production – in particular, its success in driving up the rate of exploitation. What capital does in the sphere of production comes back to haunt it in the sphere of circulation. By striving 'to reduce the relation of this necessary labour to surplus labour to the minimum', capital simultaneously creates 'barriers to the sphere of exchange, i.e. the possibility of realization – the realization of the value posited in the production process' (Marx, 1973: 422). Overproduction, Marx (1968: 468) commented, arises precisely because the consumption of workers 'does not grow correspondingly with the productivity of labour'. And, the result? Periodic crises, those 'momentary, violent solutions for the existing contradictions, violent eruptions that re-establish the disturbed balance for the time being' (Marx, 1981b: 357):

> The bourgeois mode of production contains within itself a barrier to the free development of the productive forces, a barrier which comes to the surface in crises and, in particular, in *overproduction* – the basic phenomenon in crises (Marx, 1968: 528).

Thus, capital produces its own specific barrier. It is not interested in production unless it is profitable production, production of surplus value that can be realized. If it succeeds too well in increasing surplus labour, 'then it suffers from surplus production, and then necessary labour is interrupted, because *no surplus labour can be realized by capital*'. Here we have a barrier unique to capitalist relations of production: 'capital contains a *particular* restriction – which contradicts its general tendency to drive beyond every barrier to production' (Marx, 1973: 421, 415). In this respect, 'the *true barrier* to capitalist production is *capital itself*' (Marx, 1981b: 358).

IV Barriers and limits

So, what is the story of capital we have developed so far? We see that capital contains within it both the tendency to grow and the tendency to erect barriers to growth. Unlike Ricardo (who saw only the side of growth, thereby grasping 'the positive essence of capital') and Sismondi (who, seeing only the barriers, had 'better grasped the limited nature of production based on capital, its negative one-sidedness'), Marx understood that capital by its very nature embraced both aspects and moved 'in contradictions which are constantly overcome but just as constantly posited' (Marx, 1973: 410–1). Indeed, he commented about capital that 'in as much as it both posits a barrier *specific* to itself, and on the other side equally drives over and beyond *every* barrier, it is the living contradiction' (Marx, 1973: 421).

Yet, the story is about more than the contradiction within capital. Critically, it is that capital *succeeds* in driving beyond all barriers and that its development occurs through this very process. This contradiction within capital, in short, is an essential part of its movement, impulse and activity.[6] Thus, the creation of the specifically capitalist mode of production, the growing place of fixed capital, the growth of large firms, increasing centralization of capital, development of new needs and of the world market – all these critical developments emerge as the result of capital's effort to transcend its barriers, to negate its negation. Even crises are 'not permanent' and are part of this process of development:

> Capitalist production, on the one hand, has this driving force; on the other hand, it only tolerates production commensurate with the profitable employment of existing capital. Hence crises arise, which simultaneously drive it onward and beyond [its own limits] and force it to put on seven-league boots, in order to reach a development of the productive forces which could only be achieved very slowly within its own limits (Marx, 1968: 497n; 1971: 122).

To describe capital's motion as the result of this impulse to drive 'over and beyond *every* barrier' is, of course, to suggest an endless, limitless process, an *infinite* process. Given what we know about Marx, though, how can we possibly present this as his story of capital? Capitalism as infinite? Yet, this is not at all a misreading. It was not accidental that Marx used these terms, distinguishing clearly between barriers, on the one hand, and limits and boundaries, on the other. The meaning of statements such as 'every limit appears as a barrier to be overcome' and 'every boundary [*Grenze*] is and has to be a barrier [*Schranke*] for it' is perfectly clear once one grasps the distinction between Barrier and Limit in Hegel's *Science of Logic* (Marx, 1973: 408, 334).[7]

This is not the place for an extended discussion of the relation of Marx to Hegel.[8] However, this particular point needs to be stressed here: for

Hegel, for something to be finite, it must be incapable of surpassing a particular barrier. One barrier must, in fact, be its Limit. That which has a Boundary or Limit is finite and thus must perish.[9] In contrast to Limit, the concept of Barrier by definition *can* be negated: 'by the very fact that something has been determined as barrier, it has already been surpassed' (Hegel, 1961, I: 146). Here, too, the surpassing of barriers is the way in which a thing develops: 'the plant passes over the barrier of existing as seed, and over the barrier of existing as blossom, fruit or leaf' (Hegel, 1961, I: 147).

It is obvious that Marx repeatedly uses the term, barrier, in its Hegelian sense. For example, having described the development of the specifically capitalist mode of production, he noted in *Capital* (in remarks cited partially above) that 'this mode of production acquires an elasticity, a capacity to grow by leaps and bounds, which comes up against no barriers but those presented by the availability of raw materials and the extent of sales outlets' (Marx, 1977: 579). Yet, it was very clear that Marx did not view those barriers as limits. He immediately proceeded to discuss the way in which machinery (for example, the cotton gin) increased the supply of raw materials and the part played by large-scale industry in the conquest of foreign markets and the transformation of foreign countries into suppliers of raw materials: 'a new and international division of labour springs up, one suited to the requirements of the main industrial countries...' (Marx, 1977: 579–80).

Thus, here again, we see not a limit but mere barriers – the suggestion of an infinite process, one corresponding to the concepts in Hegel's *Logic*. Underlying Marx's discussion of Growth–Barrier–Growth is Hegel's exploration of the concepts of Ought and Barrier. For Hegel, that which drives beyond Barrier is Ought, and it was in the course of exploring the Ought–Barrier relationship that he demonstrated the manner in which the concept of the Finite passed into that of Infinity: 'The finite in perishing has not perished; so far it has only become another finite, which, however, in turn perishes in the sense of passing over into another finite, and so on, perhaps ad infinitum' (Hegel, 1961, I: 149).

In conclusion, as long as we talk about mere barriers to capital, we *are* discussing an infinite process. Obviously, then, something very critical is missing from the story we've told here of capital. Marx did not think of capitalism as an endless, infinite system. *So, what is the Limit that makes capital finite?* It's not that capital gets tired or senile, unable at a certain point to drive beyond those barriers any more.[10] Rather, the answer that Marx and Frederick Engels offered throughout their lives was consistent – the working class is capital's Limit. What capital produces, they argued, 'above all, is its own grave-diggers. Its fall and the victory of the proletariat are equally inevitable' (Marx and Engels, 1848: 496). And, that is the same story Marx tells in *Capital*. With the development of the specifically capitalist mode of production, capital is more and more centralized, 'the international character of the capitalist regime' increases, and the mass of misery and exploitation grows, but 'there also grows the revolt of the working class, a class constantly increasing in numbers, and trained, united and organized by the very mechanism of the capitalist process of production'. And, the result of this revolt? 'The knell of capitalist private property sounds. The expropriators are expropriated' (Marx, 1977: 929). The conclusion: workers end capital's story.

2
Why Beyond *Capital*?

> Orthodox Marxism ... does not imply the uncritical acceptance
> of the results of Marx's investigations. It is not the 'belief' in
> this or that thesis, nor the exegesis of a 'sacred' book. On the
> contrary, orthodoxy refers exclusively to method.
>
> Georg Lukács (1972: 1)

Consider that picture of capitalism presented in the last chapter. Based upon historical experience, is there any reason to reject Marx's analysis of the nature of capital? Should we scuttle the idea that capital rests upon the exploitation of workers, that it has an insatiable appetite for surplus labour, that it accordingly searches constantly for ways to extend and intensify the workday, to drive down real wages, to increase productivity? What in the developments of world capitalism in the last two centuries would lead us to think that capital is any different?

Do we think, for example, that Marx's statement that capital 'takes no account of the health and the length of life of the worker, unless society forces it to do so' no longer holds? The case of working conditions and shortened work lives in special economic zones and *maquiladoras* suggests that what Marx wrote is as true as ever. And, is capital's treatment of the natural environment any different? Marx proposed that 'the entire spirit of capitalist production, which is oriented towards the most immediate monetary profit' is contrary to 'the whole gamut of permanent conditions of life required by the chain of human generations' and that all progress in capitalist agriculture in 'increasing the fertility of the soil for a given time is a progress towards ruining the more long-lasting sources of that fertility' (Marx, 1981b: 754n). Was he wrong? Our modern experience with chemical pesticides and fertilizers reinforces Marx's perspective on capitalism and nature, on what capitalist production does to 'the original sources of all wealth – the soil and the worker' (Marx, 1977: 638) unless society forces it to do otherwise.

Much, of course, has changed since Marx wrote *Capital*. But, not the essential nature of capital. The apparent victory of capitalism over its putative alternative, unreal socialism, does not in itself challenge the theory of *Capital*. Modern celebrants of capital can find in Marx an unsurpassed understanding of its dynamic, rooted in that self-valorization that serves as motive and purpose of capitalist production. That capital drives beyond 'all traditional, confined, complacent, encrusted satisfactions of present needs, and reproductions of old ways of life', that it constantly revolutionizes the process of production as well as the old ways of life, 'tearing down all the barriers which hem in the development of the forces of production, the expansion of needs, the all-sided development of production, and the exploitation and exchange of natural and mental forces' – all this, as we've seen, was central to Marx's conception of production founded upon capital. Thus, if capital today compels nations to adopt capitalist forms of production, creates a world after its own image and indeed shows once again that all that is solid (including that made by men of steel) melts into air, this in itself cannot be seen as a refutation of Marx.

Nor, further, in these days of the increasing intensity of capitalist competition, growing unemployment and devaluation of capital around the world, can we ignore the contradictory character of capitalist reproduction that Marx stressed – his reminder that capital's tendency towards the absolute development of productive forces occurs only in 'the first act' and that the realization of surplus value produced requires a 'second act' in which commodities must be sold 'within the framework of antagonistic conditions of distribution' marked by capitalist relations of production.

Marx's *Capital*, thus, appears to have been rather successful in revealing 'the economic law of motion of modern society' (1977: 92). And, yet, there is that so-obvious caveat – that despite Marx's assurance that capitalism was doomed, despite his assertion that it would come to an end with the revolt of the working class, capital is still with us and shows no sign of taking its early departure. The 'knell' has not sounded for capitalism, and the expropriators have not been expropriated. Here, indeed, is the dilemma which Michael Burawoy (1989: 51) articulated: 'two anomalies confront Marxism as its refutation: the durability of capitalism and the passivity of its working class.'[1]

For those on the Right, the combination of the continued existence of capitalism and the failure of 'actually existing socialism' to realize

Marx's dream of a society of free and associated workers is proof enough of the error of Marxism. Yet, some on the Left have similarly concluded that capitalism's continued existence logically demonstrates that capitalism is 'optimal for the further development of productive power' (Cohen, 1978: 175). Others on the Left have responded to the absence of that revolt of the working class by concluding that Marx had it all wrong – that his privileging of workers as the subjects of social change constituted the sins of class reductionism and essentialism. For these 'post-Marxists', the multiplicity of modern democratic struggles counts as a critique of Marx's theory.

Disdain for Marxism

Criticism of Marxism is not new. 'Among intellectuals it has gradually become fashionable to greet any profession of faith in Marxism with ironical disdain', wrote Lukács (1972: 1) in 1919. Yet, this epoch has had its own reasons for ironical disdain. For some, it's been a time to say a wistful 'Goodbye to the Proletariat'. The very development of automation and computerization within capitalism is removing the presupposed agent of social change. The 'traditional working class', according to Andre Gorz, is now no more than 'a privileged minority':

> The majority of the population now belong to the postindustrial neo-proletariat which, with no job security or definite class identity, fills the area of probationary, contracted, casual, temporary and part-time employment. In the not-too-distant future, jobs such as these *will* be largely eliminated by automation (Gorz, 1982: 69).

How, indeed, can a disappearing working class perform its assigned role? But, then, for some, that 'privileged' role of the working class was *always a myth*, anyway. One of 'the least tenable postulates of the Marxist tradition', Chantal Mouffe (1983: 8–9) informs us, this focus on the unique position of workers in the struggle for socialism amounts to little more than a reduction of all that matters to the economic sphere. Even Gramsci's seemingly non-reductionist focus on the hegemonic position of the working class in a *multi-faceted* struggle for socialism must be jettisoned, it appears, if we are to go beyond economism.

Society is more complex now (or, indeed, always has been). Accordingly, rather than class division, pluralistic social grievance stands as the basis for construction of a new society. Indeed, Jean Cohen proposes that for a large body of neo-Marxist intellectuals, 'the dogma of the industrial proletariat as *the* revolutionary class and the one and only revolutionary subject has, accordingly, been more or less abandoned'. In its place, the 'new social movements', movements organized around ecology and environmental concerns, feminism and human rights, peace, democratic and decentralized forms of economic and social interaction have become either favoured or equal contenders as the source of revolutionary subjects:

> Social movements are proliferating in nearly every sector of society. New social actors are addressing an entirely original range of issues and challenging the cultural model (progress and growth) and hierarchical structures of contemporary Western society (Cohen, 1982: 1, xi).

And, further, these new social movements are not movements of the working class. Rather, their principal social base, argues Claus Offe (1985: 828–33), is the 'new middle class' (especially those in human service professions and the public sector) – along with elements of the old middle class and those peripheral to the labour market (students, unemployed, housewives), Nor is it a class politics: 'New middle class politics … is typically a politics *of* class but not *on behalf of* a class.' In short, the demands of the new social movements tend to be 'highly class-unspecific' and universalistic.

So, where does this leave Marxism, that dated expression of faith in the working class? Apparently, on the outside looking in. 'Even the socialist portions of most democratic political movements', Samuel Bowles and Herbert Gintis (1986: 10) report,

> now treat Marxism with a respect due to its past achievements, while remaining mindful of its limited relevance to the concerns of feminists, environmentalists, national minorities, or even rank-and-file workers. Just as frequently, these movements regard Marxism with hostile indifference.

Nor is this current disdain seen to be unwarranted. Bowles and Gintis call attention to a 'Marxian tendency to treat distinct aspects of social life as theoretically indistinguishable.' And, thus, the result is predictable; it is to make anything other than the class struggle between capitalist and worker invisible:

> The result is to force the most diverse forms of domination – imperialism, violence against women, state despotism, racism,

religious intolerance, oppression of homosexuals, and more – either into obscurity or into the mold of class analysis (Bowles and Gintis, 1986: 19).

Now, add to all of this the distinct aroma that Marxism took on in the countries of 'actually existing socialism'. There, crystallized as official state ideology, Marxism became anathema to many who strove for the human liberation that Marx sought. Is it any wonder, then, that 'among intellectuals it has gradually become fashionable to greet any profession of faith in Marxism with ironical disdain'?

So, is it time to say 'goodbye' not only to the working class but to Marxism as well? *Let us be frank. Not only the absence of socialist revolution and the continued hegemony of capital over workers in advanced capitalist countries, but also the theoretical silence (and practical irrelevance) with respect to struggles for emancipation, struggles of women against patriarchy in all its manifestations, struggles over the quality of life and cultural identity – all these point to a theory not entirely successful.*

II Where did the theory go wrong?

'The facts' meant something to Marx. Theory attempts to understand things not apparent on the surface, to find the inner connections. That, he noted, is a task of science – 'to reduce the visible and merely apparent movement to the actual inner movement' (Marx, 1981b: 428). And, the point of all this is to understand the real world – in order to change it. Thus, for Marx, not only is the starting point for theory the real and concrete (that is, actually existing society), but the test of the theory is how well it grasps that concrete totality, how well it reproduces that concrete in the mind through a scrupulously logical process (Marx, 1973: 100–2):

> As regards CHAPTER IV, it was a hard job finding *things themselves*, i.e., their *interconnection*. But with that once behind me, along came one BLUE BOOK after another just as I was composing the final *version*, and I was delighted to find my theoretical conclusions fully confirmed by the FACTS.[2]

From this perspective, the theory in its current state should be acknowledged as inadequate precisely because it is *not* fully confirmed by the facts. But, does this mean Marx's theory or Marxism? The two are not necessarily the same. Could it be that the imperative that theory must serve particular practice was responsible for a deformation of Marx's original theory in the twentieth century?

As Marx knew well, the fate of *any* theory at the hands of its disciples is not necessarily a happy one. The master, for whom 'the science was not something received, but something in the process of becoming', may 'fall into one or another apparent inconsistency through some sort of accommodation' (Marx, 1841: 84). These inconsistencies and contradictions themselves may testify to the richness of the living material from which the theory itself was developed. Nevertheless, as he noted in relation to Ricardo's disciples, the very effort of disciples to *resolve* these inconsistencies and unresolved contradictions can begin the process of disintegration of that theory.

Disintegration begins when the disciples are driven to 'explain away' the 'often paradoxical relationship of this theory to reality'; it begins when, by 'crass empiricism', 'phrases in a scholastic way' and 'cunning argument', they attempt to demonstrate that the theory is still correct (despite 'the facts'). In short, the disintegration of the theory begins when the point of departure is 'no longer reality, but the new theoretical form in which the master had sublimated it' (Marx, n.d.: 87; 1971: 84–5).

This suggests that the answer may be to return to the original, unadulterated Marx and to search for those inconsistencies, accommodations and unresolved contradictions behind the 'often paradoxical relationship of this theory to reality'. Perhaps the answer is a simple one – that the elements and problems that many would identify as characteristic of Actually Existing Marxism reflect the disintegration of Marx's theory at the hands of his disciples.

And, yet, some critics have argued that this would let Marx off far too easily. The kernel of the problems, they propose, can be traced to Marx himself. 'Marx's theory of the proletariat,' argues Andre Gorz (1982: 16), 'is not based upon either empirical observation of class conflict or practical involvement in proletarian struggle ... On the contrary, only a knowledge of this [its class] mission will make it possible to discover the true being of the proletarians.' Thus, in Gorz's view, the commitment to the working class for Marx (as for subsequent revolutionaries) is not *'because* the proletariat acts, thinks and feels in a revolutionary way but because it *is* in itself revolutionary by destination, which is to say: it *has to be* revolutionary; it must "become what it is"' (Gorz, 1982: 20). In short, precisely because the philosophical stance of the Young Marx rather than 'the facts' is the original source of this central concept of Marxism, 'the various theoretical and political positions among marxists can only find legitimation in fidelity to the dogma. Orthodoxy, dogmatism and religiosity are not therefore accidental features of marxism' (Gorz, 1982: 21).

For others, however, the problems have their source not in the Young Marx but in the work of the *later* Marx, the 'scientist'. Cornelius Castoriadis, for example, has proposed that class struggle is outside the bounds of *Capital* (and, thus, Marx). Arguing that Marx presents in *Capital* only capital's side of the struggle within production ('letting the worker appear as a purely passive object of this activity'), Castoriadis situates the problem in Marx's treatment of labour-power as a commodity. Since neither the use-value nor the exchange-value of this particular commodity is determinate, he declares, this 'cornerstone' of Marxian science is inherently faulty. Thus, Castoriadis concludes (in breaking with Marxism), the whole theory of *Capital*, the whole structure, is 'built on sand' (Castoriadis, 1976–7: 33, 33n; 1975: 144–5).[3]

If class struggle, however, was eliminated from *Capital*, something else replaced it – objective laws. Thus, Castoriadis (1976–7: 14) proposed:

> The theory of the capitalist economy is elaborated through the discovery of the system's objective laws, which function unbeknownst to those concerned. This conception increasingly dominates and shapes Marx's research to the exclusion of the conception of the class struggle between the capitalists and the proletariat.

A quite similar argument was made by E.P. Thompson in his *Poverty of Theory*. *Capital*, according to Thompson, is 'a study of the logic of capital, not of capitalism, and the social and political dimensions of the history, the wrath and the understanding of the class struggle arise from a region independent of the closed system of economic logic' (Thompson, 1978: 65). And, the reason is that, in the course of his critique of political economy, Marx fell into a *trap*: 'the trap baited by "Political Economy." Or, more accurately, he had been sucked into a theoretical whirlpool' (Thompson, 1978: 59).

What occurred, Thompson proposes, was that Marx's critique of political economy became a critique which remained 'within the same premises' as political economy itself: 'The postulates ceased to be the self-interest of man and became the logic and forms of capital, to which men were subordinated ... But what we have at the end, is not the overthrow of "Political Economy" but *another* "Political Economy." ' *Capital*, thus, 'was not an exercise of a different order to that of mature bourgeois Political Economy, but a total confrontation *within* that order' (Thompson, 1978: 60, 65).

None of this, though, could be said about the Young Marx. For him, as Thompson (1978: 60) notes, Political Economy appeared as 'ideology, or, worse, apologetics. He entered within it in order to overthrow it.' The Young Marx, indeed, *was* unambiguous. Political economy, he argued in 1844, proceeded in its analysis from private property, wealth and capital and considered the worker only from the perspective of capital. It looked at the proletarian only as worker, only as working animal to enrich capital; it did 'not consider him when he is not working, as a human being' (Marx, 1844c: 241–2). For political economy, the worker's need was the barest level of subsistence and the most abstract mechanical movement. It was merely the need:

> to maintain *him whilst he is working* and insofar as may be necessary to prevent the *race of labourers* from [dying] out. The wages of labour have thus exactly the same significance as the *maintenance* and *servicing* of any other productive instrument ... (Marx, 1844c: 284, 308).

Thus, denying the worker as human being – indeed, failing to grasp the denial of the human being inherent in the wage-labour relation, bourgeois political economy could not understand the place of the proletariat within capitalism. The alienation and estrangement in labour performed for capital, the indignation to which the proletariat was necessarily driven by the contradiction between its self and its condition of life, the position of wage-labourer as the negative and destructive side within the whole – all this was a closed book to political economy (Marx, 1844c: 270–82; Marx and Engels, 1845: 33–7). But, 'let us now rise above the level of political economy', the Young Marx (1844c: 241) proposed.

How ironic, then, that the mature Marx has been accused of *failing* to transcend political economy. But, is it indeed ironic? Perhaps, as Russell Jacoby (1975: 45) proposed, 'the more one studies political economy the more one falls prey to it'. Thus, the dilemma: 'The hope of the critique of political economy is that it is more than political economy; the danger is that it is only political economy' (Jacoby, 1975: 45).

But why do these critics see political economy as such as a danger? Perhaps because, as the Young Marx knew, political economy does not consider the worker 'as a human being' and does not, for example, 'recognise the unemployed worker, the workingman, insofar as he happens to be outside this labour relationship' (Marx, 1844c: 284). Perhaps, in short, it is (as Thompson proposes) that political economy 'defines its own field of enquiry, and selects its evidence in accordance with these definitions, and its findings are relevant within the terms of this discipline' (Thompson, 1978: 149). In remaining within the premises of political economy, then, the danger would be that Marx similarly would not recognize the worker outside the wage-labour relation:

> Political Economy, including Marx's 'anti' structure, had no terms – had deliberately, and for the purposes of its analytical science, *excluded* the terms – which become, immediately, essential if we are to comprehend societies and histories (Thompson, 1978: 164).

Thus, for Thompson, the problem originates in Marx's move from Political Economy 'to *capitalism* ... that is, the whole society, conceived as an "organic system". But the whole society comprises many activities and relations (of power, of consciousness, sexual, cultural, normative) which are not the concern of Political Economy, which have been *defined out of* Political Economy, and for which it has no terms' (Thompson, 1978: 62). And, the critical 'missing term' is 'human experience'. When we raise this point, 'at once we enter into the real silences of Marx' (Thompson, 1978: 164–5).

The problems of Actually Existing Marxism, accordingly, originate in the very silence of Marx on the question of 'human experience', on human beings as subjects; their source is the 'system of *closure*' in which all is subsumed within the circuits of capital, where capital posits itself as an 'organic system' (Thompson, 1978: 163–4, 167).

Jean Cohen makes the same essential criticism, describing 'the most serious problem of Marx's work' as 'that of the very project of the critique of political economy'. Thus, she argues:

> The theoretical reproduction of the logic of capitalism through the critique of the categories of political economy implies that the critic of political economy has inherited its most basic proposition – that the capitalist economy can be analyzed as a self-sufficient, albeit contradictory, system, with its own internal dynamics and reproductive mechanisms (Cohen, 1982: 192, 150).

In accepting this proposition, 'Marx simply reproduced the political economic reduction of political, cultural, normative, religious determinations as irrelevant or determined by the economy.' Thus, inherently excluded by this 'one single totalizing logic, the logic of a "mode of production"' is the possibility of

> other modes of domination than socioeconomic class relations, other principles of stratification in addition to class (nationality, race,

status, sex, etc.), other modes of historical creation and interaction than labor and revolutionary praxis, other sources for the motivations guiding social action, other forms of political interaction (participation) than hierarchical power relations, and other modes of contesting capitalist society than class struggles around radical needs emerging in the dialectic of labor (Cohen, 1982: 192–3).

For these critics, then, the paradoxical relationship of Marxism to reality, thus, can be traced to *Capital* – that is, to Marx's failure to rise above the level of political economy. The many silences of Marxism, the determinism and fatalism of its objective laws, the reductionism and economism – all are inherent in the very nature of Marx's theoretical project.

As will be seen in the following chapters, I think these criticisms are powerful and coherent. However, I accept neither the argument that Marx provided a 'closed system of economic logic' nor, indeed, that he was engaged simply in a critique of political economy. Further, I deny that Marxism is 'of limited relevance to the concerns of feminists, environmentalists, national minorities, or even rank-and-file workers'.

Nevertheless, I *agree* that there is a problem with Marx's *Capital* – that there is, indeed, a critical silence in it. It is a silence which permits the appearance that, for the scientist, the only subject (if there is one at all) is capital, growing, transcending all barriers, developing – until, finally, it runs out of steam and accordingly is replaced by scientists with a more efficient machine. *Capital*'s silence, I agree, is at the root of the deficiencies of Actually Existing Marxism.

III   Orthodox Marxism

So, what is to be done? There are many potential strategies. *Beyond Capital* offers what I consider to be an 'orthodox Marxist' attempt to resolve the problems described above. Let me explain, though, what I mean by 'orthodox'. It should not at all be confused with the 'fundamentalism' of the Two Whatevers ('whatever Marx said is true and whatever he didn't say is not true'). Rather, I mean orthodox in the sense that Lukács meant in the passage that opens this chapter – and that means a focus on the method and approach of Marx rather than the worship of a sacred text or holy passage.

But, I also mean orthodox in the sense that Antonio Gramsci used it. And, that is the view that Marxism must be 'sufficient unto itself': that it 'contains in itself all the fundamental elements needed to construct a total and integral conception of the world...' (Gramsci, 1971: 462). In short, my orthodoxy holds that Marxism as such does not come in pieces; it is, as Gramsci argued, 'a completely autonomous and independent structure of thought'.

What constitutes, then, this orthodox Marxist project? And, is it doomed to fail because, as Lukács (1972: 1) warned, 'all attempts to surpass or "improve" Marxism have led and must lead to over-simplification, triviality and eclecticism?' I would answer – *not if those attempts are from within that structure of thought*. Insofar as new elements within the theory are developed in a manner consistent with Marx's method (rather than merely added on), then what is produced is an integral development of Marxism. But, Marxism is not advanced by grafting onto it alien elements in some eclectic effort to salvage it; in such a case, we have a syncretic operation which produces not an improved Marxism – but Something Else.

As Lukács stressed, orthodox Marxism rejects the uncritical acceptance of everything that Marx wrote. The fact that Marx brilliantly discovered a new continent does not mean that he correctly mapped it all.[4] The premise of *Beyond Capital*, however, is that it is *possible* to get it right. This is an attempt to build upon Marx's method to demonstrate that Marxism contains in itself 'all the fundamental elements needed to construct a total and integral conception of the world'.

Here, then, is the test – whether we can demonstrate that Marxist theory does correspond to 'the facts'. Clearly, we must attempt to explain those 'two anomalies' that Burawoy identified – 'the durability of capitalism and the passivity of its working class'; however, we must also respond to the criticisms of Marx introduced earlier in this chapter – criticisms which relate not to Marx's analysis of capital but to his analysis of capital's 'other', its 'gravediggers'. The focus of *Beyond Capital* is the exploration of that other side, the side of the worker, a side inadequately developed in *Capital*.

The lack of correspondence of the theory of *Capital* to the facts is the most important reason to attempt to develop theoretically the side of the worker. However, there are two additional reasons. In their order of importance, they are (a) that Marx's own dialectical logic *requires* consideration of the side of workers and (b) that Marx intended to explore the side of workers in a book on wage-labour. We will consider these in reverse order in the following chapters.

3
The Missing Book on Wage-Labour

> Man is distinguished from all other animals by the limitless and flexible nature of his needs ... The level of the necessaries of life whose total value constitutes the value of labour-power can itself rise or fall.
>
> Marx (1977: 1068–9)

I The status of *Capital*

To understand *Capital*, it is necessary to grasp what it is *not*. We know that *Capital* was never completed. Nevertheless, the problems described in the preceding chapter cannot be blamed upon the unfinished state of *Capital*. After all, the basic contents of the latter two volumes were reasonably clear in Marx's mind before he completed his final draft of Volume I of *Capital*:

> I cannot bring myself to send anything off until I have the whole thing in front of me. **WHATEVER SHORTCOMINGS THEY MAY HAVE**, the advantage of my writings is that they are an artistic whole, and this can only be achieved through my practice of never having things printed until I have them before me *in their entirety*.[1]

So, was *Capital* that 'artistic whole'? Did it provide 'a fully elaborated system' or was it merely a fragment or torso of such a system?[2] It is undisputed that Marx *originally* intended *Capital* to be only one of six books. As he indicated in letters to Ferdinand Lasalle and Frederick Engels in 1858, his long-awaited 'Economics' was to be examined in the following books:

1. Capital
2. Landed Property

3. Wage Labour
4. State
5. International Trade
6. World Market[3]

These were not isolated references. Indeed, the conception of the work as a six-book whole can be found in the pages of the *Grundrisse*, the notebooks upon which Marx was working at the time. The first three books were to establish the 'inner totality' of circulation, setting out the three classes that he viewed as the presupposition of economic activity. Following this development of the internal structure of production, there was to be the 'concentration of the whole' in the State, the State externally in the volume on International Trade and, finally, the World Market (and crises). Only with the last of these books would the subject of capitalism be adequately investigated:

> the world market the conclusion, in which production is posited as a totality together with all its moments, but within which, at the same time, all contradictions come into play. The world market then, again, forms the presupposition of the whole as well as its substratum (Marx, 1973: 227–8, 264).[4]

But what happened to the six-book plan? It clearly remained in place in 1859 when Marx published his *Contribution to the Critique of Political Economy*. In his famous Preface to that volume, Marx began by indicating that the first three of the books would examine 'the conditions of the economic existence of the three great classes, which make up modern bourgeois society.'[5] Yet, the *Critique* itself contained only a portion of the material intended for the book on capital – the sections on Commodity and Money, which were the opening of Marx's consideration of 'Capital in General' (itself only part of the book on capital). And, as we know, all that came subsequently of the plan was *Capital*.

Most commentators have concluded, simply, that Marx changed his mind and incorporated the relevant material in *Capital*. Among those proposing this answer have been Karl Kautsky, Henryk Grossmann, the Soviet editors of the *Collected Works* of Marx and Engels, Ronald Meek and Ernest Mandel.[6] Mandel, for example, argues that Marx's original plan proved increasingly to be an obstacle to a rigorous development of the laws of motion of capitalism and therefore had to be discarded in the end. In his argument, he follows the lead of Roman Rosdolsky who proposed that, whereas the last three books were set aside for an 'eventual continuation' of the work, the second and third were absorbed into *Capital*:

> However, the basic themes of the books on landed property and wage-labor were incorporated in the manuscripts of Volumes I and III of the final work, which took shape between 1864 and 1866. In this way the six books which were originally planned were reduced to one – the *Book on Capital* (Rosdolsky, 1977: 11).

One of the strongest and best-known dissents from this view was that of Maximilien Rubel. Arguing that Marx never ever betrayed 'even the slightest intention of changing the plan of the "Economics" ', Rubel proposed that the problem was, rather, that the first book, *Capital*, simply assumed 'unforeseen dimensions' (O'Malley and Algozin, 1981: 163–4). Thus, he concluded, we have to recognize the 'fragmentary state' of Marx's 'Economics' and acknowledge that 'we do not have before us a Marxist bible of eternally codified canons' (O'Malley and Algozin, 1981: 181). For Rubel, the conviction that Marx abandoned his original six-book plan exempts Marxism's 'true believers' from taking up the problem 'where Marx was forced to abandon it' (O'Malley and Algozin, 1981: 218–19).

Even the most sympathetic reader must conclude, however, that Rubel failed to *prove* his case. Although there was no explicit disavowal of the six-book plan, there is equally no unequivocal evidence that Marx did not view *Capital* in itself as a 'completely elaborated system'. For this reason, after reviewing the competing arguments, Allen Oakley (1983: 114) proposed that the bibliographical evidence necessary to determine either Marx's intentions or whether there remained any books unwritten is simply insufficient to support a judgement in either direction.

Central to the argument in this book, nevertheless, is the conclusion that Rubel is correct. There *were* missing books. In particular, the intended book on wage-labour remained unwritten, and (as we will see) its absence is at the root of the problems in *Capital* identified in Chapter 2. More than bibliographical evidence, however, is required to demonstrate this point. If we are to make the case for a missing book on wage-labour, an *analytical* consideration of *Capital* and other works of this period is needed.

Let us begin by challenging Rosdolsky's argument, the most scholarly case for the incorporation of 'Wage-Labour' within *Capital*. While Marx testified to the inclusion of themes from Landed Property into *Capital*, no such admission is apparently available when it comes to the projected volume on wage-labour.[7] Indeed, in *Capital* (1977: 683), Marx referred explicitly to 'the special study of wage-labour'. Thus, it was only through a process of inference that Rosdolsky (1977: 22, 57) concluded that 'all the themes of the earlier book on wage-labour come into the scope of Volume I' of *Capital*. Yet, how solid was his case?

Rosdolsky's basic argument is that the discussion of the wage and various forms of the wage, which was not part of the original plan for the book on capital but which constitutes Part VI of Volume I of *Capital*, was the 'main part' of the proposed book on wage-labour. Sometime not before 1864, Rosdolsky (1977: 17, 61) suggests in his Appendix on 'The Book on Wage-Labour', Marx made the decision to bring this material into *Capital* and to abandon his original outline. Nevertheless, when discussing Marx's theory of wages, Rosdolsky proceeded to *undermine* his own argument that the material that appeared in *Capital* constituted 'all the themes' or even 'the basic themes' of the projected book on wage-labour. Considering Marx's treatment of the necessities entering into the value of labour-power as constant, Rosdolsky (1977: 286n) was quick to point out that this did not mean that the 'average quantity of necessary means of subsistence' could not grow: 'Marx would have first dealt with this case in his intended "special theory of wage-labour" if he had ever reached the point of carrying out this part of his plan.'

A rather significant admission. What *else* would Marx have dealt with 'if he had ever reached the point of carrying out this part of his plan'? To understand what was left out of *Capital*, we must begin at this very point – the necessities of workers.

II   Constant needs?

As noted in Chapter 1, underlying the value of labour-power for Marx is the labour-time necessary to produce 'a certain quantity' of the means of subsistence; that is, necessary labour (w) is based upon the worker's standard of necessity relative to productivity (U/q). Further, Marx treated the set of necessities entering into the value of labour-power as given: 'in a given country at a given period, the average amount of the means of subsistence necessary for the worker is a known *datum*' (Marx, 1977: 275). While this statement does not preclude change in that certain quantity in *other* periods, it was upon this basis that Marx proceeded to explore the production of surplus value.

As we have seen, in tracing the tendency of capital to drive up the rate of exploitation in production (s/w), Marx explored in turn variations in the workday (d) and the level of productivity (q) but left unchanged the subsistence bundle or real wage (*U*). The result has been one of confusion as to what Marx believed. For example, Joan Robinson's well-known 1942 essay proposed (Robinson, 1957: 36) that Marx could demonstrate a tendency for a falling rate of profit only 'by abandoning his argument that real wages tend to be constant.' Subsequently, Paul Samuelson (1972: 53–4), attempting to emphasize the 'logical incompatibility of these two laws' (the law of the falling rate of profit and the law of the immiseration of the working class), produced his own alternative – the 'Law of Increasing Real Wages', which he considered both a better extrapolation from Marx's theory and also a closer representation of historical experience.

But did Marx have an *argument* for constant real wages; and does this concept play any particular role in a theory of immiseration? Two central points have been ignored in discussions of Marx's view of wages: first, that Marx stressed the rising level of 'necessity' as capitalism develops; and, secondly, that what has often been regarded as Marx's argument was in fact no more than a methodologically sound working *assumption*.

Consider the first of these points. Let us be blunt. Nothing could be more alien to Marx than the belief in a fixed set of necessaries. From his earliest days (see, for example, Marx and Engels, 1846: 38–42), Marx rejected a concept of 'Abstract Man' and stressed the emergence of new human needs with the development of society. Perhaps this reflected the influence of Hegel. After all, in his *Philosophy of Right*, Hegel had stressed the tendency of human needs to multiply ad infinitum; for Hegel, man transcended animal restrictions: 'first by the multiplication of needs and means of satisfying them, and secondly by the differentiation and division of concrete need into single parts and aspects which in turn become different needs, particularized and so more abstract'. As social needs become preponderant, Hegel proposed, 'the strict natural necessity of need is obscured.' Indeed, 'to be confined to mere physical needs as such and their direct satisfaction' is the condition of savagery and unfreedom (Hegel, 1975: 127–8).

In contrast to Hegel's emphasis on the sub-division of needs, for Marx the key was human activity. Needs, he noted in the *Grundrisse*, 'develop only with the forces of production'. In the course of economic development, 'the producers change, too, in that they bring out new qualities in themselves, develop themselves in production, transform themselves, develop new powers and ideas, new modes of intercourse, new needs and new language' (Marx, 1973: 612n, 494).

Nor, Marx stressed, was the development of needs, per se, a Bad Thing. Rather, he asked, 'what is wealth other than the universality of individual needs, capacities, pleasures, productive forces, etc., created through universal exchange?' Thus, he argued (1973: 488, 527) that:

> the greater the extent to which historic needs – needs created by production itself, social needs – needs which are themselves the offspring of social production and intercourse, are posited as *necessary*, the higher the level to which real wealth has become developed. Regarded *materially*, wealth consists only in the manifold variety of needs.

From this perspective, then, Marx always *rejected* the tendency on the part of economists to treat workers' needs as naturally determined and unchanging. He specifically criticized the Physiocrats, for example, in his *Theories of Surplus Value* (Marx, n.d.: 45) for their 'mistake' in conceiving of the subsistence level 'as an unchangeable magnitude – which in their view is determined entirely by nature and not by the stage of historical development, which is itself a magnitude subject to fluctuations'.

Much earlier, however, Marx had sounded a theme concerning rising social needs which was always to remain with him. In 1844, he drew at length upon a statement by Wilhelm Schulz that noted, among other things, that 'just *because* total production rises – and in the same measure as it rises – needs, desires and claims also multiply and thus *relative* poverty can increase whilst absolute poverty diminishes.'[8] To this argument (which he later would adopt explicitly as his own), Marx responded only: 'But political economy knows the worker only as a working animal – as a beast reduced to the strictest bodily needs.' In short, political economy ignored the worker as a being in society.[9]

Simply stated, Marx's perspective that 'needs are produced just as are products' and that 'the producers change, too' is not compatible with a treatment of labour-power as a commodity with fixed technical (or physiological) input requirements (Marx, 1973: 527). Labour-power has a 'peculiar' feature compared to other commodities – its value is formed not only by physical requirements but also by a historical or social element; and this latter element, as Marx noted (1865b: 144–5), is related to 'the satisfaction of certain wants springing from the social conditions in which people are placed and reared up'.

III   The nature and growth of workers' needs

Let us consider, then, the nature of the needs of workers within the specific social conditions characteristic of capitalism. Here we will concern ourselves only with needs for use-values in a commodity-form, a restriction that will be removed in later chapters.

In the very definition of a commodity with which *Capital* begins, Marx indicates that a commodity must satisfy 'human needs of whatever kind' and that the *nature* of such wants makes no difference, 'whether they arise, for example, from the stomach or from the imagination' (Marx, 1977: 125). Thus it is not simply a physical requirement or the natural properties of an object that give it use-value. A use-value may be purely imaginary (Marx, 1973: 769). Its essence is to be found in human beings rather than in things: 'the product supplied is not useful in itself. It is the consumer who determines its utility' (Marx, 1847a: 118).

Yet those consumers who determine the utility or use-value of products (that is, determine that products *are* use-values) are themselves beings within a particular society. Rather than considering their judgements as totally subjective and emanating from an eternal human nature, Marx argued that the reference point was necessarily society itself:

> The consumer is no freer than the producer. His estimation depends upon his means and his needs. Both of these are determined by his social position, which itself depends on the whole social organisation. True, the worker who buys potatoes and the kept woman who buys lace both follow their respective estimations. But the difference in their estimations is explained by the difference in the positions which they occupy in society, and which themselves are the product of social organisation (Marx, 1847a: 118–19).

What, then, is central to the social position of workers in capitalism? Simply that they are separated from the means of production and, to obtain the use-values they need, must sell their capacity to perform labour to capitalists, the owners of those means of production. What the worker secures in this way is 'a means of subsistence, objects for the preservation of his life, the satisfaction of his needs in general, physical, social etc'. What he yields, on the other hand, is the right of disposition over his '*creative power*, like Esau his birthright for a mess of pottage' (Marx, 1973: 284, 307).

Under these circumstances, the worker's labouring activity is an external, forced labour, a means rather than an end in itself. 'Labour capacity's own labour is as alien to it,' and it necessarily appears as sacrifice and toil. As Marx noted in the *Grundrisse* (1973: 462, 470):

> Hence, just as the worker relates to the product of his labour as an alien thing, so does he relate to the combination of labour as an alien

combination, as well as to his own labour as an expression of his life, which, although it belongs to him, is alien and coerced from him, and which A. Smith, etc. therefore conceives as a *burden, sacrifice*, etc.

There is more, however, than alienated labour as such. Insofar as the wage-labourer has relinquished the right of disposition over her labour-power to a capitalist whose goal is surplus value, she must perform surplus labour in order to engage in necessary labour. Having surrendered all claim to the use-value of labour-power in order to realize its exchange-value, the wage-labourer produces a commodity in which she has no property rights. It is the property of another, an alien commodity; and that commodity, as capital, confronts her as an alien power over her.

Thus, the worker emerges not only not richer, but emerges rather poorer from the process than he entered. He 'necessarily impoverishes himself... because the creative power of his labour establishes itself as the power of capital, as an *alien power* confronting him' (Marx, 1973: 453, 307).

Under these circumstances (i.e., within this relation), every increase in the productive power of labour directly enriches those who have purchased the *right* to this power and its products; it 'enriches not the worker but rather *capital*' (Marx, 1973: 308). Thus, the very growth of capitalist production brings with it an increase in the subjective poverty, need and dependence of the worker. As Marx commented in materials originally drafted for Volume I of *Capital* (1977: 1062):

> And just as the social productive forces of labour develop in step with the capitalist mode of production, so too the heaped-up wealth confronting the worker grows apace and confronts him as *capital*, as *wealth that controls him*. The world of wealth expands and faces him as an alien world dominating him, and as it does so his subjective poverty, his need and dependence grow larger in proportion. His *deprivation* and its *plenitude* match each other exactly.

Marx here returns to themes set out much earlier in his *Economic and Philosophic Manuscripts of 1844*. There, too, he had argued that 'the worker becomes all the poorer the more wealth he produces, the more his production increases in power and size'; that the worker is 'related to the *product of his labour* as to an *alien* object'; that the worker's labour is a '*forced labour*' and 'merely a *means* to satisfy needs external to it'. And, there as well, Marx stressed the growing need for money accompanying the extension of the realm of alien products (Marx, 1844c: 271–2, 274, 306).

Thus, Marx was consistent in pointing out the alienating nature of capitalist production which itself generates needs for commodities. The worker seeks to annihilate the alien and independent object by bringing it (back) within herself, by consuming it. Only by direct possession can the object be *hers*; her need is for the object that is the possession of another (Marx, 1844c: 299–300, 314). The worker's needs (an alien compulsion to her) and alienating production (which makes labour appear to be a sacrifice and the product of labour an alien object) reciprocally interact upon each other as parts of a whole. Accordingly, the level and nature of workers' needs are not to be found in the intrinsic qualities of things. *The very expansion of capitalist production provides the foundation for the growth of workers' needs.*

But the manner in which these needs are generated, the specific mediation, is critical. And here not only the production of capital but also its circulation plays a central role. As we have seen in Chapter 1, one of the most important aspects of Marx's description of capitalism is his account of the constant striving of capital to go beyond the barriers to its growth by expanding the market, the sphere of circulation. In order to ensure the realization of surplus value, there is a constant effort by capital to discover new use-values and to create new needs:

> Hence exploration of all of nature in order to discover new, useful qualities in things; universal exchange of the products of all alien climates and lands; new (artificial) preparation of natural objects, by which they are given new use values. The exploration of the earth in all directions, to discover new things of use as well as new useful qualities of the old; such as new qualities of them as raw materials, etc; the development, hence, of the natural sciences to their highest point; likewise the discovery, creation and satisfaction of new needs arising from society itself (Marx, 1973: 409)

Although capitalists may preach the importance of thrift and moderation to workers, that is not their interest as sellers of commodities. 'To each capitalist, the total mass of all workers, with the exception of his own workers, appear not as workers, but as consumers, possessors of exchange values (wages), money, which they exchange for his commodity' (Marx, 1973: 419). And, as the seller of a commodity, what the capitalist wants from the possessor of money is not saving but spending: 'He therefore searches for means to spur them on to consumption, to give his wares new charms, to inspire them with new needs by constant chatter, etc' (Marx, 1973: 287).

As Marx had noted earlier (1844c: 306–7), the capitalist producer 'puts himself at the service of the other's most depraved fancies, plays the pimp between him and his need, excites in him morbid appetites, lies in wait for each of his weaknesses – all so that he can demand the cash for this service of love'. The effect is to create a '*new* need in another, so as to drive him to fresh sacrifice, to place him in a new dependence and to seduce him into a new mode of *enjoyment* and therefore economic ruin'.[10]

Thus, inherent in the impulse to expand capital is the attempt to expand the means of *realizing* capital, of selling commodities. The sales effort, the attempt to create new needs and a new mode of gratification, expands with the growth of capital. There is more, then, than simply alienating production which fosters the growth of workers' needs.

Yet, we cannot treat the needs of workers in isolation; their position in capitalist society is a relative position. While our concern here is with the needs of workers, the context of capitalist society requires that we explore the needs and consumption of at least one other class – capitalists.

Since Marx's main interest is in the capitalist as a personification of capital, there is only a limited account of the capitalist as consumer.[11] However, there was certainly no assumption that capitalists were motivated solely by the desire to accumulate. It is ironic that Marx's famous phrases, 'Accumulate, accumulate! That is Moses and the prophets!' and 'accumulation for the sake of accumulation', were not intended as *his* description of the capitalist's behaviour but rather as an observation on how classical political economy (the object of his critique) treated the capitalist.

In contrast, Marx emphasized that, in addition to the desire for limitless wealth (manifested in accumulation), there was *also* the 'desire for enjoyment' (Marx, 1977: 738–43). Alongside of – and in conflict with – the desire for accumulation, there was a capitalist desire for prodigality and luxury expenditure. Although it fell short of the drive to 'raise consumption to an imaginary boundlessness' of an earlier 'consumption-oriented wealth,' this passion for consumption was one of 'two souls' dwelling within the capitalist's breast (Marx, 1977: 741; 1973: 270). Of course, to the capitalist as such, 'pleasure-taking' was necessarily subordinate to capital-accumulating; and when he enjoyed his wealth, he did also 'with a guilty conscience, with frugality and thrift at the back of his mind'. To do otherwise was to negate the function of capital itself: 'The industrial capitalist becomes more or less unable to fulfill his function as soon as he personifies the enjoyment of wealth, as soon as he wants the accumulation of pleasures instead of the pleasure of accumulation' (Marx, n.d.: 274; 1844c, 316).

There is no suggestion in Marx, however, that the capitalist is restricted to a fixed set of needs; rather, his consumption requirements tend to rise with the growth of capital: 'this expenditure nevertheless grows with his accumulation, without the one necessarily restricting the other' (Marx, 1977: 741).[12] And here we have an additional reason for the growth of workers' needs. There is a definite relationship between the perception of capitalist consumption and the development of workers' needs which Marx (1849: 216) vividly identified in *Wage Labour and Capital*:

> A house may be large or small; as long as the surrounding houses are equally small it satisfies all social demands for a dwelling. But let a palace arise beside the little house, and it shrinks from a little house to a hut. The little house shows now that its owner has only very slight or no demands to make; and however high it may shoot up in the course of civilisation, if the neighbouring palace grows to an equal or even greater extent, the occupant of the relatively small house will feel more and more uncomfortable, dissatisfied and cramped within its four walls.

Thus, again, it is not the intrinsic properties of an object that determine whether it meets social needs; only within society can the judgement be made. 'Our desires and pleasures spring from society; we measure them, therefore, by society and not by the objects which serve for their satisfaction. Because they are of a social nature, they are of a relative nature' (Marx, 1849: 216).[13] *Keeping up with the Joneses)*

Capitalist consumption (the palace in the parable) thus has the effect of setting social standards for workers. Even if wages were to rise, Marx (echoing Schultz) argued that the rising social standard would limit any gain in satisfaction: *look this up*

> The rapid growth of productive capital brings about an equally rapid growth of wealth, luxury, social wants, social enjoyments. Thus, although the enjoyments of workers have risen, the social satisfaction that they give has fallen in comparison with the increased enjoyments of the capitalist, which are inaccessible to the worker, in comparison with the state of development of society in general (Marx, 1849: 216).

Alienating production, the sales effort, the growth of capitalist consumption with accumulation – the entire course of development of capitalist society involves the creation of new needs for workers. Workers' needs expand as a function of the growth of capital. As Marx noted in the *Grundrisse*, these are 'historic needs – needs created by production itself, social needs – needs which are themselves the offspring of social production and intercourse'. With capitalist development what previously appeared as a luxury now becomes necessary: 'the transformation of what was previously superfluous into what is necessary, as a historically created necessity – is the tendency of capital'.

Thus, the old standards of necessity and luxury are replaced by *new* standards:

> *Luxury* is the opposite of the *naturally necessary*. Necessary needs are those of the individual himself reduced to a natural subject. The development of industry suspends this natural necessity as well as this former luxury – in bourgeois society, it is true, it does so only *in antithetical form*, in that it itself only posits another specific social standard as necessary, opposite luxury (Marx, 1973: 527–8).

In short, capitalism turns what had been the limits of earlier modes of production into mere barriers to be transcended. Capital drives beyond 'all traditional, confined, complacent, encrusted satisfactions of present needs, and reproductions of old ways of life'. It constantly revolutionizes these old ways of life, 'tearing down all the barriers which hem in the development of the forces of production, the expansion of needs, the all-sided development of production, and the exploitation and exchange of natural and mental forces'. And, this process of going-beyond the existing standard of needs plays a part in producing a new social being:

> the discovery, creation and satisfaction of new needs arising from society itself; the cultivation of all the qualities of the social human being, production of the same in a form as rich as possible in needs, because rich in qualities and relations – production of this being as the most total and universal possible social product, for in order to take gratification in a many-sided way, he must be capable of many pleasures, hence cultured to a high degree – is likewise a condition of production founded on capital (Marx, 1973: 409–10).

Marx saw this development of real wealth (regarded *materially*), the development of the many-needed social being, as part of the historic role of capital. Further, just as capital fosters the emergence of a new social being rich in needs, it also produces a being rich in labouring potential who is no longer the bearer of one specialized social function – 'the totally developed individual, for whom the different social functions are different modes of activity he takes up in turn' (Marx, 1977: 618).

Nevertheless, this universal tendency of capital to develop productive forces faces barriers inherent to capital; it is restricted by the social relations of production of capital. This new social being requiring many-sided gratification emerges in a particular social situation: her new needs create a new dependence and require fresh sacrifices.

Assume, for example, that the needs of workers were indeed constant. In that case, the development of social productivity would lead to a reduction in necessary labour and to the possibility of the emergence of 'free time'. The growing gap between total labour-time (d) and necessary labour-time (w) would point toward 'the realm of freedom,' for which the shortening of the workday is a prerequisite, where the development of human energy can become 'an end in itself' (Marx, 1981b: 958–9). The possibility of labour for itself, without external compulsion, would be manifest.

In contrast, the constant generation of new needs for commodities means that each new need becomes a new requirement to work, adds a new burden. *Each new need becomes a new link in the golden chain that secures workers to capital.* The creation of new needs for workers, this side of the relation of capital and wage-labour, Marx concluded, 'is an essential civilizing moment, and on which the historic justification, but *also the contemporary power of capital rests*' (Marx, 1973: 287; emphasis added).

IV   Necessary needs and social needs

Marx's comment about 'the contemporary power of capital' is extremely important – not only because of its insight but also because this entire discussion (and, indeed, this side of the relation of capital and wage-labour) is missing from *Capital*. Much of it, we see, comes from the *Grundrisse* upon which Marx was working at the time of the formulation of his six-book plan. How, then, does his argument about growing needs fit in with his discussion in *Capital*?

It would be wrong to identify these growing social needs (on which 'the contemporary power of capital rests') directly with those that form the standard of necessity underlying the value of labour-power. Rather, there are *three* levels of workers' needs for articles of consumption that Marx articulates at various points:

A. *Physiological needs.* This is the set of needs for use-values required to produce the worker as a natural subject. It represents the 'physical minimum', the lower limit, and is 'formed by the value of the physically indispensable means of subsistence' (Marx, 1977: 276–7).

B. *Necessary needs*. This is the level of needs which is rendered necessary by habit and custom. It includes the use-values that are 'habitually required' and normally enter into the consumption of workers. This is the level of needs that underlies the concept of the value of labour-power in *Capital* (Marx, 1977: 655).

C. *Social needs*. This is the level of needs of the worker as a socially developed human being at a given point; it constitutes the *upper* limit in needs for use-values in a commodity-form.

Now, both of the first two categories of need are familiar enough. But, what permits us to speak specifically of this third category, social needs? For, it is certainly not a familiar (or apparent) category.

Consider the capitalist structure of need – a concept proposed by Agnes Heller (although in a faulty manner). Reflecting capitalist relations of production, the capitalist structure of needs is defined by the need of capital, on the one hand, and the need of wage-labourers, on the other; and, it is characteristic that the need of the former – the need for valorisation, the need for surplus value – leads to the *non-realization* of the needs of workers.[14]

Thus, Marx continually points to the inability of workers to realize their needs, to the restriction of the consuming power of workers by capital:

The consumption capacity of the workers is restricted partly by the laws governing wages and partly by the fact that they are employed only as long as they can be employed at a profit for the capitalist class.

Since capital's purpose is not the satisfaction of needs but the production of profit, ... there must be a constant tension between the restricted dimensions of consumption on the capitalist basis, and a production that is constantly striving to overcome these immanent barriers (Marx, 1981b: 615, 365).

There is, in short, 'a lack of demand for those very goods that the mass of the people are short of'. Production is determined by a 'certain rate of profit' and not by 'the proportion between production and social needs, the needs of socially developed human beings'. Capitalist production is set 'not at the point where needs are satisfied, but rather where the production and realization of profit impose this' (Marx, 1981b: 367; 1968: 527).

Thus, without question, it was inherent in the very nature of capitalism for Marx that there are needs which are *not* satisfied, needs whose realization is not customary – that is, needs which exceed the level of necessary needs. This is, in fact, the identification of a critical failing in capitalism – the existence of capitalist limitations on the satisfaction of needs. The standard of necessity would rise, Marx noted, if freed from: 'its capitalist limit and expanded to the scale of consumption that is both permitted by the existing social productivity...and required for the full development of individuality' (Marx, 1981b: 1015–16).

There is a level, then, of needs which is *hidden* – needs which conform to the requirements of 'socially developed human beings', needs whose realization is required for 'the full development of individuality'. It is a level of needs not manifest on the surface at any given point. Noting that it *appears* that at a given point there is 'a certain quantitatively defined social need on the demand side, which requires for its fulfilment a definite quantity of an article on the market', Marx emphasized that behind this level of needs there was a hidden level of need: 'Its fixed character is mere illusion. If means of subsistence were cheaper or money-wages higher, the workers would buy more of them, and a greater "social need" would appear...'.

There is, thus, a critical difference, a *gap*, between the needs for commodities in the market at a given point and: 'the *genuine social need*... the difference between the quantity of commodities that is demanded and the quantity that would be demanded at other money prices or with the buyers being in different financial and living conditions' (Marx, 1981b: 289–90).

Hidden from the surface of society, these social needs are nevertheless part of the very nature of those workers: 'the need of a thing is the most evident, irrefutable proof that the thing belongs to *my* essence, that its being is for me' (Marx, 1844b: 213). They are not separate from the worker: 'if I am determined, forced, by my needs, it is only my own nature, this totality of needs and drives, which exert a force upon me' (Marx, 1973: 245).

Not to satisfy those social needs, then, is a denial of self. It is to produce dissatisfaction – 'so long as the need of man is not satisfied, he is in *conflict* with his needs, hence with himself' (Marx, 1879–80: 191). *This gap between social needs (SN) and necessary needs (NN), then, is a measure of the misery of the worker, a measure of his deprivation and poverty; and we can define 'the degree of immiseration' as the relation (SN − NN)/NN.*

This is not a gap, however, between a customary standard of life and an infinite level of wants. Social needs at any given point are finite. 'Use value in itself does not have the boundlessness of value as such. Given objects can be consumed as objects of need only up to a certain level'

(Marx, 1973: 405). There is a *definite* quantity of commodities that would be 'demanded at other money prices or with the buyers being in different financial and living conditions'.

This gap, however, is 'very different for different commodities' (Marx, 1981b: 290). Why? Because workers *rank* their needs, because at any given point there exists a 'hierarchy' of needs:

> Since man stamps certain things of the external world ... as '*goods*', he comes by and by to compare these 'goods' with one another and, corresponding to the hierarchy of his needs, to bring [them] into a certain rank-ordering ...

> Since the commodity is purchased by the buyer, not because it has value, but because it is 'use-value' and is used for determinate purposes, it is completely self-evident, 1. that use-values are 'assessed', i.e., their *quality* is investigated ...; 2. that if different sorts of commodities can be substituted for one another in the same useful employment, this or that is given preference etc., etc. (Marx, 1879–80: 195, 202).

The level of real wages (the cost of means of subsistence and the level of money-wages) and the worker's hierarchy of needs, then, determine at any given point those needs which will be satisfied normally (*NN*) – and those which are *not*. As a consumer, the worker's 'judgement depends on his means and his needs'.

The higher the real wage ('if means of subsistence were cheaper or money-wages higher'), the more that workers 'can extend the circle of their enjoyments, make additions to their consumption fund of clothes, furniture, etc., and lay by a small reserve fund of money' (Marx, 1977: 769). Previously 'latent needs' can be satisfied – both those 'necessities' which are now accessible in increased quantities and also 'luxuries' previously beyond the worker's reach (Marx, 1968: 553, 558; 1971: 220).[15] Increased real wages permit more social needs to be fulfilled:

> as a result of rising wages the demand of the workers for necessary means of subsistence will grow. Their demand for luxury articles will increase to a smaller degree, or else a demand will arise for articles that previously did not enter the area of their consumption (Marx, 1981a: 414).

Thus, every increase in wages means a reduction in the degree of immiseration – *as long as social needs remain constant*. We can observe

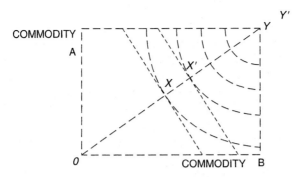

Figure 3.1   The degree of immiseration

this in Figure 3.1 in which social needs are represented as the 'bliss point' (Y) on an indifference map – to which indifference curves are concave. If 'means of subsistence were cheaper, or money wages higher,' new bundles of use-values would be purchased and the gap between necessary needs and social needs would decline. The reduction in the degree of immiseration occurs with the shift from OY/OX to OY/OX'.

Yet, as we have seen, social needs are *not* constant. Their increase is inherent in the very growth of capitalist production. Thus, the bliss point itself tends to move outward (changing, in its course, slopes of indifference curves). In Figure 3.1, an increase of social needs to Y' (along with the increase in real wages to X') demonstrates the *compatibility of increasing immiseration and growing real wages*.[16] And, of course, this is exactly what Marx had argued:

> The rapid growth of productive capital brings about an equally rapid growth of wealth, luxury, social wants, social enjoyments. Thus, although the enjoyments of workers have risen, the social satisfaction that they give has fallen in comparison with the increased enjoyments of the capitalist, which are inaccessible to the worker, in comparison with the state of development of society in general (Marx, 1849: 216).

Thus, capitalism constantly produces new unsatisfied needs. But, what is the place of those unsatisfied needs? Social needs, those essential but hidden requirements, are not mere wishes in the heads of workers. They are a real moment of economic life insofar as they pre-exist purposeful activity on the part of workers to posit those social needs as necessary, that is, insofar as they determine the actions of wage-labourers.

The existence of unfulfilled social needs underlies the worker's need for more money, her need for a higher wage.

We can now situate the necessary needs that underlie the value of labour-power. They depend 'not only on physical needs but also on historically developed social needs, which become second nature' (Marx, 1981b: 999). And, those necessary needs can move upward or downward: 'the level of the necessaries of life whose total value constitutes the value of labour-power can itself rise or fall' (Marx, 1977: 1068–9). What determines that movement? Struggle:

> The fixation of its actual degree [that of profit] is only settled by the continuous struggle between capital and labour, the capitalist constantly tending to reduce wages to their physical minimum and to extend the working day to its physical maximum, while the working man constantly presses in the opposite direction (Marx, 1865b: 146).

In short, to satisfy those growing social needs constantly generated by capital requires struggle in the 'opposite direction' to capitalists. There is, however, no discussion in *Capital* about the struggle for higher wages – and, there *cannot* be because *Capital* assumes the standard of necessity given, i.e., that 'in a given country at a given period, the average amount of the means of subsistence necessary for the worker is a known *datum*'.

V   The critical assumption

Whenever Marx stressed that the value of labour-power contained a historical and social element and depended on historically developed social needs, he was *also* quick to point out that:

> The quantity of the means of subsistence required is given at any particular epoch in any particular society, and can therefore be treated as a constant magnitude (Marx, 1977: 275, 655).

But, why make such an important assumption?

Let us note what such an assumption permits. As we saw in Chapter 1, assuming a given subsistence bundle (U) is critical to determining necessary labour (w) and, thus, the performance of surplus labour (s). The conception that labour-power, as a commodity, has a value different from the value which that labour-power creates allows us to locate the origin of surplus value in production. Thus, despite his criticisms of the Physiocrats, Marx praised them as 'the true fathers of modern political economy' for their ground-breaking work in the analysis of capital. By placing the 'minimum of wages', 'the equivalent of the necessary means of subsistence', as the pivotal point in their theory, 'the Physiocrats transferred the inquiry into the origin of surplus-value from the sphere of circulation into the sphere of direct production, and thereby laid the foundation for the analysis of capitalist production':

> Therefore the foundation of modern political economy, whose business is the analysis of capitalist production, is the conception of the *value of labour-power* as something fixed, as a given magnitude – as indeed it is in practice in each particular case (Marx, n.d.: 44–5).[17]

With this starting point, the Physiocrats were able to formulate the concept of surplus value and to identify a productive worker as one producing surplus value – even though they identified this as a surplus of use-values originating only in agriculture. For this understanding, all that was necessary was the concept of the 'minimum of wages', the '*strict necessaire*', for a given period. If the Physiocrats 'made the mistake of conceiving this *minimum* as an unchangeable magnitude', Marx (n.d.: 45) noted that 'this in no way affects the abstract correctness of their conclusions'. In short, the Physiocrats developed a central concept in political economy, that of the subsistence wage; and, in this respect, Adam Smith followed their lead, 'like all economists worth speaking of' (Marx, n.d.: 44, 68, 296).

For the analysis of capital, therefore, it is easy to understand why Marx made this critical assumption of a given subsistence level – and also why, in contrast to the Physiocrats, he stressed that this referred to a given period, a given time, a given epoch. This was not an unusual practice for Marx – assuming a factor constant for the moment for the purpose of analysis was a method he employed throughout *Capital*. (His discussion of the rate of profit is one of the clearest examples.) Indeed, in his consideration of the magnitude of the value of labour-power in Volume I of *Capital*, he noted explicitly:

> A large number of combinations are possible here. Any two of the factors may vary and the third remain constant, or all three may vary at once ... The effect of every possible combination may be found by treating each factor in turn as variable, and the other two constant for the time being (Marx, 1977: 664).

As we have seen, however, Marx did *not* consider 'every possible combination' affecting the value of labour-power. The one factor that Marx did not treat in its turn as variable was the given set of necessaries. There is a simple explanation – *he never finished his work and never wrote the book in which he would remove the assumption of a fixed set of necessaries.*

We are now at the point where we can talk about the question of the 'missing book on wage-labour'. Since this issue is most likely to perturb those whom Rubel called Marxism's 'true believers', we need to set out the case carefully.

Consider Marx's reasoning at the time of the *Grundrisse*, when he explicitly envisioned a separate book on Wage-Labour. In his letter to Engels on 2 April 1858, Marx described his six books on political economy and, in particular, indicated his intentions for the book on 'Capital': 'Throughout this section [*Capital in general*] wages are invariably assumed to be at their minimum. Movements in wages themselves and the rise or fall of that minimum will be considered under wage labour' (Marx and Engels, 1983b: 298). By 'minimum' (as he subsequently spelled out), Marx meant the average wage, the existing standard: 'we understand by minimum not the extreme limit of physical necessity but the average daily wage over for example one year, in which are balanced out the prices of labour capacity during that time, which now stand above their value, and now fall below it' (Marx, 1988: 52). Marx made the same assumption explicitly at the time in the *Grundrisse*: 'For the time being, necessary labour supposed as such; i.e., that the worker always obtains only the minimum of wages' (Marx, 1973: 817).

As Marx explained to Engels, 'only by this procedure is it possible to discuss one relation without discussing all the rest'. Again, he made the same point in the *Grundrisse*:

> All of these fixed suppositions themselves become fluid in the further course of development. *But only by holding them fast at the beginning is their development possible without confounding everything.* Besides it is practically sure that, for instance, however the standard of necessary labour may differ at various epochs and in various countries, or how much, in consequence of the demand and supply of labour, its amount and ratio may change, at any given epoch the standard is to be considered and acted upon as a fixed one by capital. *To consider those changes themselves belongs altogether to the chapter treating of wage labour* (Marx and Engels, 1983b: 298; Marx, 1973: 817; emphasis added).

Accordingly, here at this point when it is undisputed that Marx intended a Book on Wage-Labour, we know at least one thing he intended for that book – removal of the assumption that the standard of necessity is given and fixed. Marx's reference to the site for considering these changes as a 'chapter' need not concern us since it occurs in his 'chapter' on capital, which comprises pages 239 to 882 in this edition; further, as mentioned at the beginning of the chapter, he continued to refer to a book on wage-labour subsequently in 1859 in the Preface to his *Contribution to the Critique of Political Economy*.

But, what about after 1859? Unfortunately, since there is no letter written by Marx indicating his regrets at not being able to write his intended book on wage-labour, the best we can do is to weigh the balance of probabilities. We can make inferences, in short, from the evidence we *do* have. What probability can we assign to Marx's continued recognition of the need for a separate book on wage-labour, given the bits of evidence that do exist?

Certainly if Marx's references to the issues noted above had ceased after the *Grundrisse*, it might lend support to the position that he abandoned the idea of a book separate from *Capital* which would focus on wage-labour. However, this was definitely not the case. Marx returned to these questions in his *Economic Manuscript of 1861–63* and explicitly distinguished there between material properly belonging to the book on Capital and material that belongs in Wage-Labour. Taking up the discussion of 'Capital in General' where it was left in his *Contribution to the Critique of Political Economy*, Marx called attention to differences in 'natural needs' between countries, changes in needs which are a product of history and also movements in the market price of labour-power above and below its value. However, he noted:

> The problem of these movements in the level of the workers' needs, as also that of the rise and fall of the market price of labour capacity above or below this level, do not belong here, where the general capital-relation is to be developed, but in the doctrine of the wages of labour. It will be seen in the further course of this investigation that whether one assumes the level of workers' needs to be higher or lower is completely irrelevant to the end result. The only thing of importance is that it should be viewed as given, determinate. All questions relating to it as not a given but a variable magnitude belong to the investigation of wage labour in particular and do not touch its general relationship to capital (Marx, 1988: 44–5).[18]

Here we see several points. Firstly, given that the subject of study is capital, to understand the nature of capital, it is necessary to treat the level of workers' needs as given and determinate. This is the same point he made both in the *Grundrisse* and in his letter to Engels, and it is consistent with his comments on the Physiocrats. Secondly, changes in workers' needs are not part of the study of capital. All questions relating to changes in the level of needs 'belong to the investigation of wage labour in particular'. Accordingly, the needs of workers are assumed unchanging where the general capital-relation is explored. Marx continued on this point, noting that in practice the level of workers' needs did change – for example, could be driven downward (thereby affecting the value of labour-power):

> In our investigation, however, we shall everywhere assume the amount and quantity of the means of subsistence, and therefore also the extent of needs, at a given level of civilisation, is never pushed down, because this investigation of the rise and fall of the level itself (particularly its artificial lowering) does not alter anything in the consideration of the general relationship (Marx, 1988: 45–6).

Again, why explore questions of changes in the level of needs immediately when the first requirement was to understand the nature of capital and the capital-relation? For this purpose, 'the only thing of importance' for determining the value of labour-power is that the level of needs is treated 'as given, determinate'. As Marx proceeded to comment, 'it was naturally of the highest importance for grasping the capital-relation to determine the *value of labour capacity*, since the capital-relation rests on the sale of that capacity' (Marx, 1988: 47).

Finally, the *Economic Manuscript of 1861–63* provides some additional evidence supporting the argument that Marx wanted to leave certain specific matters to a book on wage-labour. As we have seen above, Marx's clear intent was to treat the standard of necessity as given, thereby leaving only one reason for changes in the value of labour-power – changes in productivity in the production of items entering into the worker's consumption bundle. This allowed him to focus on the link between increases in productivity and the development of relative surplus value (a link which, as we will see later in the book, becomes somewhat problematic once the assumption of a fixed consumption bundle is relaxed). He addressed this point as follows:

> In so far as machinery brings about a direct reduction of wages for the workers employed by it, by e.g. using the demand of those rendered unemployed to force down the wages of those in employment,

it is not part of our task to deal with this CASE. It belongs to the theory of wages. In our investigation we proceed from the assumption that the *labour capacity* is paid for *at its value*, hence wages are only reduced by the DEPRECIATION of that labour capacity, or what is the same thing, by the cheapening of the means of subsistence entering into the workers' consumption (Marx, 1994: 23).

We see here that Marx was quite consistent in indicating what was to be left to the study of wages (or of wage-labour) and what belonged in the investigation of capital. He continued in the same vein in his manuscripts of 1864–5. In the section called 'The Results of the Immediate Process of Production', Marx again stressed the importance of assuming workers' needs to be constant: 'for the analysis of capital it is a matter of complete indifference whether the level of the worker's needs is assumed to be high or low'. Further, he once again indicated that consideration of variations in the standard of necessity belonged in the 'investigation of wage labour in particular': 'The level of the necessaries of life whose total value constitutes the value of labour-power can itself rise or fall. The analysis of these variations, however, belongs not here but in the theory of wages' (Marx, 1977: 1068–9).

We now have a consistent thread from the *Grundrisse* (1857–8) to the 'Results' (1864–5). Does it extend as well to *Capital*? Well, we know that Marx followed the guideline as to what was appropriate to the study of capital and what belonged in the investigation of wage-labour in particular. In *Capital*, he did exactly what he planned to do – hold the standard of necessity constant. The closest he comes to breaching his planned divide between the two books is where he refers to the effect of machinery in displacing workers and thereby driving wages down. Even here, however, he does not consider changes in the level of workers' needs but focuses upon movements of the price of labour-power above and below the existing value: 'the oscillation of wages is confined within limits satisfactory to capitalist exploitation' (Marx, 1977: 935).

Where, then, is the place for that discussion of rising social needs for workers, the needs that become second nature? Where is the exploration of the struggle by workers to satisfy more of those 'historic needs – needs created by production itself, social needs – needs which are themselves the offspring of social production and intercourse'? Where is the place that the assumption about a constant standard of necessity is removed? When *Capital* excludes the basis for 'the contemporary power of capital', how could anyone view *Capital* as providing 'a fully elaborated system'?

Indeed, how much *else* was not incorporated into *Capital*? *In short, what belongs in the book on Wage-Labour?* Rubel proposed that the book was 'destined to reveal in detail the historical and dialectical process of the "negation" of capital' (O'Malley and Algozin, 1981: 223). Similarly, based upon his spirited reading of the *Grundrisse*, Antonio Negri (1991: 5, 18–19, 127–51 passim) argues that *Capital* is only one part in the totality of the Marxian thematic; he finds the corrective to the objectivism in *Capital* in the *Grundrisse* (and, in particular, in the latter's elaboration of the material for the book on wage-labour). Negri argues that the theme of that missing book is *'from the wage to the subject, from capital relation to the class struggle'* (Negri, 1991: 134). Both Rubel and Negri, in short, have proposed that the material for the book on wage-labour is essential for understanding Marx's theory.

So was Marx's silence in *Capital* on critical issues the source of the problems identified in the preceding chapter? The evidence seems to suggest that the concept of a separate book on wage-labour remained alive and well in *Capital* – that he continued to view the 'investigation of wage labour in particular' as outside the scope of *Capital*. At the beginning of Chapter 20 of Volume I of *Capital*, when noting the various forms that wages take, he commented: 'An exposition of all these forms belongs to *the special study of wage-labour, and not, therefore, to this work*' (Marx, 1977: 683; emphasis added). Marx's last word on the subject, in short, was that there was a separate work required on wage-labour.

Let me close this discussion on the missing book, however, with a statement whose basis should become clearer in the following chapter. The central issue is not at all whether Marx intended to write a book on wage-labour. If he had not mentioned it, we would still need to write it.

4
The One-Sidedness of *Capital*

> It is impossible completely to understand Marx's *Capital*, and especially its first chapter, without having thoroughly studied and understood the *whole* of Hegel's *Logic*. Consequently, half a century later none of the Marxists understood Marx!!
>
> V.I. Lenin (1961: 180)

Capital, we have seen, does not explore the side of the capital/wage-labour relation that involves the creation of new social needs for workers (and upon which 'the contemporary power of capital rests'). It doesn't consider changes in the standard of necessity, those which can emerge when the worker 'presses in the opposite direction' to the capitalist in the course of wage struggles. Nor, indeed, does it take up the question of struggles over wages. These are the kinds of questions that relate not to the analysis of capital as such but, rather, were relegated to the 'investigation of wage labour in particular'.

How serious a problem is that? Is it a minor deficiency that can be remedied simply by a process of addition – that is, by adding these missing aspects to *Capital*? There's a problem in doing that – it potentially creates an eclectic amalgam in which premises and deductions are intermingled in the kind of 'witches' circle' which Hegel (1961: II, 87–9) identified in one of his criticisms of prevailing scientific practice. Don't we have to understand the *presuppositions* of wage struggles if we are to incorporate wage struggles into Marx's arguments? Knowing how and when to introduce specific categories was a matter to which Marx was very sensitive and which is central to his method: to understand capital, we first must understand money; and to understand money, we first must understand the commodity. What we cannot do (and remain consistent with Marx's method), however, is to juxtapose categories externally without exploring their inner connections.

To understand, then, the implications of the missing elements and to explore any resulting inadequacies of *Capital*, it is first of all necessary to consider the method that Marx utilized in *Capital*.

I   The method of *Capital*

'If ever the time comes when such work is again possible', Marx wrote to Engels in January 1858, 'I should very much like to write 2 or 3 sheets making accessible to the common reader the *rational* aspect of the method which Hegel not only discovered but also mystified.' Working on the *Grundrisse* at that point, Marx had recently re-read Hegel's *Logic* which he had found 'of great use to me as regards *method* of treatment' (Marx and Engels, 1983b: 249). The time for such work, however, never did come (even though ten years later Marx was still hoping).[1] Thus, a text which might allow us to consider the methodological implications of a missing book on Wage-Labour is unfortunately not available.

In its absence, we have to make do with what we have – utilizing for glimpses into Marx's method not only *Capital*, as (1961: 319) proposed, but also Marx's other works (and, indeed, Lenin's own comments on Hegel's *Logic*).[2] And, because a full discussion is beyond both our purpose here and our competence, it must be far shorter than the roughly 40 pages (at 16 printed pages per printer's sheet) that Marx judged necessary to explain his method (O'Malley and Algozin, 1981: 196).

So, what is that method? Firstly, it is an emphasis on the 'whole'. Marx's goal was to understand bourgeois society as a totality, as an interconnected whole. Why? Because, like every other society, it really *was* such a whole: 'The production relations of every society form a whole' (Marx, 1847a: 166) Thus, like ancient society and feudal society before it, bourgeois society was a 'totality of production relations': 'The relations of production in their totality constitute what are called the social relations, society, and, specifically, a society at a definite stage of historical development, a society with a peculiar distinctive character' (Marx, 1849: 212).

For Marx, a society is a particular complex of interconnected elements, a whole composed of various aspects which 'stand to one another in a necessary connection arising out of the nature of the organism' (Marx, 1843: 11). And, those elements are differing limbs of an organic system, a 'structure of society, in which all relations coexist simultaneously and support one another' (Marx, 1847a: 167). Rather

than 'independent, autonomous neighbours' extrinsically or acciden-
tally related, the elements 'all form the members of a totality, distinctions within a unity' (Marx, 1973: 99).

In this emphasis upon the organic interconnection of parts, we have
precisely the concept of the totality that Marx took from Hegel, the idea
that Lenin (1961: 146–7) described as 'the universal, all-sided, *vital* connection of everything with everything':

> A river and the *drops* in this river. The position of *every* drop, its rela-
> tion to the others; its connection with the others; the direction of its
> movement; its speed; the line of the movement – straight, curved, cir-
> cular, etc. – upwards, downwards. The sum of the movement ... There
> you have a peu pres [approximately] the picture of the world accord-
> ing to Hegel's *Logic*, – of course minus God and the Absolute.

The whole, that totality of interconnections, then, is the framework
within which Marx examines and understands the parts. As Lukács
(1972: 27) commented: 'The category of totality, the all-pervasive
supremacy of the whole over the parts is the essence of the method
which Marx took over from Hegel and brilliantly transformed into the
foundations of a wholly new science.'

Whereas 'bourgeois thought', Lukács (1972: 28) noted, proceeds 'consistently from the standpoint of the individual', Marx rejected an
approach that leads from the individual parts, atomistic individuals, to
the whole. His perspective in this respect was diametrically opposed to
the 'methodological individualism' characteristic of much non-Marxist
work (including, in particular, neoclassical economics) – that 'Cartesian'
heritage so well described by Richard Levins and Richard Lewontin as
follows: 'The parts are ontologically prior to the whole; that is the parts
exist in isolation and come together to make wholes. The parts have
intrinsic properties, which they possess in isolation and which they lend
to the whole.'

In contrast, for Marxism the parts have *no* prior independent existence as parts. They 'acquire properties by virtue of being parts of a particular whole, properties they do not have in isolation or as parts of
another whole' (Levins and Lewontin, 1985: 269, 273, 3).

Proceeding from the perspective of the whole means a break with
many habits of thought that flow from the Cartesian perspective. If we
think of the individual parts, for example, not as independent and indifferent to each other but, rather, as 'members of a totality', then a view
of change as the result of exogenous stimuli is difficult to sustain.

To understand society as a totality is to understand that its change and development is not a simple relationship of cause and effect, of independent and dependent variables. Rather, 'mutual interaction takes place between the different moments. This [is] the case with every organic whole' (Marx, 1973: 100). Indeed, as Lenin (1961: 159) noted in his reading of Hegel, 'the all-sidedness and all-embracing character of the interconnection of the world...is only one-sidedly, fragmentarily and incompletely expressed by causality.' There is 'reciprocal action of these various sides on one another'; and, as a result, there is movement and change within the whole (Marx and Engels, 1846: 53). In this respect, the motion and direction of bourgeois society may be seen as a 'self-movement', an organic development inherent in the nature of the system.

Thus, the point of view of totality is at the core of a Marxian world-view. It compels us always to think about the connections, to recognize that on the surface of society we do not see the 'obscure structure of the bourgeois economic system' – that is, the 'inner core, which is essential but concealed' (Marx, 1968: 65; 1981b: 311). Understanding the world as an interconnected whole, however, is only one aspect of Marx's method. There remains the critical matter of *how* precisely Marx develops an understanding of that whole. How, in short, does one come to grasp the nature of the totality in question?[3]

We cannot hope to understand a real society with its interconnections by starting from an abstract model, and we cannot simply 'apply an abstract ready-made system of logic to vague presentiments of just such a system' (Marx and Engels, 1983b: 261). Rather, we must begin with careful study of that real society – this is 'the point of departure for observation and conception'. For Marx, though, mere observation and empirical study cannot possibly grasp the interconnections of that concrete totality. If that were the case, there would be no need for science, no need for abstract thought. Indeed, all that results from observation is a 'chaotic conception of the whole' (Marx, 1973: 100–1). Accordingly, the method of inquiry 'has to appropriate the material in detail, to analyse its different forms of development and to track down their inner connection' (Marx, 1977: 102). And, that appropriation of the material in detail is a precondition for bringing 'a science to the point at which it admits of a dialectical presentation'.

Having studied the concrete, Marx argued, we need to develop an understanding of that totality logically. And the way to do this, he proposed, is to begin from simple concepts that are the result of the analysis of the concrete. One must begin with the 'simplest determinations' and concepts and proceed to deduce logically a conception of the whole 'as a rich totality of many determinations and relations.' This, Marx stressed, was the 'scientifically correct method' (Marx, 1973: 100–1).

In describing this 'method of rising from the abstract to the concrete' as 'the way in which thought appropriates the concrete, reproduces it as the concrete in the mind,' Marx was following Hegel's prescription:

> it is easier for Cognition to seize the abstract simple thought-determi-nation than the concrete, which is a manifold concatenation of such thought-determinations and their relations: and this is the manner in which the concrete is to be apprehended, not as it is in intuition.

> The abstract must everywhere constitute the beginning and the ele-ment in which and from which the particularities and rich shapes of the concrete spread out (Hegel, 1961: II, 443–4).

But, what was the method of deduction by which one moves from the simple abstract to the rich totality of many determinations and rela-tions? While both Hegel and Marx engaged in a process of dialectical derivation, their terrains differed. Hegel's journey in his *Science of Logic* takes place purely in the realm of thought; it is a movement from con-cept to concept propelled only by the revelation of logical connections. In contrast, Marx always has the real totality before him as what is to be understood. Nevertheless, as Marx and Lenin recognized, there was more than mystification in Hegel; there also was the discovery of a method.

Not only the 'necessity of connection' but also 'the immanent emer-gence of distinctions' was central, as Lenin noted, to Hegel's *Logic* (Lenin, 1961: 97; Hegel, 1961: I, 66). To the extent that a concept can be shown to imply a further concept, it can be said to contain within it a distinction, a negation, which demonstrates that it is not adequate in itself. The 'dialectic moment' with respect to the first term, then, is the grasping of 'the *distinction* that it implicitly contains', the Other which is latent within it. Accordingly, as we first encounter the second term, it is understood merely as the opposite of the first, as that which stands outside the first. Yet, upon further interrogation of this second term, we come to understand the relation of the two terms, their unity: 'The sec-ond term on the other hand is itself the determinate entity, distinction or relation; hence with it the dialectic moment consists in the positing of the *unity* which is contained in it' (Hegel, 1961: II, 477).[4]

Thus, having developed the concept of its opposite from the first or immediate term, Hegel proceeded to demonstrate that the second term (although encompassing the content of the first term) was also deficient in itself; further progress in understanding occurs only by grasping fully the relation of the two terms, by understanding the unity of these specific opposites. The third term (the negation of the negation) contains and preserves within it the content of the first two terms while at the same time transcending the one-sidedness of each. In this respect, the third term is clearly a richer, fuller concept.

Yet, this is not a stopping point. Since this new understanding in its turn can be shown to contain within it a distinction, Hegel proposed that 'cognition rolls forward from content to content. This progress determines itself, first, in this manner, that it begins from simple determinatenesses and that each subsequent one is richer and more concrete.' In this way, every step of the process is one of dialectical progress that 'not only loses nothing and leaves nothing behind, but carries with it all that it has acquired, enriching and concentrating itself upon itself' (Hegel, 1961: II, 482–3).

How long does this process of reasoning go on? For Hegel, the stopping point could only be where there no longer are any deficiencies in concepts – that is, the Absolute Idea, the whole that is sufficient unto itself.[5] Having begun with his discussion in the *Logic* with Pure Being, the starting point selected initially as devoid of presuppositions, Hegel reveals at the end that the Absolute Idea is Pure Being – that is, that the presupposition is itself a result. Thus, 'the science is seen to be a circle which returns upon itself': 'The method thus forms a circle, but, in a temporal development, it cannot anticipate that the beginning as such shall already be derivative … ' (Hegel, 1961: II, 483–4).

While Marx's object clearly differed from Hegel's, he similarly uses the method of dialectical derivation as his means of 'tracking down' the inner connections within the concrete totality. Indeed, he succeeds so well in grasping and presenting the real logically that his method slips into the background – it appears 'as if we have before us an *a priori* construction' (Marx, 1977: 102). Here, however, we want to look specifically for that method.

As Lenin (1961: 146) noted, to understand the concrete totality, that 'universal, all-sided, *vital* connection of everything with everything', it is necessary to develop concepts that 'likewise must be hewn, treated, flexible, mobile, relative, mutually connected, united in opposites, in order to embrace the world.' And, this is what Marx did. Beginning with simple concepts, Marx proceeded to deduce new categories and concepts. He takes pains to introduce no categories exogenously and stresses the absolute necessity not to omit 'essential links'; indeed, omission of the intermediate terms was an important aspect of Marx's methodological criticism of Ricardo and classical political economy (Marx, 1968: 164–5, 190–1; 1971: 500).[6]

Yet, for Marx (in contrast to Hegel) this process of deduction was not a matter of 'thought concentrating itself, probing its own depths, and unfolding itself out of itself, by itself'. Nor was that 'totality of thoughts', the 'product of thinking and comprehending', itself 'a product of the concept which thinks and generates itself outside or above observation and conception.' Rather, that totality of thoughts is a product of 'the working-up of observation and conception into concepts.' It is 'a product of a thinking head, which appropriates the world in the only way it can' (Marx, 1973: 101–2).

As noted above, for Marx the reference point for his process of dialectical derivation is always the real society. Without encroaching on the subject matter of the next section (which explores the derivation of the totality in *Capital*), we can illustrate this method by considering Marx's discussion of value-forms in his chapter on the Commodity in *Capital*. Having identified the 'insufficiency of the simple form of value', Marx noted that this form of value 'automatically passes over into a more complete form', that of the Expanded Form of Value. In its turn, the 'defects' of the latter become the basis for consideration of the General Form of Value which, to acquire 'general social validity', passes into the Money Form of Value (Marx, 1977: 154, 156, 162).

Similarly, consider Marx's discussion in the opening section of Volume II of *Capital*; there, in the course of showing the insights available by exploring the various forms of the circuit of capital (those of money capital, productive capital and commodity capital), he brought out as well the deficiencies inherent in each separate representation of the circuit. Nevertheless, each form is shown to contain within it a further form. Precisely because all of the forms in themselves were found to be inadequate and one-sided, Marx proceeded to find that 'only the unity of the three forms' of the circuit of capital adequately expresses the continuity of the process of capital (Marx, 1981a: 141–2, 172, 179–80, 184).

In these cases, the deficiencies, defects and insufficiencies that Marx identifies are not the result of thought acting upon itself. Rather, the measure of their inadequacy is the real – the concrete processes and relations that they fail to express conceptually. In short, rather than engaging in a dialectic of pure thought, for Marx it is the defect in the theory *relative to the concrete totality* which propels the discussion forward. As long as something critical to understanding the concrete is not contained within the thought-totality, then dialectical deduction must continue.

Thus, the specific subject, society, is always present as the premise of this theoretical process; and, as Lenin (1961: 320) noted with respect to *Capital*, 'Testing by facts or by practice respectively, is to be found here in *each* step of the analysis.'

Of course, if there is a category remaining outside the thought-complex that has been developed, it has been outside all along. (Early in the logical excursion, almost all categories are outside; they are only appropriated in the course of this dialectical derivation.) The critical question accordingly thus is to determine at what point the category is to be introduced.[7] For this process of dialectical reasoning to demonstrate the *logical interconnection* of all parts of the whole, the answer is clear: no category can be introduced before all its premises have been developed, and no category should be introduced until it is implicit and its incorporation is necessary for the further development of the thought-totality. No categories, in short, can drop from the sky; they must be developed from within the system when required. Thus, it is essential to proceed deductively on a step-by-step basis in order to ensure that no elements are external, extrinsic, independent, indifferent, exogenous to the system.

Obviously, then, the historical order (that is, the order in which the real itself came into being) cannot dictate the logical order. Marx, indeed, insisted that it is 'unfeasible and wrong to let the economic categories follow one another in the same sequence as that in which they were historically decisive.' Rather, the order and sequence of categories is necessarily determined 'by their relation to one another in modern bourgeois society', by their precise interconnections within the whole (Marx, 1973: 107). Thus, in contrast to Hegel, for Marx there was no necessary relation between the historical order and the logical order.[8] As he had asked 20 years earlier (Marx, 1847a: 167), 'How, indeed, could the single logical formula of movement, of sequence, of time, explain the structure of society, in which all relations coexist simultaneously and support one another?'

At the end of Marx's process of dialectical derivation, the 'prize' is representation of the connected whole, the 'totality of production relations'. We understand precisely how these categories are interconnected. In the end, we arrive at not the 'chaotic conception of the whole, but ... a rich totality of many determinations and relations' (Marx, 1973: 100). We have a concept of that organic system 'in which all relations coexist simultaneously and support one another': 'in the completed bourgeois system every economic relation presupposes every other in its bourgeois economic form, and everything posited is thus also a presupposition, this is the case with every organic system' (Marx, 1973: 278). And, if we cannot demonstrate that all its presuppositions are the result of capitalism's own doing? Have we grasped the concrete totality? For Marx, all capital's presuppositions must be explained as produced by it itself, as developed and shaped within the whole, 'and everything posited is thus also a presupposition'. As we will see, this was a point that he repeatedly stressed in his development of the totality in *Capital*.

II The derivation of the totality

While we cannot here trace in detail all the steps involved in the derivation of the totality in *Capital*, let us review the key moments in the process. Beginning with the commodity, the elementary form of wealth in capitalist society, Marx proceeded to analyse this particular concrete, a product of labour which was sold, and discovered that it contained a distinction – that it was, on the one hand, a use-value and, on the other, a value. Reasoning further, he concluded that the very concept of the commodity contained latent within it the concept of money – that the commodity was in and for itself only in exchange, only by passing into money, the independent expression of value.

For the commodity as such to exist, it required that value take an independent form, and this is 'achieved by the differentiation of commodities into commodities and money' (Marx, 1977: 181). The distinction between use-value and value, inherent in the commodity, thus was expressed externally by the opposition between commodity and money (Marx, 1977: 199).

As independent value, money (the Other of Commodity) is also use-value, the power to represent and realize the value of all commodities, to be exchanged for all commodities; it is this which permits it to act as mediator for commodities (*C-M-C*). Yet, latent in money is that it can be an end in itself, that money as wealth can be a goal – for which the commodity is mediator and vanishing moment. Money for itself (*M-C-M'*), however, is merely value; in the movement of money as wealth, value is common and present in all forms: 'both the money and the commodity function only as different modes of existence of value itself' (Marx, 1977: 255).

Commodity and money thus are opposites – both mutually exclusive and also necessary to each other. But, they are also united in the concept of capital. Thus, value-for-itself moves through the forms of money and commodity in this process and, indeed, is the subject of the process. For self-expanding value, *both* commodity and money are mediators, vanishing moments, mere forms in a specific unity which is capital. Money, thus, is for itself only by passing into capital, self-expanding value; it differentiates itself into money which is spent and money which is advanced, into money as money and money as capital.

Considering capital, Marx concluded that it *too* contained a distinction. Encountered initially as a unity of commodity and money, as capital in the sphere of circulation, capital was shown to require (in order to exist as self-expanding value) a process that lay beyond circulation itself – a process of production. Capital, thus, differentiates into capital in circulation and capital in production. It must leave the sphere of circulation and enter into that of production; and, it is in this latter sphere that we see capital, as self-valorising value, generate the production of surplus value and secure the production of commodities containing surplus value.

However, this surplus value in the commodity-form is only latent; to be made real, capital must return to the sphere of circulation and the commodity must be exchanged for money. Capital must always return to circulation, the point of departure. Capital in production is a mediator for capital in circulation (*Kc-Kp-Kc*). Yet, in turn, capital in circulation is a mediator for capital in production (*Kp-Kc-Kp*); capital can only grow by passing through circulation.

The two processes are opposites, are mutually exclusive, are necessary to each other – and, indeed, are a specific unity, capital as a whole (Lebowitz, 1976b). Taking the forms of capital in circulation and capital in production – just as it takes those of commodity and money, capital as a whole is the totality that Marx constructs in *Capital* (and whose moments can be seen in Figure 4.1). Nothing could be clearer – it is this very unity of production and circulation whose central moments are announced in the titles of the three volumes of *Capital*.

Seen as a whole, we recognize that capital must move through a continuing circuit, which can be expressed in several ways. In the circuit of money-capital, we begin with money-capital (*M*) purchasing as commodities (*C*) both means of production (*Mp*) and labour-power (*Lp*); there is an intervening process of production (*P*) during which commodities containing surplus value are produced (*C'*) which must be sold (*C'-M'*) in order to return to the money-capital form:

$$M\text{-}C(Mp, Lp)\ldots P\ldots C'\text{-}M'.$$

Alternatively, the circuit may be viewed as one of productive capital (beginning and ending with *P*) or as one of commodity-capital (beginning and ending with *C'*). However, as noted, all particular forms of the circuit were inadequate and one-sided: the circuit of capital had to

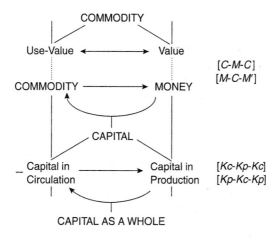

Figure 4.1 The construction of capital as a totality

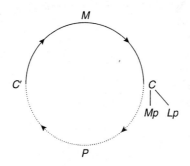

Figure 4.2 The circuit of capital as a whole

be understood as all three forms simultaneously and was best conceived as a 'circle' (as depicted in Figure 4.2).

Considering, then, the circuit of capital as a whole, Marx stressed that 'all the premises of the process appear as its result, as premises produced by the process itself. Each moment appears as a point of departure, of transit, and of return' (Marx, 1981a: 180). His choice of language is by no means incidental. *All presuppositions, all preconditions, all premises are themselves results within the circuit of capital – that is precisely the nature of capital understood as a totality, capital as process of reproduction*:

> In a constantly revolving orbit, every point is simultaneously a start-
> ing point and a point of return ... The reproduction of capital in each
> of its forms and at each of its stages is just as continuous as is the

metamorphosis of these forms and their successive passage through the three stages (Marx, 1981a: 180–1).

In short, reproduction (understood as the reproduction both of material products and of relations of production) is the central concept of the organic whole, of capital as totality. Even the reproduction models with which Marx ends Volume II of *Capital* are none other than a demonstration of the way in which the two departments of production (means of production and articles of consumption) produce the necessary material presuppositions for reproduction. As Marx noted, that very discussion showed 'that the capitalist production process, taken as a whole, is a unity of the production and circulation processes' (Marx, 1981b: 117).

It is essential in this respect to recognize that the very concept of simple reproduction introduced by Marx in *Capital* is that of the organic whole. As he noted in the opening lines of Chapter 23 in Volume I, the chapter on 'Simple Reproduction':

> Whatever the social form of the production process, it has to be continuous, it must periodically repeat the same phases. A society can no more cease to produce than it can cease to consume. When viewed, therefore, as a connected whole, and in the constant flux of its incessant renewal, every social process of production is at the same time a process of reproduction (Marx, 1977: 711).

Thus, capital understood as a totality, an interconnected whole, produces and reproduces material products and social relations – which are themselves presuppositions and premises of production. 'Those conditions, like these relations, are on the one hand the presuppositions of the capitalist production process, on the other its results and creations; they are both produced and reproduced by it' (Marx, 1981b: 957). In short, we have in capital as a whole a closed social input–output system in which nothing is exogenous.

Or do we? There is an obvious question (perhaps not so obvious unless the logical structure of *Capital* is clear): do we *really* have an adequate totality in capital as a whole? Is it really an organic whole in which all presuppositions are results, in which all points of departure are points of return? Or, *does capital as a whole itself contain a distinction*, one that will not permit us to stop here (or, rather, one that permits us to pause only for a moment).

The answer to this question is also obvious. Yes, there is an element that is not part of capital, which is not produced and reproduced by capital, which is a point of departure but not one of return in the circuit of capital, a presupposition that is not a result of capital itself. And, it is one that is necessary for the reproduction of capital, which is required for the very existence of capital itself. The point is made quite clearly in Marx's chapter on Simple Reproduction: 'The maintenance and reproduction of the working class remains a necessary condition for the reproduction of capital. But the capitalist may safely leave this to the worker's drives for self-preservation and propagation' (Marx, 1977: 718).

Thirty-two words – and, then, theoretical silence. *The totality presented in* Capital *remains incomplete – incomplete at the very point that the reproduction of capital is revealed to require something outside of capital.*

Yet, this point – that capital depends on something outside it, the production of the worker – is too important to rest solely on the extrinsic evidence of a single quotation (although there are others). If capital as a whole is not an adequate totality, then this should be clear from a closer examination of its reproduction, from an examination of its reproduction model and of the circuit of capital.

III Capital as inadequate

Consider first the model of simple reproduction in Volume II of *Capital*. Here we are presented with two departments of production: Department I (Means of Production) and Department II (Articles of Consumption). There are two inputs into production in each department – means of production (*Mp*) and labour-power (*Lp*) – and, thus, two component sources of value (past labour and living labour). And, there are two outputs – means of production (*Mp*) and articles of consumption (*Ac*). One output, means of production, is also an input; it is both a result and a presupposition of production. The other output, articles of consumption, however, is not here an input; and, the other input, labour-power, is not here an output. The model, in fact, is not closed in itself: there are three variables (*Mp, Ac, Lp*) and only two processes of production.

As is well-known, the balance condition for simple reproduction, for equilibrium, which may be derived from this model is that $C2 = V1 + S1$: the value of means of production consumed in Department II must equal the value added in Department I. *However, this condition does not meet the requirements for reproduction if we specify that reproduction must entail the reproduction of a given number of required workers (N).* This is easily demonstrated if we recognize that variable capital (*V*) is the product of the number of workers and the value of labour-power (*Nw*):

$$C2 = V1 + S1.$$
$$V2(C2/V2) = V1(1 + S1/V1).$$

$$V2/V1 = (1 + S1/V1)/(C2/V2).$$
$$N2/N1 = (1 + S1/V1)/(C2/V2).$$

Thus, all that the balance equation reveals is the required ratio of workers in Department II relative to those in Department I. Nothing, however, requires that $N1 + N2 = Nt$, where Nt represents the total number of workers. The reproduction condition is consistent with different levels of total employment – with full employment equilibrium, below full employment equilibrium, and so on. In short, there is a 'degree of freedom' which results precisely from the fact that the model is not closed (and requires a scalar), from the fact that a closed system would require a 'third' department.

The same essential point may be demonstrated graphically in relation to the circuit of capital as depicted in the form of a circle. First, we must recognize that the circuit as illustrated in Figure 4.2 is *inadequate* because it does not distinguish the two different types of commodities produced under capitalist relations – means of production and articles of consumption. This distinction, necessary for reproduction, must be introduced into the circuit if it is to represent truly the process of reproduction.

Now, we see that the circuit includes both an exchange of money for means of production (M-Mp) and an exchange of means of production for money (Mp-M) – which are the same act viewed from different sides. Means of production are clearly both a presupposition and a result within the circuit of capital. However, this point merely underlines the *asymmetry* (which has been hidden) between labour-power and articles of consumption: there is an exchange of money for labour-power (M-Lp) and an exchange of articles of consumption for money (Ac-M). Thus, again we see that labour-power is *only* a presupposition, and articles of consumption are *only* a result within the circuit of capital.

Clearly, to have all presuppositions results and all results presuppositions, an additional relationship must be identified – that between articles of consumption and labour-power. The first step in closing this system must be to recognize explicitly the metamorphosis within circulation that occurs as labour-power is exchanged for money which is in turn exchanged for articles of consumption (Lp-M-Ac). Both parts of this metamorphosis have already been implied by the movements of capital within *its* circuit (M-Lp, Ac-M); they are transactions that are the mirror-image of those already considered.

Yet, this step is *still* inadequate because labour-power remains here a presupposition but not a result. We have here the consumption of labour-power but not its production and the production of articles of

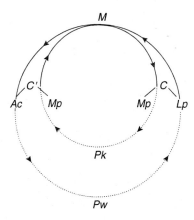

Figure 4.3   The circuit of capital and wage-labour

consumption but not their consumption. *In short, the system can only be complete by positing explicitly another process of production, a second moment of production (Pw), distinct from the process of production of capital – one in which labour-power is produced in the course of consuming articles of consumption.* Thus, the circuit of capital *necessarily* implies a second circuit, the circuit of wage-labour (which is depicted in Figure 4.3).

The necessary existence of this second moment of production, the production of the worker (*Pw*), clarifies Marx's comment in the *Grundrisse* regarding the division of the entire circuit of capital into four moments: 'each of the two great moments of the production process and the circulation process appears again in a duality.' Two of these four moments were the moments of circulation (*M-C, C'-M'*), and a third was the capitalist production process. These three moments will be recognized as the moments within capital as a whole, within the circuit of capital. *But, what was the fourth moment – the other process of production?*

Marx's comment was that this moment was to be seen as separate: it involved the exchange of variable capital for living labour capacity and here population was the 'main thing'. And, where was this second moment of production to be analysed? 'Moment IV belongs in the section on wages, etc' (Marx, 1973: 520–1). It belonged, in short, in the missing book on Wage-Labour.

Capital as a whole, as a totality, accordingly does not include within it that which is a 'necessary condition for the reproduction of capital' – the maintenance and reproduction of the working class. 'The constant existence of the working class, however, is necessary for the capitalist class, and so, therefore is the consumption of the worker mediated by M-C' (Marx, 1981a: 155). But, this individual consumption of the labourer does not fall within the circuit of capital. Only the productive consumption, the process of production of capital, does.

Thus, by Marx's own standard, capital as a whole is not the adequate totality in which all presuppositions, all premises, are shown to be results. Upon examination, it is shown not to exist on its own without a necessary relation to an Other. At the very point when we have an apparent totality in capital as a whole, in the concept of its reproduction, it turns out to contain a distinction – capital as a whole must posit the wage-labourer outside it in order to exist as such.

We see, then, that it is necessary to consider the wage-labourer insofar as she exists *outside* capital. Recall Marx's early comment about political economy – a political economy which considered the worker only as a working animal and not 'when he is not working, as a human being': 'Let us now rise above the level of political economy' (Marx, 1844c: 241). It is time to rise above the level of the political economy of capital, which constitutes only a moment within an adequate totality.

IV   Situating wage-labour

Capital as a whole, it develops, is not a stopping point but differentiates into capital, on the one hand, and wage-labour, on the other. We have considered initially the side of capital, and now we must examine that of wage-labour.

Thus far, we have seen wage-labour insofar as it is a moment within capital, as it exists for capital. In *Capital*, we are first introduced to wage-labour in itself as the worker separated from means of production, who stands opposite capital as not-capital, who is the possessor of a use-value for capital – the only use-value for capital as such, labour-power. Labour-power as use-value confronts money, just as money as value confronts labour-power in the sphere of circulation (M-Lp). Capital, value-for-itself, posits here an independent use-value outside it.

With the completion of the process of exchange (the buying and selling of labour-power), we enter into the process of capitalist production (Pk) where the use-value which capital has purchased is consumed, where the exercise of labour-power (labour) is brought within capital. Here we see the wage-labourer compelled to work, subordinated to the will of capital in order to achieve the goal of capital, valorization (self-expansion). And, finally, we see the wage-labourer once again in the sphere of circulation (C'-M') as capital seeks to realize the surplus value contained in the commodities that have been produced.

Thus, wage-labour is present in every moment of capital. It exists for capital as a necessary means for the growth of capital; it is the mediator for capital (K-WL-K). Value-for-itself posits an independent use-value in order to be for self. Yet, *within the circuit of capital, there is already a distinction that points beyond that circuit.* Capital does not *only* confront the wage-labourer who is the possessor of a use-value; it also necessarily faces the wage-labourer as one who possesses *value* in the sphere of circulation (C'-M'). For the capitalist, here workers 'appear as consumers, possessors of exchange values (wages), money, which they exchange for his commodity' (Marx, 1973: 419). Thus, capital is not only value in relation to wage-labour; it is also, in its commodity-form, use-value for wage-labour.

The wage-labourer thus approaches capital in its commodity-form as value in relation to use-value (M-Ac). Capital indeed *must* be a use-value in order to be realized as value. The question then becomes – what is a use-value for the wage-labourer in this sphere of circulation? And, this question cannot be answered by reference solely to the sphere of circulation any more than the similar question posed with respect to capital. For capital in commodity-form to be a use-value for the worker, it must be so in the sphere of production of wage-labour.

Let us, then, leave behind the sphere of circulation and enter into this hidden abode of production upon whose threshold there hangs the notice 'no admittance for business', the sphere of production of wage-labour. Considered *abstractly*, a necessary starting point, the process of production of the worker appears as a natural process of production; considered as a whole, however, it will be seen as a process of reproduction of a specific relation – that of wage-labour.

Firstly, this process of production is immediately a process of consumption:

> It is clear that in taking in food, for example, which is a form of consumption, the human being produces his own body. But this is also true of every kind of consumption which in one way or another produces human beings in some particular aspect (Marx, 1973: 90–1).

The process of production of the worker, in short, is a process of consuming use-values; and, these use-values are not limited to those associated with physiological subsistence, but include any which produce the worker in 'some particular aspect'.

Secondly, the *result* of this process of production is the worker himself. 'Now, as regards the worker's consumption, this reproduces one thing – namely himself, as living labour capacity' (Marx, 1973: 676). We have here the 'reconversion' of means of subsistence into 'fresh labour-power'; in short, 'the product of individual consumption is the consumer himself' (Marx, 1977: 718, 290).

Finally, the process of production of the worker is a *labour process*. There are two aspects in this designation. First, this process is an activity – that is to say, the process of consuming use-values in order to produce the worker is not passive but active. Time spent in this activity cannot be contrasted to time spent in the direct labour process of capital as non-producing time, as free time compared to direct labour time: 'It goes without saying, by the way, that direct labour time itself cannot remain in the abstract antithesis to free time in which it appears from the perspective of bourgeois economy' (Marx, 1973: 712).

On the contrary, what occurs during 'free time' is a process of production, a process in which the nature and capability of the worker is altered. It is 'time for the full development of the individual, which in turn reacts back upon the productive power of labour as itself the greatest productive power' (Marx, 1973: 711). This second process of production, which political economy does not see, is precisely the process of producing the worker: 'From the standpoint of the direct production process [of capital] it can be regarded as the production of *fixed capital*, this fixed capital being man himself' (Marx, 1973: 711–12).

In the course of this activity, thus, the human being is altered. He acts upon that which is external to him and 'simultaneously changes his own nature' (Marx, 1977: 283). 'Free time – which is both idle time and time for higher activity – has naturally transformed its possessor into a different subject, and he then enters into the direct production process as this different subject' (Marx, 1973: 712). In this activity, accordingly, which is simultaneously an exercise and a cultivating of labour-power, the worker produces herself as a specific type of labour-power (Marx, 1973: 712). *Every act of consumption of a use-value produces her in a particular aspect; every process of activity alters her as the subject who enters into all activities*. We have here one of Marx's central propositions:

> Man himself is the basis of his material production, as of any other production that he carries on. All circumstances, therefore, which affect man, the *subject* of production, more or less modify all his functions and activities, and therefore too his functions and activities as the creator of material wealth, of commodities (Marx, n.d.: 280).

The process of production of the worker, considered as a labour process, may be represented as follows:

$$U, Lp \ldots Pw \ldots Lp,$$

where labour-power (Lp) is both an input and an output and use-values (U) are means of production which are consumed in this process of production. We may note that these use-values, which significantly are not also outputs of this process, include both those produced directly as commodities and others that may not be produced under capitalist relations. For the moment we will restrict ourselves to considering only use-values produced as articles of consumption within the circuit of capital.[9]

The second aspect of the production of the worker considered as a labour process is that the activity involved in this process is 'purposeful activity'. In other words, there is a preconceived goal, a goal that exists *ideally*, before the process itself; and, this particular labour process is a process of realizing this goal by the subordination of the will of the worker to that purpose (Marx, 1977: 284).

And, what is this goal that exists latently before the process of production of the worker? It is the worker's conception of self – as determined within society. It is this that 'creates the ideal, internally impelling cause for production'; it is this which '*ideally posits* the object of production as an internal image, as a need, as drive and as purpose' (Marx, 1973: 91–2). That preconceived goal of production is what Marx described as 'the worker's own need for development' (Marx, 1977: 772). This goal, determined within society – since the *category*, 'Man', has no needs – is a presupposition of this process of production (Carver, 1975: 189).

Thus, just as the process of production of capital has as its goal the valorization of capital, the process of production of the worker has that of 'the worker's own need for development'. On the one hand, we have capital for itself, value for itself; on the other hand, we have labour-power for itself, use-value for itself. In the process of production of the worker, 'Man makes his life activity itself the object of his will and of his consciousness ... (H)is own life is an object for him' (Marx, 1844c: 276) The worker here 'belongs to himself' (Marx, 1977: 717).

The process of production of the worker, considered as labour process, is accordingly a labour process of the 'simple' type in which human beings employ means of production in order to realize their own preconceived goal; here, they dominate the conditions and results of their labour, and their labour is not distinct from selves but is indeed activity for self, activity in 'his own interest' (Marx, 1977: 718).

But, what are the requirements of this particular labour process? First, the necessary means of production must be accessible to the worker; she must be able to secure the use-values required in order to realize her goal. These are use-values not in themselves but only use-values insofar as they correspond to the goal of production; this is what generates 'needs' for particular use-values – they are use-values that conform to the requirements of socially developed human beings. Those needs, which are part of the very nature of the worker, include among them the 'social needs' discussed in our last chapter. Rather than being restricted to physiological requirements or even those normally satisfied, they encompass: 'the worker's participation in the higher, even cultural satisfactions, the agitation for his own interests, newspaper subscriptions, attending lectures, educating his children, developing his taste, etc.' (Marx, 1973: 287).

Yet another requirement of this particular labour process is labour-power itself. Since the labour process is a process of activity, there must be the *capacity* to carry out this activity. Both the energy (the 'strength, health and freshness') – since there is only a certain quantity of 'vital force' to expend – and the particular quality and capability (which is itself a product of previous activity) must be available (Marx, 1977: 341, 343).

Similarly (but distinct from capacity itself), there must be *time* for this labour process. 'Time is the room of human development. A man who has no free time to dispose of, whose whole lifetime, apart from the mere physical interruptions by sleep, meals, and so forth, is absorbed by his labour for the capitalist, is less than a beast of burden' (Marx, 1865b: 142). As Marx (1977: 341) noted in his chapter on the workday: 'The worker needs time in which to satisfy his intellectual and social requirements, and the extent and number of these requirements is conditioned by the general level of civilization.'

In short, in this process of production in which the goal is the development of the worker, the worker needs time ('free time') for his full development: 'Time for education, for intellectual development, for the fulfillment of social functions, for social intercourse, for the free play of the vital forces of his body and his mind' (Marx, 1977: 375).

What, then, are the prospects that the worker will be able to realize her goals? Consider this process of production of the worker – not only what is produced but also what is *not* produced. The process has as its result the worker, as living labour capacity; it is its *only* product. The use-values, necessary as presuppositions, are not produced, are not results. Thus, this labour process by itself cannot be a system of reproduction.

Indeed, the presuppositions *cannot* be produced within this process – because the wage-labourer *by definition* is separated from the means of production necessary to produce them. Given this separation, labour-power 'can be directly used neither for the production of use-values for its possessor nor for the production of commodities which he could live from selling' (Marx, 1981a: 114). And, not only does the worker not produce the use-values he requires – he necessarily *annihilates* them in the process of production, which is a process of consumption, a process that 'simply reproduces the needy individual' (Marx, 1977: 719).

In short, this particular labour process is not *at all* a natural process of production but is the production of a particular social relation, the production of wage-labour:

> (It) reproduces the individual himself in a specific mode of being, not only in his immediate quality of being alive, and in specific social relations. So that the ultimate appropriation by individuals taking place in the consumption process reproduces them in the original relations in which they move within the production process and towards each other; ... (Marx, 1973: 717n).

Thus, in order to produce for self, the wage-labourer must secure use-values from outside his own process of production. Under the prevailing circumstances, he must take the only potential commodity he has, living labour capacity, and must re-enter the sphere of circulation; To be for himself, the worker must treat his labour capacity as something distinct from himself, as his *property*.[10] In the sphere of circulation, 'the worker is thereby formally posited as a person who is something for himself *apart from his* labour, and who alienates his life-expression only as a means towards his own life' (Marx, 1973: 289). He must find the buyer for whom his property, labour-power, is a use-value – capital. *Thus, to be for self, the wage-labourer must be a being for another.* We have here the worker as wage-labourer for self – as one who approaches capital as a *means*, a means whose end is the worker for self. *Capital faces not a wage-labourer for capital but a wage-labourer for self.*

There is a parallel here to the consideration of capital. We were first introduced to capital in the sphere of circulation and noted its necessary entry into the sphere of production and then its re-entry into the sphere of circulation. Capital as a whole, it developed, was a specific unity of production and circulation. In the same way, we see that the wage-labourer must secure articles of consumption in the sphere of circulation, consumes and annihilates these in the process of his own production and thus must re-enter the sphere of circulation as the seller of labour-power. Wage-labour as a whole is a specific unity of production and circulation.

Yet, there is more than an identity in form here. There is also a critical inversion. In the first case, we consider the relation of capital and wage-labour as one of *K-WL-K*, where wage-labour is a mediator for capital, where the end is capital. *Yet we now see that there is also WL-K-WL, where capital is a mediator for the wage-labourer, where the wage-labourer is the end in itself, where labour for capital is a mere means and not an end at all.* Capital here is a moment in the reproduction of wage-labour.

However, for capital to be a mediator for wage-labour, wage-labour must be a mediator for capital. As the young Marx (1844c: 283) noted, 'the worker exists as a worker only when he exists *for himself* as capital; and he exists as capital only when some *capital* exists *for him*'. Similarly, Marx commented in the *Grundrisse* that if capital cannot realize surplus value by employing a worker, then: 'labour capacity itself appears outside the conditions of the reproduction of its existence; it exists without the conditions of its existence, and is therefore a mere encumbrance; needs without the means to satisfy them; ... ' (Marx, 1973: 609).

However, the worker does not merely posit his living labour capacity as separate from self in the sphere of circulation; this separation necessarily is realized as such when capital consumes labour-power in the process of production of capital. Here, the worker expends himself in accordance with the goal of capital and under the direction and control of capital; here, there is an 'inverted' labour process in which 'it is not the worker who employs the conditions of his work, but rather the reverse, the conditions of work employ the worker' (Marx, 1977: 548).

Thus, the worker must engage in activity that is not for self. 'The worker, instead of working for himself, works for, and consequently under, the capitalist' (Marx, 1977: 448). And, precisely because the wage-labourer's activity in the capitalist labour process is in accordance with the purpose of capital and is not enjoyed by him 'as the free play of his own physical and mental powers', the worker's will must be subordinated to that of capital (Marx, 1977: 284). Thus, the capitalist production process is one in which the worker resists 'the domination of capital', where 'capital is constantly compelled to wrestle with the insubordination of the workers' (Marx, 1977: 449, 489–90).

Similarly, workers struggle to 'set limits to the tyrannical usurpations of capital' – they struggle over the length and intensity of the workday in order to have time and energy for themselves (Marx, 1865b: 142). Thus, we see that *underlying* the discussion of the struggle over the workday in

Capital is what has *not* been established in *Capital* – the wage-labourer as being-for-self. These struggles are themselves latent in the process of production of the wage-labourer.

Finally, this process of production of capital, a process of 'sacrifice' – which 'correctly expresses the *subjective relation of the wage worker to his own activity*', is an activity which itself produces the wage-labourer as a particular socially developed human being, as one with the 'need to possess' (Marx, 1973: 614). Thus, capitalist production, which produces both the alien commodity and the alienated worker, constantly generates new needs for workers. *The goals of wage-labour, initially considered as a presupposition of its own labour process, are seen here as themselves results.*

As we have seen in the last chapter, those inputs required to produce the worker in accordance with her conception of self, however, cannot be fully realized – because capitalist production is limited by capital's goal of valorization and not by 'the proportion between production and social needs, the needs of socially developed human beings'. The existence of 'capitalist limitations' to the satisfaction of needs, that gap between necessary and social needs, means that the worker produces himself as *deprived*: 'So long as the need of man is not satisfied, he is in *conflict* with his needs, hence with himself' (Carver, 1975: 191). Inherent in the wage-labourer as being-for-self is the struggle for higher wages.

Thus, what emerges from consideration of wage-labour is – *class struggle from the side of the wage-labourer*. There is not merely capital for itself but also wage-labour for itself. Contrary to the picture presented in *Capital*, there are *two* 'oughts' – not merely capital's need for valorization but also 'the worker's own need for development'. A two-sided struggle, in which each attempts to reduce the other to dependence, is present in every aspect of the relation of capital and wage-labour.

Latent, for example, in the wage-labourer as being-for-self are her struggles over the workday (where 'between equal rights, force decides') in order to secure the time and energy required for her own development. And, similarly latent are her struggles for higher wages in order to secure those use-values that correspond to 'the requirements of socially developed human beings'. We see, then, the two oughts in struggle:

> The fixation of its actual degree [that of profit] is only settled by the continuous struggle between capital and labour, the capitalist constantly tending to reduce wages to their physical minimum, and to extend the working day to its physical maximum, while the working man constantly presses in the opposite direction.

The matter resolves itself into a question of the respective powers of the combatants (Marx, 1977: 344; 1865b: 146).

Between two 'oughts', force decides.

It must be stressed that we are not suggesting that *Capital* is one-sided because it excludes wage-labour as such. Obviously, wage-labour *in itself* could not be absent from *Capital* – because we could not even talk about the development of capital without it. Wage-labour is present as the barrier which capital transcends in its attempt to grow. But, not as the ought that has capital as *its* barrier! *Capital* is one-sided and inadequate precisely because the worker is not present as the subject who acts for herself against capital.

Thus, even where the struggles of workers were noted by Marx (as in the case of the workday), the logical presupposition from the side of wage-labour, wage-labour for itself, is absent. *It is only with the development of the side of wage-labour, the side absent from* **Capital***, that we have an adequate basis for considering the struggle of workers to realize their own goals.*

After considering wage-labour, we have before us not only the goals of capital but also those of wage-labour – *which imply the non-realization of capital's goals.* Certainly, we can no longer assume 'necessary needs,' the level of needs customarily satisfied, constant – that working assumption in *Capital* that was to be removed in the book on Wage-Labour. Not when we explicitly recognize the existence of the ought of wage-labour, when we see that against the thrust and tendency of capital 'the working man constantly presses in the opposite direction'; not when we posit workers struggling to reduce the gap between their existing standard and their social needs – just as they press in the direction of plowering the workday.

Rather, the level of necessary needs is itself revealed to be a product, a result – the result of class struggle.[11] That is the historical and social element in the value of labour-power. Indeed, Volume I of *Capital* introduces the level of necessary needs as an unexplained historical presupposition, as 'prehistory'. An adequate totality, however, requires the consideration of wage-labour-for-itself in order to show necessary needs as a result of its own existence, as developed and shaped anew within the whole. By itself, *Capital* cannot explain logically the level of necessary needs.

Our examination of wage-labour began as an investigation of the distinction present in capital as a whole, as that which stood outside of but which was necessary for capital. It remains now to complete the second 'dialectical moment', the positing of its unity with capital.

V The unity of opposites

Consider the process of production of capital and that of wage-labour. Firstly, these processes are *opposites*. In the first, labour-power is consumed by capital, exists for capital; in the second, labour-power is consumed by the worker and exists for the worker. In the first, the means of production possess and dominate the worker; in the second they are possessed and dominated by the worker. The distinction thus is one of the worker for capital vs the worker for self.

Further, these processes *exclude* each other. The worker cannot be for capital and self simultaneously. The more time the worker exists for capital, the less time there is for herself. Similarly, the greater the intensity of work for capital, the more energy consumed by capital, the less which is available for self. Thus, labour for capital is distinct from labour for self; it is labour alienated from self. The worker is only for self when she is not a worker for capital.

Finally, these processes, which are opposites and exclude each other, are also *necessary to each other*. If the worker does not produce for capital, she does not produce for herself; if she does not produce for herself, she is not available for capital. If capital does not go through its circuit, the worker cannot go through hers; if the worker does not go through her circuit, capital cannot proceed through its. The reproduction of capital requires the reproduction of wage-labour as such; the reproduction of wage-labour as such requires the reproduction of capital. The two processes of production thus presuppose each other. They are a unity.

Capital and wage-labour, thus, exist as opposites that are united within the capital/wage-labour relation. Each serves the other in this:

> reciprocity in which each is at the same time means and end, and becomes a means only insofar as he posits himself as end, that each thus posits himself as being for another, insofar as he is being for self and the other as being for him, insofar as he is being for himself.

Each posits self as dominant and serves as means 'only in order to posit the self as an end in itself' (Marx, 1973: 244). Only one side of this relationship, however, was presented in *Capital* – capital as being-for-self.

We have here now an organic totality in which all presuppositions are results and all results are presuppositions – the unity of capital and wage-labour, capital*ism* as a whole. It is a unity of opposites in which there is both *K-WL-K* and *WL-K-WL* and which has as its very nature two-sided class struggle. (This further development is illustrated in Figure 4.4.)

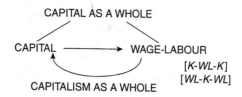

Figure 4.4 Capitalism as a whole as a totality

Is it *really*, though, an adequate totality? Does it adequately reflect the concrete totality? And, does it stand by itself with no external presuppositions? *In short, can we stop here?* We will put these questions aside for a moment. First, it is critical to explore the implications when we explicitly recognise the existence of this second ought, the side of wage-labour for itself.

5
The Political Economy
of Wage-Labour

> Owing to this *alien mediator* – instead of man himself being the
> mediator for man – man regards his will, his activity and his
> relation to other men as a power independent of him and
> them. His slavery, therefore, reaches a peak.
>
> Marx (1844b: 212)

I Capitalism as a whole

For the Young Marx, who remains dear to some of us, there was not one
subject – but two. Whatever the shortcomings of his early conceptions,
capitalism for him was clearly characterized by two sides and their relations. The relations of capitalism contained within them the relations of
capitalism as capital, the same relations as wage-labour and the mutual
relations of these two to one another.

Capital and wage-labour (wealth and the proletariat) thus were understood as antitheses – and, as such, constituted a whole (as represented in
Figure 5.1). They presupposed each other, reciprocally fostered and
developed each other as positive conditions and actively related to each
other as two sides of the same relation. Indeed, for the Young Marx, capital and wage-labour stood (and acted) in inimical mutual opposition;
and, the struggle between these two inseparable opposites, these elements in a two-sided and contradictory whole, constituted a dynamic
relationship, class struggle, driving it inexorably to its resolution (Marx,
1844c: 285, 289, 294; 1975c: 35; 1849: 214–15, 220).

Political economy, argued the Young Marx, could not grasp this. As we
have seen in Chapter 2, he criticized political economy because it looked
at the worker only from the perspective of capital. But isn't this
Marx's own position in *Capital*? The wage-labourer is considered as the

Figure 5.1   Capitalism as a whole

mediator for capital, as the means by which capital grows. She is not, on the other hand, considered as subject; and capital is not developed as the mediator for wage-labourers, as the means by which they satisfy their needs. One side of the relation of capital and wage-labourer is left undeveloped.

Nevertheless, that omission should not lead us to conclude that Marx changed his mind and abandoned his conception of capitalism as a whole. Let me offer two arguments in support of the position that Marx *retained* his early view – one logical and the other textual.

First, the side of wage-labour is present in *Capital* – *latently*. It is not incidental that much of our discussion in the preceding chapter has been drawn from the language of *Capital* itself. In this respect, the ability to develop the concept of capitalism as a whole (i.e., the completion of the 'inner totality') by incorporating material from *Capital* suggests an essential continuity between the thought of the Young Marx and that of the mature Marx, between the young Hegelian and the old scientist. That concept of capitalism as a whole as totality is *always present* – but its presence has been obscured by a silence, the completion of only *Capital*.

This does not at all imply, on the other hand, that there were no significant developments, no 'epistemological breaks' between the position of the Young Marx and the mature Marx. On the contrary, it is essential to understand that there *was* such a rupture, coinciding with the re-reading of Hegel's *Science of Logic*, which is manifested in the *Grundrisse*. But, it is not a shift in the view of capitalism as a totality; rather, the *Grundrisse* represents the development of a new understanding of the side of *capital* within that totality.

Whereas previously Marx had proceeded from labour to capital, he now emphasized that 'to develop the concept of capital it is necessary to begin not with labour but with value' (Marx, 1973: 279). In the *Grundrisse*, we trace the emergence of an adequate concept of capital, the concept of capital as self-valorization, as value-for-itself. We see Marx argue that the concept of capital itself must contain within it all its later developments; and we see him explicitly reject an analysis that would explain developments in capital by reference to its external forms of manifestation – i.e., by reference to the results of the competition of many capitals on the surface of society.

To try to explain the inner laws of capital as the result of competition, he asserts now, 'means to concede that one does not understand them' (Marx, 1973: 752). In short, no more do we find Marx explaining the movement of capital as the result of the external movements of the individual capitals (their repulsion and attraction) – as he had in his writings (such as *Wage Labour and Capital*) before the *Grundrisse*. With this 'break' – a rupture that has not been recognized adequately (as we see in the manifest variety of Marxian economists who dwell mainly in the sphere of competition) – Marx announced as a first principle the necessity to grasp *fully* the inner nature of capital.

Thus, with the *Grundrisse*, a new concept of capital now existed. And, of course, it really *does* affect our understanding of capitalism as a whole. Consider Figures 4.1 and 4.4 in the preceding chapter. Before the *Grundrisse*, we could not say that capital vs wage-labour is value-for-itself vs use-value-for-itself, money vs labour-power, money vs commodity, value vs use-value – indeed, that the opposition of capital and wage-labour is contained latent within the commodity, the celebrated starting point.

As Marx (1973: 248) noted in the *Grundrisse*, 'already the simple forms of exchange value and of money latently contain the opposition between labour and capital.' And, as Lenin, who observed in his private notes on Hegel that it was impossible to understand *Capital* 'without having thoroughly studied and understood the *whole* of Hegel's *Logic*', commented in those same notes: 'the simple form of value, the individual act of exchange of one given commodity for another, already includes in an undeveloped form *all* the main contradictions of capitalism' (Lenin, 1961: 180, 178–9).

The concept of capitalism as a whole thus is developed adequately only with this new understanding of capital which emerged in the *Grundrisse* – for which we have to thank (or blame as the case may be) Freiligrath's present to Marx of a few volumes of Hegel which were apparently of no use to Bakunin (Marx and Engels, 1983b: 249).

Why, then, don't we see this new conception of capitalism as a whole in Marx's mature work? Why is *Capital* one-sided? The problem is that, after putting aside his 'investigation of wage-labour in particular' in order to develop 'the general capital-relation', Marx never even completed his book on capital. Not only did he continue to discover theoretically new sides of capital but he was also delighted to be able to support theoretical conclusions with the 'FACTS' (Marx and Engels, 1987b: 407–8).[1] Given the importance in particular of Volume I of *Capital* (as we will see in Chapter 8), there is a definite logic to Marx's choice. Nevertheless, Marx's failure to set out the side of wage-labour in a logical and analytical manner equivalent to that developed for the side of capital has meant that there is a silence that yields a certain one-sidedness to the entire project. Wage-labour for itself and capitalism as a whole may be present – but they are there *only* 'in an undeveloped form'.

If this logical case does not appear compelling by itself, however, there is a second reason for us to believe that Marx retained his early conception of capitalism as a two-sided whole. His *other* writings at the time reveal that his ideas went beyond what we can find in *Capital*. We have already seen that Marx recognized the existence of more than one 'ought' at the time of his work on *Capital* in his classic statement in *Value, Price and Profit*:

> The fixation of its actual degree [that of profit] is only settled by the continuous struggle between capital and labour, the capitalist constantly tending to reduce wages to their physical minimum and to extend the working day to its physical maximum, *while the working man constantly presses in the opposite direction* (Marx, 1865b: 146; emphasis added).

Yet, that is by no means the only place where Marx revealed that he did not conceive of workers only insofar as they exist for capital. Nowhere is it more apparent that he himself went beyond *Capital* than in the 'Inaugural Address' of the First International (which also dates from the time that he was working on *Capital*). In that text, Marx called attention to the existence of *not one political economy but two* – the political economy of capital and the political economy of the working class.

'Two great facts', Marx noted, went counter to the general pattern of decline in the English workers' movement after 1848. Two victories had been achieved for 'the political economy of the working class'. In the case of one, the Ten Hours' Bill, not only was there a practical success – the effect of the shorter workday upon the 'physical, moral and intellectual' conditions of workers; but, 'there was something else to exalt the marvellous success of this working men's measure.' And, this something else was that the Ten Hours' Bill involved a victory over the 'the blind rule of the supply and demand laws which form the political economy of the middle class'. It was 'the victory of a principle', the first time that 'in broad daylight the political economy of the middle class succumbed to the political economy of the working class'.

'A still greater victory of the political economy of labour over the political economy of property', however, was the emergence of the co-operative movement, especially the co-operative factories. These demonstrated in practice that modern large-scale production could 'be carried on without the existence of a class of masters employing a class of hands' (Marx, 1864: 10–11).

Except for those who see all victories this side of socialism as victories for capital, the description of the 'two great facts' seems reasonable enough. Yet, a critical question has been begged. If Marx's purpose was a critique of political economy as such, how could he speak with obvious approval of the political economy of the working class? And, if he was really stuck within the logic and forms of capital in that 'trap baited by "Political Economy"', how could he hail the victories of an alternative logic? *What, in short, is this political economy of workers which contests the political economy of capital – and which encompasses both 'victories'?*

There is always a great danger in taking selected quotations from Marx at face value without grasping the inner core that informs them. Our purpose here, then, is to attempt to reconstruct and unveil by analysis that core, the alternative political economy, and to indicate the intrinsic connection between the two aspects identified in the Inaugural Address. The starting point for analysis is Marx's description of 'the blind rule of the supply and demand laws' as the basis of the political economy of capital.

II Competition and wage-labour

Underlying Marx's comment about the political economy of capital was his conception of the relation between the analysis of 'capital in general' and the phenomena of 'many capitals' in competition. Before one could understand the behaviour and movements of capital on the surface, Marx considered it necessary to grasp the inner nature, the essential character, of capital. Thus, his concept of 'capital in general' – 'an abstraction which grasps the specific characteristics which distinguish capital from all other forms of wealth – or modes in which (social) production develops' – abstracts from surface phenomena in order to comprehend the inner laws, immanent tendencies and intrinsic connections of capital (Marx, 1973: 449; 1968: 106; Lebowitz, 1985b).

Only *then* could one proceed to consider capital as it really exists – as individual capitals, as many capitals, as capitals in competition. Why? Because we need to distinguish between what is necessary (that is, that which flows from the concept of capital) and what is contingent: 'the general and necessary tendencies of capital must be distinguished from their forms of appearance'. Only after developing an understanding of those inner tendencies can one understand the apparent movements on the surface:

> a scientific analysis of competition is possible only if we can grasp the inner nature of capital, just as the apparent motions of the heavenly bodies are intelligible only to someone who is acquainted with their real motions which are not perceptible to the senses (Marx, 1977: 433).

Thus, Marx developed an understanding of the inner nature of capital and its tendencies through an analysis in which 'capital in general' appears as the actor. As we have seen in the account in Chapter 1, it is 'capital' which drives up the workday, drives down real wages, increases productivity – and always in order to increase surplus value. With that understanding, it was now possible to analyse the movements of capitals on the surface. Competition, he proposed, 'is nothing more than the way in which the many capitals force the inherent determinants of capital upon one another and upon themselves' (Marx, 1973: 651). What occurs at the level of competition, the real existence of capital as many capitals, is the execution and manifestation of the inner laws of capital in general: 'the immanent laws of capitalist production manifest themselves in the external movement of the individual capitals, assert themselves as the coercive laws of competition' (Marx, 1977: 433).

Not content with asserting this methodological principle, Marx provided glimpses into exactly how the inner tendencies of capital are expressed through competition. Capital's tendency to increase the workday (extensively and intensively) and to increase productivity – that is to increase the rate of surplus value – is manifested through the efforts of individual capitals to lower their costs of production relative to other individual capitals in the context of competition. *The competition of individual capitals to expand, their effort to act in their individual self-interest by seeking market advantages, is the way in which the inner tendencies of capital to grow are realized.* Precisely for this reason, Marx described the laws of competition, 'the blind rule of the supply and demand laws', as forming the political economy of capital.

Yet, consider capital's opposite – the side of wage-labour. As we have seen, *Capital* does not have as its object the examination of the movement when 'the workingman presses in the opposite direction' to capital. Even where Marx examines the struggle over the workday, rather than a theoretical exploration of the inherent tendency of workers to struggle for a reduction of the workday, he focuses upon the effort of workers to retain the 'normal' workday (that is, a defensive action against capital's initiative). And, of course, there is (as noted earlier) no discussion at all about workers struggling to increase the standard of life – which is precluded by the assumption that the standard of necessity is *given* in *Capital*, the assumption which was to be removed in the missing book on Wage-Labour.

In general, while we see capital's tendency to increase the rate of surplus value, there is no treatment of wage-labour's tendency to *reduce* the rate of surplus value. The very tendencies of wage-labour in general which emerge from 'the worker's own need for development' and that are the basis of the struggles of workers *for themselves* are absent. Silent, then, on the theoretical basis for class struggle *from the side of the worker* (that is, on *why* the worker 'constantly presses in the opposite direction'), it is not surprising that *Capital* similarly does not reveal the precise nature of the political economy of workers.

Return, however, to the relation between the tendencies of capital in general and their execution through competition. *Are the inner laws of wage-labour similarly executed in competition?* Marx's answer was a consistent 'NO!' As the General Council of the First International (in an address adopted unanimously at a meeting which Marx attended) declared, 'What the lot of the labouring population would be if everything were left to isolated, individual bargaining, may be easily foreseen. The iron rule of supply and demand, if left unchecked, would speedily reduce the producers of all wealth to a starvation level ...' (Marx, 1867: 137).

The logic was quite clear: competition between workers 'allows the capitalist to force down the price of labour'; it brings with it an increase in the length and intensity of the workday of employed workers, forcing them 'to submit to overwork' (Marx, 1977: 689, 789, 793). When workers compete among themselves, they press in the *same direction* as capital – the tendency is to *increase* the rate of surplus value!

In contrast to the side of capital, the efforts of wage-labourers *as individuals* to act in their self-interest run counter to the interests of wage-labour *as a whole*. Consider the effect of piece-work:

> the wider scope that piece-wages give to individuality tends to develop both that individuality, and with it the worker's sense of

liberty, independence and self-control, and also the competition of workers with each other. The piece-wage therefore has a tendency, while raising the wages of individuals above the average, to lower this average itself (Marx, 1977: 697).

Further, the self-interest of the individual wage-labourer engaged in piece-work similarly leads to the intensification of labour: 'Given the system of piece-wages, it is naturally in the personal interest of the worker that he should strain his labour-power as intensely as possible; this in turn enables the capitalist to raise the normal degree of intensity of labour more easily' (Marx, 1977: 695). Thus, acting in their individual interest and competing among themselves, workers do not express the inner tendencies of wage-labour but, rather, the inner tendencies of *capital*. Insofar as wage-labour competes, it does so as part of capital, as a component of capital: 'the competition among workers is only another form of the competition among capitals' (Marx, 1973: 651).

So, then, *how* does the worker 'constantly press in the opposite direction' to capital? How does the worker prevent capital from reducing 'wages to their physical minimum' and extending the workday to 'its physical maximum'? *Only by negating competition*, only by infringing upon the 'sacred' law of supply and demand and engaging in 'planned co-operation' (Marx, 1977: 793).

In short, only when wage-labourers struggle against competition do they go against the inner laws of capital and manifest the inner laws of wage-labour. Rather than separation and competition, only combination and cooperation yields the optimum solution for workers. The struggle between capital and wage-labour, the essential contradiction, assumes the form on the surface of a struggle between competition and combination.

III   Cooperation and separation

The recognition that capital and wage-labour stand in inimical opposition with respect to competition and its negation is critical but is insufficient to reveal the basis for the political economy of wage-labour. For that, we must delve deeper and ask *why*? What is it in the essence of wage-labour that yields the result that it is only through cooperation and combination that wage-labour acts in its own interest? Why is it that workers must negate competition in order that the worker's 'ought', the 'worker's own need for development', can be realized? Our enquiry necessarily takes us beyond the question of wage-labour as such to the consideration of relations that are not unique to the capitalist form of production.

Two specific propositions implicit in *Capital* are relevant to our investigation. The first proposition is that *any cooperation and combination of labour in production generates a combined, social productivity of labour that exceeds the sum of individual, isolated productivities.* Thus, when producers cooperate by working together side by side performing similar operations or engage in different but connected processes or where they produce differing use-values which correspond to social requirements (the division of labour within society), the effect of their combined, social labour is increased productivity. Their cooperation results in 'the creation of a new productive power, which is intrinsically a collective one' (Marx, 1977: 443).

This greater productivity of social labour had been noted in the *Grundrisse* where Marx (1973: 528) commented that the combination of individuals to build a road is more than just an addition of their individual labour capacities: 'The unification of their forces increases their *force of production*'. This 'association of workers – the cooperation and division of labour as fundamental conditions of the productivity of labour' is independent of any particular form of production (Marx, 1973: 585). Even earlier, however, he had called attention to 'the multiplied productive force, which arises through the co-operation of different individuals as it is caused by the division of labour' (Marx and Engels, 1846: 48).

This division and cooperation of labour which yields increased productivity in any society extends beyond a particular workplace to the division of labour within society. For example, insofar as some producers are active in the production of means of production that increase the productivity of others who work with those means of production, total social productivity is higher than it would be in the absence of this division (or, more appropriately, combination) of labour within society. Indeed, the growth of social productivity increasingly depends upon the extent that science, intellectual labour, 'the general productive forces of the social brain' are embodied in means of production (Marx, 1973: 694, 704–6). Here, too, the unification of different workers yields higher productivity for the producers as a whole, which is a social productivity:

> This development in productivity can always be reduced in the last analysis to the social character of the labour that is set to work, to the division of labour within society, and to the development of intellectual labour, in particular of the natural sciences (Marx, 1981b: 175).

In this proposition that social productivity is dependent upon the degree of combination among producers, Marx expressed a principle quite similar to Adam Smith's emphasis on the relation of productivity to the division of labour (Smith, 1937: 3). By expressing the principle as one of the cooperation and combination of labour, however, division of labour is understood as significant only insofar as that 'divided' labour is subsequently combined. In short, these parts have significance only as parts of a whole, parts of social labour as a whole.[2]

Nor is it simply the combination of labour as such which increases social productivity – there is, further, the enhancement of individual productivity occurring when producers work side by side which 'originates from the fact that man ... is at all events a social animal': 'When the worker co-operates in a planned way with others, he strips off the fetters of his individuality, and develops the capabilities of his species' (Marx, 1977: 444, 447). Thus, we begin with the proposition that the social productivity of labour is a positive function of the degree of cooperation in production, that is, of social production.

The second proposition in question is concerned with the *distribution* of the gains from the socially productive power of labour. It states that, in any society, *separation and division in social relations among producers allow those who mediate among the producers to capture the fruits of cooperation in production*. For example, in simple commodity production, profit is 'derived from the two-fold advantage gained, over both the selling and the buying producers, by the merchant who parasitically inserts himself between them' (Marx, 1977: 267). The merchant's mediation between the extremes, the various producers, allows him to secure the gains from cooperation and is the basis for the formation of capital (Marx, 1981b: 442–3, 447). Similarly, within pre-capitalist production, those who 'round-up' individual producers secure the surplus products which are the effect of the combined labour. Thus, the palaces and temples of early societies resulted from the ability to direct large numbers of producers in cooperation (Marx, 1973: 528; 1977: 451–2)

The same benefit accruing to the mediator among producers clearly holds true within capitalist production, where capital mediates between 'individual, isolated' owners of labour-power 'who enter into relations with the capitalist, but not with each other' (Marx, 1977: 451). In this process, 'the individual workers or rather labour capacities are paid, and paid as separate ones. Their cooperation, and the productive power which arises therefrom, is not paid for'; i.e., the increase in productive power resulting from cooperation 'costs the capitalist nothing' (Marx, 1988: 260, 321). Thus, having purchased labour-power and thereby secured the property rights to the products of labour, the capitalist captures the fruits of cooperation in production. 'The social productive power which arises from cooperation is a *free gift*' (Marx, 1988: 260).

In capitalism, the productive forces of social labour – collective unity in cooperation, combination in the division of labour, the use of the forces of nature and the sciences – appear as the productive forces of capital, the mediator (Marx, 1977: 1054, 451; 1973: 585). What capital secures is the productive power of socially combined labour, which appears as 'a productive power inherent in capital'; those productivity gains resulting from the social character of labour accrue to the capitalist: 'What the capitalist makes use of here are the benefits of the entire system of the social division of labour' (Marx, 1977: 451; 1981b: 175).

Why are the producers themselves not able to capture the fruits of cooperation in production? Marx's answer is clear: their situation depends upon the degree of separation among them. For example, comparing rural and urban workers within capitalism, he pointed out that 'the dispersal of the rural workers over large areas breaks their power of resistance, while concentration increases that of the urban workers' (Marx, 1977: 638). Similarly, he noted that 'in the so-called domestic industries this exploitation is still more shameless than in modern manufacture, because the workers' power of resistance declines with their dispersal' (Marx, 1977: 591). This second proposition implies that the *extent* of the surplus extracted by those who mediate among producers (i.e., the extent of exploitation) is a function of the degree to which producers are separated.

In this context, 'planned cooperation' among wage-labourers in capitalism (and the struggle against competition) is no chance or contingent aspect of the side of wage-labourers-for-themselves. Rather, only by struggling to reduce their degree of separation can workers achieve their goals. The struggle against the existence of a mediator between (and above) them is inherent in the 'worker's own need for development'. Thus, Marx did more than develop a critique of the political economy of capital; he also revealed its antithesis, the political economy of the working class, which stresses *the combination of labour as the source of social productivity and the separation of workers as the condition for their exploitation*. Precisely how that political economy is manifested within capitalism (and the situation of the two aforementioned victories) remains to be shown.

IV The struggle against capital as mediator

The positive side of capitalism is that it socializes production and creates an interdependence within production far exceeding pre-existing levels. Capital has the tendency, thus, to create a collective worker – wage-labourers who are part of a productive organism and, as such, are One within production. Of course, the resulting increase in social productivity is not capital's goal as such but is merely the means to appropriate relative surplus value. Nevertheless, it is one side of capital's tendency.

The other side is that capital requires separation and division among wage-labourers as a condition of its ability to capture the fruits of cooperation in production. (Thus, the tendency to 'divide and conquer' wage-labour is inherent in capital.) As wage-labour is present in every moment within the circuit of capital, separation and division of workers in each moment is necessary if capital is to realize its goal.

This necessary separation is present initially insofar as each wage-labourer is an individual, isolated owner of labour-power for whom capital is the possessor of value (M-Lp). Within production, however, the very process of cooperation brings workers together; thus, in order to enforce the production of surplus value (P), capital must develop ways (such as division of labour, piece-work, etc.) to foster separation and to assert its authority. Finally, as owner of the products of labour, capital separates the producers from those who consume – both individually and productively; the division of labour within society is mediated by capital as owner of means of production and articles of consumption (C'-M').

Just as capital is the mediator for wage-labour, separating the worker from her labour-power as property, from her labour as activity and from the product of her labour – so also is capital the mediator between wage-labourers in each moment of the circuit of capital.

A   The co-operatives

In this context, the significance of co-operative factories was quite clear in that they involved the *replacement* of capital as a mediator in all phases – in the purchase of labour-power, in the direction and supervision of production, and in the ownership of the products of labour. Rather than selling their labour-power as isolated owners, the particular co-operating producers combined it. Rather than characterized by the despotism of capital, the supervision and direction required of combined labour on a large scale lost its 'antithetical character'. And, rather than the products of labour embodying the power of capital, they signified the communal relation between the particular co-operators – which was presupposed from the outset (Marx, 1973: 171–3; 1981b: 512). In this sense, the co-operative factories represented the 'first examples of the emergence of a new form' (Marx, 1981b: 571). Their great merit was: 'to practically show, that the present pauperising, and despotic system of the *subordination of labour* to capital can be superseded by the republican and beneficent system of the *association of free and equal producers'* (Marx, 1866: 346).

Nevertheless, Marx was emphatic that those co-operative factories, as they existed, necessarily reproduced the 'defects of the existing system'. They did not go beyond profit-seeking and competition; co-operative production here remained an isolated system 'based on individual and antagonistic interests', one in which the associated workers had 'become their own capitalist', using the means of production to 'valorize their own labour' (Marx, 1981b: 571).[3] Further, in the 'dwarfish forms' inherent in the private efforts of individual workers, the co-operatives would 'never transform capitalistic society':

> To convert social production into one large and harmonious system of free and co-operative labour, *general social changes* are wanted, *changes of the general conditions of society*, never to be realised save by the transfer of the organised forces of society, viz., the state power, from capitalists and landlords to the producers themselves (Marx, 1866: 346).

In this context, focus on co-operatives as the means by which the working class could emancipate itself necessarily remained a 'sham and a snare'. The experience of 1848 to 1864 had 'proved beyond doubt' that, within their narrow circle, the co-operatives could not succeed in transforming capitalism (Marx 1871b: 76; 1864: 383). Nevertheless, Marx *still* declared those co-operative factories as a great 'victory' – they had shown that wage-labour was 'but a transitory and inferior form' of labour, 'that the capitalist as functionary of production has become just as superfluous to the workers as the landlord appears to the capitalist with regard to bourgeois production', and 'that to bear fruit, the means of labour need not be monopolized as a means of dominion over, and of extortion against, the labouring man himself' (Marx, 1864: 383; 1981b: 511; 1971: 497).

The very existence of co-operative factories, then, was a practical demonstration that capital was not necessary as a mediator in social production. This 'victory of the political economy of labour over the political economy of property' was an *ideological* victory.

3 Against capital in the labour market (*M–Lp*)

The significance of the co-operative factories is that they pointed to the alternative to capital in each moment of its circuit. Within these moments, however, workers were *directly* confronting the power of capital. The first and foremost task was the struggle against capital as a mediator in the labour market; the necessity here was to end their own disunion as sellers of labour-power – a disunion 'created and perpetuated by their *unavoidable competition amongst themselves*' (Marx, 1866: 347).

Unchecked, capital's power is the power of a buyer in a buyer's market: each seller of labour-power, the weaker side in the labour market, 'operates independently of the mass of his competitors, and often directly against them' (Marx, 1981b: 295). That relative weakness of workers is not accidental. Its basis is the existence of unemployment, a reserve army of labour which capital inherently reconstitutes through the cessation of accumulation or the substitution of machinery. This relative surplus of workers, then, is 'the background against which the law of the demand and supply of labour does its work' (Marx, 1977: 770, 784, 792). It is the basis for a tendency of the price of labour-power to be driven downward. The result, as Engels (1881b: 104) argued, is that in 'trades without organization of the work-people':

> wages tend constantly to fall and the working hours tend constantly to increase … Times of prosperity may now and then interrupt it, but times of bad trade hasten it on all the more afterwards. The work-people gradually get accustomed to a lower and lower standard of life. While the length of working day more and more approaches the possible maximum, the wages come nearer and nearer to their absolute minimum …

Thus, if workers are to be able to satisfy their needs – both their customary needs and those new needs generated within capitalist society – they must negate their disunity as competing commodity-sellers. Their need for self-development, the workers' 'ought', requires them to develop new social relations among themselves that allow them to go beyond barriers to the realization of their needs. Thus, Marx argued that, through the formation of trade unions ('whose importance for the English working class can scarcely be overestimated'), workers attempt to check that competition; they attempt to 'obviate or weaken the ruinous effects of this natural law of capitalist production [competition among workers] on their class' (Marx, 1977: 1069, 793). This action is necessary and can not be 'dispensed with so long as the present system of production lasts' (Marx, 1866: 348).

The point, then, of the trade unions was precisely to counter capital's tendency and to 'prevent the *price* of labour-power from falling below its *value'* (Engels, 1881b: 106; Marx, 1977: 1069). And, insofar as the organized worker 'measures his demands against the capitalist's profit and demands a certain share of the surplus value created by him', there is the possibility of success in resisting capital's tendency. The workers here do not permit wages 'to be reduced to the absolute minimum; on the contrary, they achieve a certain quantitative participation in the general growth of wealth' (Marx, 1973: 597; 1971: 312). As Engels (1881a: 102) commented, the great merit of the trade unions is that 'they tend to keep up and to raise the standard of life'.[4]

For their success in expressing the interests of wage-labourers as commodity-sellers, the trade unions were viewed by political economy as an infringement upon personal freedom and competition (Marx, 1977: 793–4, 1070n). (The standard here, of course, is the political economy of *capital*, which rests upon individual self-interest and competition – rather than the *separate political economy of the working class* apparent in the social forms of cooperation that workers create in their own interest.) Yet, Marx saw that success as necessarily limited – precisely because of the power of capital within production.

C   Against capital in production (*P*)

What about the struggle against capital as a mediator in production, where capital attempts to exercise the property right it has purchased in the labour market, the right of disposition over labour-power? The central issue here is the struggle against capital's 'will' – and, in particular, against the capitalist character of direction and supervision within the labour process. Precisely because capital's goal is surplus value and not the worker's own need for development, the worker's own will must be subordinated to that of capital within the capitalist labour process. Thus, capital strives to ensure 'that the worker does his work regularly and with the proper degree of intensity' (Marx, 1977: 424).

Given that workers enter into the capitalist process of production as 'isolated, mutually independent commodity owners' and that they are placed into a relation within production which belongs to capital, it might seem that capital's ability to enforce its will cannot be checked (Marx, 1988: 261). Since capital owns the right to command the exercise of their labour-power, doesn't this imply the maximum intensity of work?

Yet, recall that this is a peculiar commodity that capital has purchased. The seller, a human being whose own goals include the time and energy for herself, enters the process of production along with the commodity she has sold. Further, nothing in this particular contract specifies precisely how hard the workers must work. (The contract in this respect is incompletely specified.) Accordingly, the potential exists within production for workers to retain energy for themselves by pressing in the opposite direction to the capitalist. In Marx's discussion of manufacturing, he notes (1977: 458) that the specialized workers learn 'by experience how to attain the desired effect with the minimum of exertion'. They jealously guard their skills and secrets through methods such as long apprenticeship periods 'even where it would be superfluous' (Marx, 1977: 489). All of this was the result of the combination of workers – in particular, within craft unions.

In short, even though they are initially assembled by capital for its own goals and their 'relation therefore confronts them as a relation of capital, not as their own relation', workers do proceed to create their own relations within production (Marx, 1988: 261). They come to recognize their unity as producers and to understand their power against capital. As they are brought together by capital in larger numbers, their degree of separation diminishes and their 'power of resistance' rises. Indeed, 'as the number of the co-operating workers increases, so too does their resistance to the domination of capital'. And, the greater the opposition of workers to the rule of capital in production, the 'greater the role that this work of supervision plays' in order to subject the worker to capital's purpose (Marx, 1977: 449; 1981b: 507).

Thus, Marx observed that within manufacturing 'capital is constantly compelled to wrestle with the insubordination of the workers'. Standing against the despotism of the capitalist workplace and capital's tendencies were 'the habits and the resistance of the male workers' (Marx, 1977: 489–90). And, despite 'the pressure put on by capital to overcome this resistance' (and all others), 'the complaint that the workers lack discipline runs through the whole of the period of manufacture' (Marx, 1977: 449, 490). As we saw in Chapter 1, manufacture as a mode of production was a barrier to the growth of capital – but not simply because of its technical limitations.

Thus, capital drove beyond this barrier. Modern industry and the factory system brought a new form of competition for workers – competition with the result of past labour, the machine. Not only did the machine substitute for the work of many wage-labourers, but it also became 'the most powerful weapon for suppressing strikes, those periodic revolts of the working class against the autocracy of capital' (Marx, 1977: 562). As well as freeing capital from dependence upon the skills of specialized workers (and breaking 'the resistance which the male workers had continued to oppose to the despotism of capital'), the machine became the objective basis for the intensification of labour and for the emergence of a 'barrack-like discipline' in the factory (Marx, 1977: 526, 536, 549). Not only did the conditions of labour come to dominate labour technologically, but they also came to 'replace it, suppress it and render it superfluous in its independent forms' (Marx, 1977: 1055). Thus, capital, by restructuring production, could defeat the resistance of workers in production.

But not quite. Marx *overestimated* capital's victory from the machine at the time and underestimated the ability of workers to 'set limits to the tyrannical usurpations of capital' by pushing in the opposite direction. In part, the problem results from the rather significant gap between the 'real' machine and its concept (what is *latent* in the machine). Were the worker *really* reduced to 'watchman and regulator to the production process itself,' the potential and form of opposition within production would be quite delimited (Marx, 1973: 705). As long, however, as the machine-operator has not yet 'been deprived of all significance', the potential for opposition to capital within production is obviously still present (Marx, 1977: 549).

To this extent, there was an important counter-tendency inherent in the machine as fixed capital. The very growth in fixed capital makes the continuity of the production process all the more necessary; 'every interruption of the production process acts as a direct reduction of capital itself, of its initial value'. The development of machine industry makes capital *more*, rather than less, vulnerable to the weapon of strikes: capital is in a form in which 'it loses both use-value and exchange-value whenever it is deprived of contact with living labour' (Marx, 1973: 703, 719; 1977: 529). Thus, the potential for workers to assert their own will within production was *not* automatically removed with the emergence of large-scale industry. Why else would capital introduce means of dividing workers (such as piece-work and various forms of labour segmentation) if not to overcome the workers' own strength within the production process?[5]

Yet, this was not Marx's only point about the significance of the machine. Central to Marx's judgement about the weakness of trade unions was his recognition of the critical feed-back and interpenetration between developments in the sphere of production and those in the buying and selling of labour-power. In opposition to the sanguine view of the political economists of capital, Marx stressed machinery's tendency to displace workers and, thus, to add to the size of the reserve army of labour – leading to falling wages.

Outsourcing
offshoring

In turn, this meant a tendency for workers to supply additional labour 'to secure even a miserable average wage' – a process which, under the Factory Acts, occurred through intensification of labour (via the mechanism of piece-wages). The effect was to make 'the supply of labour to a certain extent independent of the supply of workers'; wages dropped even more – which 'completes the despotism of capital' on the basis of the blind laws of supply and demand (Marx, 1977: 687–8, 699, 793).

Thus, precisely because of capital's power as owner of the means of production, in their struggles over wages trade unions *necessarily* were 'fighting with effects, but not with the causes of those effects' – causes emanating from capital's power outside the labour market as such. And, they necessarily were fighting a *losing* battle ('retarding the downward movement, but not changing its direction') because the 'general tendency of capitalistic production' was to drive down the standard of wages 'more or less to its *minimum limit*' (Marx, 1865b: 148).[6]

D   Against capital as owner of products of labour ($C'-M'$)

What gives capital the power to cast people off by replacing them with machines? Simply, because capital owns the process of production and, having seized possession of production, exercises its ownership to pursue its own particular goal – surplus value. Capital has this power because, having purchased labour-power, it is the owner of the products of labour and, accordingly, the immediate beneficiary of all the social wealth produced by the collective worker.

As owner of articles of consumption, capital decides how much of what particular use-values shall be produced and the terms on which they shall be transferred to those with needs. For capital, only a use-value which is C' (i.e., a commodity containing surplus value) – and, indeed, only one whose surplus value can be *realized* (i.e., which can make the mortal leap from C' to M') – shall be produced. Thus, restricting the production of use-values to those that satisfy its own needs, capital determines both the extent and the particular nature of the needs of human beings that shall be satisfied.

Similarly, as owner of the means of production, capital has the power to determine how or whether the means of production shall be used and the power to exclude others from their use. Having acquired the results of past social labour, capital can determine both the extent and the particular nature of the labour that shall be performed. Just as it mediates between individuals as isolated sellers of labour-power and as parts of a productive organism, as owner of the products of labour, capital mediates between the producer and the consumer, between the worker who produces means of production and the worker who uses them, between the social brain and the social hand. It rules over the division of labour within society. All the power of the collective worker is capital's; it is the dictator over society.

But, the power of capital is mystified. As the owner of articles of consumption, capital's power is hidden by the mystification that attaches to the product of labour as a commodity. Capital appears here simply as the individual seller of a commodity and wage-labour as the individual buyer – as participants in a relation of simple exchange (C-M-C); thus, capitalist relations of production are not at all apparent here: in C'-M', all distinction between the contracting parties as capitalist and wage-labourer is extinguished (Marx, 1973: 246, 639).

Rather than as the result of capital's mediation between producers, the existing social division of labour appears in the market as 'an objective interrelation, which arises spontaneously from nature'. The relations of individuals to one another appear as an autonomous power over them – 'although created by society, [they] appear as if they were *natural conditions*, not controllable by individuals' (Marx: 1973: 196–7, 164). In short, the unity and mutual complementarity in the division of social labour exist 'in the form of a natural relation, as it were, external to the individuals and independent of them' (Marx, 1973: 158).

It is as *individuals* that wage-labourers experience their powerlessness in this realm – and that powerlessness (their inability to satisfy needs, etc.) does not appear foremost as the result of the power of capital as mediator within society. Rather, it appears as a powerlessness of the individual with respect to society – a powerlessness that is expressed as the absence of a thing, *Money*. Capital's separation of producer from product ensures the dependence of the wage-labourer upon capital as the possessor of money, 'social power in the form of a thing' (Marx, 1973: 158).

Similarly, as owner of the means of production, capital 'confronts society as a thing, and as the power that the capitalist has through this thing' (Marx, 1981b: 373). The material conditions of production of the community of labour appear 'as something independent of the workers and intrinsic to the conditions of production themselves' (Marx, 1977: 1053). They 'confront the individual workers as something *alien, objective, ready-made*, existing without their intervention, and frequently even hostile to them' (Marx, 1977: 1054). This becomes especially true with the development of machine industry, where 'objectified labour confronts living labour as a ruling power,' and where knowledge appears as alien and external to the worker (Marx, 1973: 693, 695).

Since the productive forces of social labour are the property of capital and thus 'the development of the *social* productive forces of labour and the conditions of that development come to appear as the *achievement of capital*', it seems like common sense that the worker is dependent upon capital for the production of wealth (Marx, 1977: 1054–5). How insignificant the individual worker must appear to herself: the 'elevation of direct labour into social labour appears as a reduction of individual labour to helplessness in face of the communality represented by and concentrated in capital' (Marx, 1973: 700).

Capital's power as owner of the products of labour is, accordingly, both absolute and mystified. Yet, since its power as owner underlies (and continually reproduces) its power as both purchaser of labour-power and director of labour, only a challenge to its power as owner of the products of labour can satisfy the workers' own need for development. But, capital's power in this sphere is not only mystified but also qualitatively different. There is no direct arena of confrontation between *specific* capitalists and *specific* wage-labourers in this sphere comparable to that which emerges spontaneously in the labour market and the workplace. *The power of capital as owner of the products of labour and as mediator of the division of labour within society appears as the dependence of wage-labour upon capital-as-a-whole.*

Indicative of capital's power as mediator within society is that it transcends the ability of trade unions as such to combat it. How can specific groups of workers compel capital to produce use-values that will not realize surplus value? Or to use its property in means of production, the product of social labour, to satisfy the needs of socially developed human beings? To demand as much is to demand that capital be not-capital. It is to demand that capital relinquish its claim as owner of property.

Further, what is the medium through which such a demand could be made? Trade unions act in opposition to specific and particular capitals. *Yet, the power to be confronted is that of capital as a totality – and only insofar as it is a totality.* In the absence of such a total opposition, the trade unions fight the effects within the labour market and the workplace but not the causes of the effects.

Thus, the character of existing relations among workers may itself emerge as a barrier to the workers' drive for self-development. Precisely for that reason, Marx criticized the trade unions for restricting themselves to a guerrilla war against capital. They had failed, he argued, to recognize their potential power 'of acting against the system of wages slavery itself. They therefore kept too much aloof from general social and political movements.' Trade unions, 'apart from their original purposes', now had to learn to act as organizing centres of the working class 'in the broad interest of its *complete emancipation*'. They had to go beyond purely economic struggles for that purpose: 'They must aid every social and political movement tending in that direction' (Marx, 1866: 348–9). What Marx was stressing was the need for greater unity of workers as a class.

It is in this context that we should consider the significance of the Ten Hours' Bill. What precisely was the victory? Certainly, it revealed in broad daylight the class struggle of capital and wage-labour over the workday; similarly, like the organization of trade unions, it suppressed competition among workers over the length of the workday. But, its *real* victory is that it revealed clearly that wage-labour required political struggle and the use of the State to achieve success in this case! The Ten Hours' Bill, after all, was a legislative act – which it *had* to be:

> As to the *limitation of the working day* in England, as in all other countries, it has never been settled except by *legislative interference*. Without the working men's continuous pressure from without that interference would never have taken place. But at all events, the result was not to be attained by private settlement between the working men and the capitalists. This very necessity of *general political action* affords the proof that in its merely economic action capital is the stronger side (Marx, 1865b: 146).

In short, only by going beyond 'a purely economic movement' to act as a class *politically* could the working class coerce capital 'by pressure from without' to achieve a goal which was not to be attained by private settlement. Only through a '*political* movement, that is to say, a movement of the *class*, with the object of enforcing its interests in a general form, in a form possessing general, socially coercive force.'[7] To enforce the interests of wage-labour in such a form meant, of course, to use the State, *within capitalism*, in the interests of workers. The Ten Hours' Bill proved 'in broad daylight' that it was possible for the political economy of the working class to triumph over that of capital when workers went beyond guerrilla warfare.

That victory in the case of the Ten Hours' Bill demonstrated what was necessary to challenge capital's power as owner of the products of labour and mediator within society. For, precisely where we have the power of capital as a totality in opposition to the separate individual interests of workers, the interests of workers as a whole have to be enforced in a 'form possessing general, socially coercive force'. Private settlements 'between the working men and the capitalists' cannot suffice. Indeed, since such efforts are contrary to the interests of workers as a whole, socially coercive force is necessary to bind not only capital but *also wage-labourers as individual self-seekers*.

In the case of the limitation of the workday, for example, Marx noted that 'the workers have to put their heads together and, as a class, compel the passing of a law, an all-powerful social barrier by which they can be prevented from selling themselves and their families into slavery and death by voluntary contract with capital' (Marx, 1977: 416).

Similarly, the struggle against existing child labour and for public education involved saving children not only from capital but also from the individual acts of their parents. Children, Marx noted, 'are unable to act for themselves. It is, therefore, the duty of society to act on their behalf.' Since the future of society depended upon the vindication of the rights of children and their formation, Marx's 'instructions' to the delegates of the First International stressed the necessity for political action by workers:

> This can only be effected by converting *social reason* into *social force*, and, under given circumstances, there exists no other method of doing so, than through *general laws*, enforced by the power of the state. In enforcing such laws, the working class do not fortify governmental power. On the contrary, they transform that power, now used against them, into their own agency. They effect by a general act what they would vainly attempt by a multitude of isolated individual efforts (Marx, 1866: 344–5).

The same logic that calls for workers to 'put their heads together' and act as a class to compel passage of a law limiting the workday, though, also applies to a struggle to make the state serve the interests of wage-labourers by, for example, legalizing and supporting the existence of trade unions or by engaging in policies that reduce the level of unemployment. General political action aimed at making the state the workers' own agency is necessary since 'in its merely economic action capital is the stronger side'.

At the root of capital's power in general is its power as owner of the products of labour – which workers can challenge only by acting politically as a class. This, of course, was the message of the First International: 'To conquer political power has therefore become the great duty of the working classes' (Marx, 1865b: 384). And, this was the message that Marx and Engels continued to stress in the *Communist Manifesto*: 'the first step in the revolution by the working class is to raise the proletariat to the position of ruling class, to win the battle of democracy' (Marx and Engels, 1848: 504).

V The political economy of wage-labour

Those who mediate among producers have an interest in maintaining and increasing the degree of separation, division and atomization among producers in order to continue to secure the fruits of cooperation in production. Capital achieves this by fostering competition – between workers in one firm, between workers in different firms, between past and living labour; its power depends on the appearance that particular individuals and particular groups of individuals, by acting in their individual self-interest, can succeed in advancing their own particular interests. Individual self-seeking and competition constitutes the political economy of capital.

The political economy of wage-labour, by contrast, begins from the recognition that social productivity results from the combination of social labour, from the cooperation of the limbs and organs of the collective worker. And, it stresses that only by reducing the degree of separation, that only through combination and unity can wage-labourers capture the fruits of cooperation *for themselves* and realize their 'own need for development'. That political economy focuses on the necessity to remove capital as mediator between workers *as a whole* – and thus on the intrinsic nature of both purely economic and political struggles against capital. The two victories for the political economy of the working class revealed the goal (the 'new form' of production) and the means to achieve it.

The full dimensions of the political economy of wage-labour are clarified only in relation to consideration of capital as a whole. As we move through the circuit of capital, different aspects of the struggle against capital as mediator become apparent. From sellers of labour-power, whose assertion of selves as commodity-sellers does not transcend the capital/wage-labour relation; to producers within the workplace, whose assertions of their needs as producers implicitly go beyond capitalist direction; to wage-labour *as a class* which politically asserts the needs of workers as human beings in opposition to the rights of capital as property – each moment contains the preceding and represents a *higher* level of struggle against capital.

Thus, the explicit consideration of the side of wage-labour for itself reveals that there is an integral relation between the 'purely economic' analysis of *Capital* and the political struggle against capital, one inherent in Marx's political economy. For this reason, Marx had little patience with the position of the Proudhonists within the First International:

> They spurn all *revolutionary* action, i.e. arising from the class struggle itself, every concentrated social movement, and therefore also that which can be achieved by *political means* (e.g., such as limitation of the working day by *law*) (Marx and Engels, 1987b: 326).

Once we understand Marx's conception of the political economy of the working class, it is obvious that it goes well beyond the trade union issues characteristic of the first two moments (*M-Lp* and *P*) of the circuit of capital. We are not yet at the point, however, where we can consider fully that political economy and the political struggle it encompasses – one reason why this chapter has the more restricted title of 'The Political Economy of Wage-Labour'. We need to understand, for example, the limits of the capitalist state for going beyond capital. Indeed, we have yet to explore at all how workers can go beyond capital – as opposed to pursuing their interests within capitalism.

6
Wages

> The level of the necessaries of life whose total value constitutes the value of labour-power can itself rise or fall. The analysis of those variations, however, belongs not here but in the theory of wages.
>
> Marx (1977: 1068–9)

The political economy of wage-labour discussed in our last chapter stipulates that, just as capital benefits directly from the competition of workers, in turn the ability of workers to capture the gains from social production depends upon their success in reducing the separation and division in social relations among themselves. By forming trade unions and by attempting to turn the state 'into their own agency' (Marx, 1866: 344–5), workers struggle to satisfy unrealized social needs and to 'achieve a certain quantitative participation in the general growth of wealth' (Marx: 1971: 312). They press in the opposite direction to capital in order to increase the level of their wages. Class struggle, it appears, is critical in the determination of wages.

But, where does class struggle fit into *Capital*'s discussion of the value of labour-power? Chapter 1 introduced the concepts of necessary labour and the value of labour-power. There we noted that the hours of labour (w) necessary to produce the daily requirements (U) of the worker depend upon the productivity of labour (q):

$$w = U/q \tag{1.1}.$$

In value-terms, 'the value of labour-power [the value-form of necessary labour] can be resolved into the value of a definite quantity of the means of subsistence. It therefore varies with the value of the means of subsistence, i.e. with the quantity of labour-time required to produce them' (Marx, 1977: 276).

As Chapter 3 demonstrated, however, Marx assumed in *Capital* that this 'definite quantity of the means of subsistence' was given and fixed. Rather than explore the effects of class struggle on wages, he set aside anything to do with changes in real wages or in the level of needs that workers are able to satisfy as a subject for a later work:

> The problem of these movements in the level of the workers' needs, as also that of the rise and fall of the market price of labour capacity above or below this level, do not belong here, where the general capital-relation is to be developed, but in the doctrine of the wages of labour (Marx, 1988: 44–5).

Accordingly, with respect to wages, Marx explicitly analysed in *Capital* only the effect of productivity increases upon the value of labour-power. 'In our investigation', he indicated in his notebooks, 'we proceed from the assumption that the *labour capacity* is paid for *at its value*, hence wages are only reduced by the DEPRECIATION of that labour capacity, or what is the same thing, by the cheapening of the means of subsistence entering into the workers' consumption.' Beginning, in short, from that 'definite quantity of means of subsistence', Marx's focus in *Capital* is upon changes in the quantity of labour required to produce that given set of necessaries.

Of course, Marx knew that there were other reasons for a change in wages:

> In so far as machinery brings about a direct reduction of wages for the workers employed by it, by for example using the demand of those rendered unemployed to force down the wages of those in employment, it is not part of our task to deal with this CASE. It belongs to the theory of wages (Marx, 1994: 23).

So, can we infer from these passages elements in the theory of wages? What is the link between the value of labour-power and changes in the price of labour-power? Does the introduction of machinery drive the price of labour-power below the value of labour-power, leading to a fall in the value of labour-power? As the following passages suggest, a prima facie case could be made for this line of reasoning:

> As to the *limits* of the *value of labour*, its actual settlement always depends upon supply and demand. I mean the demand for labour on the part of capital, and the supply of labour by the working men (Marx, 1865b: 146).

however the standard of necessary labour may differ at various epochs and in various countries, or *how much, in consequence of the demand and supply of labour, its amount and ratio may change*, at any given epoch the standard is to be considered and acted upon as a fixed one by capital (Marx, 1973: 817; emphasis added).

The standard of necessity (*U*) *may* change; thus, labour market conditions may produce changes in the market price of labour-power, and these may lead to changes in the value of labour-power – once the assumption that the quantity of the means of subsistence is 'definite' is dropped.

Recall our discussion in Chapter 3. There, we noted that *Capital* analyses the magnitude of the value of labour-power and surplus value by taking different factors and treating them in turn as constant and variable:

A large number of combinations are possible here. Any two of the factors may vary and the third remain constant, or all three may vary at once…The effect of every possible combination may be found by treating each factor in turn as variable, and the other two constant for the time being (Marx, 1977: 664).

Given that Marx did not complete this analysis (that is to say, he did not treat the standard of necessity as variable), let us continue Marx's project by considering the combinations that he did not explore. This will allow us to take account of various sides of the matter.[1]

I Standard of necessity constant; productivity constant

Begin with the case of both the standard of necessity and productivity constant. Following (1.1), accordingly, we commence with the assumption that necessary labour and the value of labour-power are given and fixed. From this starting point, we can examine the concept of the value of labour-power that Marx presents.

The value of labour-power, Marx proposes, is determined by the '*value of the necessaries* required to produce, develop, maintain, and perpetuate the labouring power' (Marx, 1865b: 130). Yet, as Bob Rowthorn observed, this definition 'is really no different from that given by classical economists such as Ricardo' (Rowthorn, 1980: 206). It is a view of the worker as working animal, as piece of machinery. Simply stated, the value of labour-power must be sufficient to maintain this particular machine, to compensate for its 'wear and tear' and to provide for its ultimate replacement (in the desired quality).

Given that *Capital* looks upon the worker from the perspective of capital (that is, as an object for capital rather than as a subject for herself), it is not surprising that the concept of the value of labour-power focuses not upon the worker's ability to satisfy her socially determined needs but, rather, upon the cost of a productive input for capital. However, the implications are significant: once you approach the value of labour-power as the cost to capital of securing this peculiar instrument of production with a voice, a particular logic seems to develop. If, for example, the length of the working day were to be extended, extended beyond its normal duration, then obviously there will be *accelerated depreciation* in this machine – 'the amount of deterioration in labour-power, and therefore its value, increases with the duration of its functioning' (Marx, 1977: 686). The increase in the workday leads to 'premature exhaustion' of this input; and the result is that:

> the forces used up have to be replaced more rapidly, and it will be more expensive to reproduce labour-power, just as in the case of a machine, where the part of its value that has to be reproduced daily grows greater the more rapidly the machine is worn out (Marx, 1977: 376–7).

This is a perspective in which the side of workers and the struggle of workers to satisfy their needs have no place. *Capital's* proposition that an increased workday leads to an increase in the value of labour-power directly contradicts Marx's understanding in *Value, Price and Profit* that 'the respective power of the combatants' determines if wages fall and the workday increases. Rather than that inverse relation between wages and the workday (flowing from class struggle), *Capital* here posits a *direct* relation. While this might make sense to a neoclassical economist who links wages to the quantity of labour performed, this argument seems quite out of place for Marx; yet, it is totally consistent with treating workers as comparable to lifeless instruments of production.[2]

So, how does this perspective differ from the position of political economy which the Young Marx criticized – the position that the 'wages of labour have thus exactly the same significance as the *maintenance* and *servicing* of any other productive instrument?' The answer is – *it does not differ*; it is the same perspective, the one-sided perspective of capital! The individual consumption of the worker, Marx noted in *Capital*, 'remains an aspect of the production and reproduction of capital, just as the cleaning of machinery does.' Indeed, 'from the standpoint of society', Marx commented (in the one-sided language of political economy), the working class 'is just as much an appendage of capital as the lifeless instruments of labour are' (Marx, 1977: 718–19).

Since this wonderful working machine unfortunately not only depreciates but has a limited life, it follows that the maintenance of its use-value includes expenditures both to redress its daily wear and tear and also for those 'means necessary for the worker's replacements, i.e., his children' (Marx, 1977: 275). 'The man, like the machine', Marx proposes, 'will wear out, and must be replaced by another man.' Accordingly, there must be sufficient necessaries 'to bring up a certain quota of children that are to replace him on the labour market and to perpetuate the race of labourers' (Marx, 1865b: 129).

The similarity between Marx's position (with its focus on the need for a definite quantity of children) and that of classical political economy is underlined by his own citation and quotation of the authority of Robert Torrens, whose definition of the value of labour-power ('natural price' of labour) included the necessities which would enable the worker 'to rear such a family as may preserve, in the market, an undiminished supply of labour.' Marx's only criticism of Torrens here was that he wrongly used the term, 'labour' instead of 'labour-power' (Marx, 1977: 275n). As Rowthorn points out, Marx's view (like that of political economy) in this case was clearly 'demographic in inspiration' (Rowthorn, 1980: 206).

Indeed, nowhere is Marx's subjection to the premises of political economy more obvious than in his treatment of the relation between the value of labour-power and population theory.[3] The idea that there is a natural price of labour that ensures that capital has the labour force it requires runs throughout classical political economy, and Marx's emphasis upon the need 'to perpetuate the race of labourers' demonstrates that this is a place where his break with that political economy was not complete.

Consider the relation between a variable price of labour-power and a constant value of labour-power. For classical political economy, the relationship between the market price and the natural price of labour as a commodity was perfectly symmetrical with its treatment of other commodities. If the market price for products of capital exceeds what we may (inaccurately) designate as 'value', then an increased profit rate in such sectors will stimulate flows of capital and thereby generate subsequent supply increases such that prices are brought back into accord with 'values'. In short, via supply shifts, the tendency is for 'value' (natural value or natural price) to be the long-run average around which chance fluctuations of market price revolve; it is 'law' in relation to contingency.

In the classical view of workers, the same mechanism applied: if the price of labour-power increased (due to a rise in the demand for labour), then a wage in excess of subsistence would lead to an increase in the supply of labour-power via population increases; the resulting tendency would be to bring the price of labour-power back to the level of the value of labour-power (subsistence). Thus, the value of labour-power (natural price of labour) was the wage that would maintain a constant labouring population for capital. Of course, this is familiar as the classical (Malthusian) population theory – the price of labour-power adjusts to the value of labour-power via supply shifts.

Like the classicals, Marx understood quite well that market prices are determined by supply and demand and that the price of labour-power is determined in the market. His chapter on 'The General Law of Capitalist Accumulation' describes how wages rise as the demand for workers increases – how relative to the rate of accumulation, 'the rate of wages is the dependent, not the independent variable' (Marx, 1977: 763, 770). Similarly, he understood that 'relatively high wages' in North America were the result of the supply and demand for workers there (Marx, 1865b: 146; Marx, 1977: 935–6).

Also consistent with the classicals is the fact that Marx acknowledged the relationship between higher wages and a real increase in population: 'Periods of prosperity facilitate marriage among the workers and reduce the decimation of their offspring.' The effect was the same 'as if the number of workers actually active had increased' (Marx, 1981b: 363). Where Marx broke with classical theorists, however, was over the *efficacy* of population increases for capital. He argued that capital could not be *content* with what the natural increase in population yielded: 'It requires for its unrestricted activity an industrial reserve army which is independent of these natural limits' (Marx, 1977: 788). Thus, Marx criticized the proposition that increased wages will generate a 'more rapid multiplication' of population and will thereby lead to a reduction of wages to their normal level primarily because the gestation period for production of this particular input, 'the population really fit to work', is *too long*. Capital cannot and will not wait for an absolute surplus population.[4] Accordingly, capital substitutes a *different* productive input, machinery, and thereby produces unemployment – a *relative* surplus population that lowers wages because of increased competition among workers. Thus, 'the general movements of wages are exclusively regulated by the expansion and contraction of the industrial reserve army' (Marx, 1977: 790).

The scenario that Marx offered in place of the classical emphasis upon population movements, consequently, is one where, in response to rising wages, the increase in the technical composition of capital (that is, the

machinery not population (increase)

use of machinery) releases workers and drives down the price of labour-power as required. This is 'the great beauty of capitalist production':

> Thus the law of supply and demand as applied to labour is kept on the right lines, the oscillation of wages is confined within limits satisfactory to capitalist exploitation, and lastly, the social dependence of the worker on the capitalist, which is indispensable, is secured (Marx, 1977: 935).

This is a better theory – but one still from the side of capital. Marx's emphasis upon the role of machinery in restoring the price of labour-power to its customary level remains entirely within the bounds of classical political economy (especially Ricardo). Supply shifts continue to bring about the adjustment of price to value, with the difference only that the surplus population is relative rather than absolute. Significantly, too, this modification did not lead Marx to reject the formulation of the value of labour-power as containing provision for the generational replacement of labour-power *because capital requires* that 'certain quota of children' for future recruits.[5]

Given the assumption of fixed real wages and productivity, despite the introduction of machinery, neither the values of commodities nor the value of labour power changes; all we can talk about here, accordingly, is an oscillation of prices around values.

II Standard of necessity constant; productivity variable

Let us return to the basic case that Marx examines in *Capital*. By assuming the standard of necessity constant, Marx was able to focus specifically upon the effect of increases in productivity upon the value of labour-power and surplus value. *Capital*'s story of relative surplus value and of the drive of capital to revolutionize the process of production revolves around the tendency of the value of labour-power to fall as the result of increases in productivity. How plausible, however, is this story?

Increases in productivity in the production of wage goods mean that the quantity of social labour necessary to produce the average worker (that is, the value of that given wage bundle) falls. Society, in short, now purchases that definite quantity of the means of subsistence with less of its labour; less money – the representative of that social labour – is required by workers to purchase that given set of necessities. Doesn't this mean, all other things equal, that workers have additional money at their disposal? Unless we can demonstrate that this increase in productivity means that the money wage that workers receive has *also* fallen, don't we have to conclude that workers are the immediate beneficiaries of this increase in productivity?

After all, the exchange of labour-power for means of subsistence has two quite separate and distinct moments: the exchange of labour-power for money (*Lp-M*) and the exchange of money for articles of consumption (*M-Ac*). At any given point, we may assume that labour-power has been sold at its value – that is, the worker receives the equivalent in money of the value of that definite quantity of means of subsistence; in other words, the price of labour-power is equal to its value. Now, with the increase in productivity (*q*), the value of that set of means of subsistence has fallen; assuming the standard of necessity (*U*) constant, necessary labour (*w*) and its value-form, the value of labour-power, fall. 'Although labour-power would be unchanged in price', Marx (1977: 659) comments, 'it would have risen above its value.' So, why aren't workers – rather than capitalists – the beneficiaries of productivity increases? To assume that the reduced quantity of money required to secure a definite quantity of means of subsistence translates into a reduced quantity of money which workers receive for the sale of their labour-power is to assume what must be demonstrated.

Is it possible, in short, to construct a scenario in which the value of labour-power falls in accordance with increased productivity in the production of means of subsistence – that is, where workers do not benefit? (We explicitly abstract here from the effect of machinery on the labour market noted in the previous section in order to consider only the side of increased productivity.) These are the conditions of the problem: productivity increases (which can be assumed to drop from the sky), a fixed standard of necessity, falling value of labour-power and rising relative surplus value. As Marx (1977: 269) posed his challenge, '*Hic Rhodus! Hic Salta!*'

On their face, two scenarios appear to satisfy these stated conditions. Given the central assumption that the standard of necessity is fixed, the premise of these scenarios is that workers either do not purchase more means of subsistence or that any additional expenditures they may make are incidental and do not alter their conceptions of normal requirements. In both cases, a change in the labour market is required such that money wages fall in accordance with the values of means of subsistence.

In the first scenario, insofar as a reduced value of articles of consumption leads to no additional consumption by workers, then by definition the effect of rising real income for workers will be the growth of their savings. (Rather than life-cycle savings, these funds would be set aside to permit workers to extract themselves from the status of wage-labourers.) As Marx pointed out, however, general savings by workers would be damaging to production (that is, to the demand for the output of those necessities) and 'thus also to the amount and volume of the exchanges which they [workers] could make with capital, hence to themselves as workers.' In short, the inability of capitalists to realize surplus value because of reduced consumption-spending by workers would lead to lower production, a reduced demand for labour, rising unemployment, and a falling price of labour-power:

> If they all save, then a general reduction of wages will bring them back to earth again; for general savings would show the capitalist that their wages are in general too high, that they receive more than its equivalent for their commodity, the capacity of disposing of their own labour; ... (Marx, 1973: 285–6).

Thus, in this scenario, the price of labour-power falls to the appropriate level because rather than spending what they get, the restriction on consumption expenditures means that workers get what they spend. The fall in the value of means of subsistence leads to a fall in the price of labour-power and, accordingly, a constant real wage.

Yet, Marx would have been the first to point out that this is not a very realistic scenario. Workers spend what they get. Given their unsatisfied needs, when their income increases, they purchase more of the means of subsistence and satisfy needs previously unrealized: 'if means of subsistence were cheaper, or money-wages higher, the workers would buy more of them' (Marx, 1981b: 289–90). If this occurs, this first scenario could not work.

In a second scenario, the combination of fixed commodity needs and reduced monetary requirements provides workers with the ability to marry earlier and maintain larger families. Thus, in this situation, rising population would bring about a falling price of labour-power (until such time that the fall in money-wages corresponds to the fall in the values of means of subsistence). This, of course, is a familiar scenario – classical political economy's population theory, and we have already seen that Marx rejected the effectiveness of population growth in reducing the price of labour-power.

These two scenarios based upon productivity increases combined with a standard of necessity fixed by definition, thus, don't stand up. It leaves, though, an alternative scenario in which a given standard of necessity is enforced by class struggle; for example, with the decline in the value of wage-goods providing slack in the workers' budget, capitalists could be emboldened to attempt to drive down money-wages to capture the gain for themselves in the form of surplus value. However, once we allow class struggle to determine the set of necessaries entering into the worker's consumption, we are implicitly treating the latter as variable (which means that a fixed standard is only one of several possible outcomes).

III Standard of necessity variable; productivity constant

By specifying constant productivity and a variable standard of necessity, we can focus upon struggles over distribution of a given output.[6] Given constant productivity, an increase in the standard of necessity, all other things equal, means an increase in necessary labour and thus a reduction in surplus labour. Similarly, capital may attempt to drive down real wages in order to increase surplus value; it is a zero-sum game. In short, class struggle in the labour market is the focus of this section.

As we have seen earlier in this chapter, the prices of wage goods or of labour-power may oscillate as the result of shifts in supply and demand without this in itself producing a change in the standard of necessity. Under these conditions, despite changes in money-wages, necessary labour and the value of labour-power remain unchanged. Thus, if the price of labour-power exceeds its value, it means that workers are receiving more than the equivalent of their necessary labour; although still compelled to work longer than necessary (as defined with reference to a definite quantity of means of subsistence), the worker 'appropriates a part of his surplus labour for himself' (Marx, 1973: 579). The worker here 'gains in enjoyment of life, what the capitalist loses in the rate of appropriating other people's labour': 'an increase in wages over their normal average level is, on the part of the workers, a sharing in, an appropriation of, a part of his own surplus labour (similarly assuming the productive power of labour remains constant)' (Marx, 1988: 235).

With those higher wages, workers receive back 'in the shape of means of payment' a portion of their 'own surplus product'. As a result, 'they can extend the circle of their enjoyments, make additions to their consumption fund of clothes, furniture, etc., and lay by a small reserve fund of money' (Marx, 1977: 769). Such occasions are an opportunity for the worker to widen 'the sphere of his pleasures':

> the worker's participation in the higher, even cultural satisfactions, the agitation for his own interests, newspaper subscriptions, attending

lectures, educating his children, developing his taste, etc., his only share of civilization which distinguishes him from the slave, is economically only possible by widening the sphere of his pleasures at the time when business is good ... (Marx, 1973: 287).

Implicit, though, is the corollary that when business is 'bad', the price of labour-power will fall and the sphere of the worker's pleasure will narrow – a quite significant narrowing if the price of labour-power is oscillating around a constant value of labour-power.

Yet, as we have noted, Marx did acknowledge that 'in consequence of the demand and supply of labour', the standard of necessity and thus necessary labour *may* change (Marx, 1973: 817). But, how do changes in market wages produce changes in the standard of necessity (and, thus, in the value of labour-power)? We have already seen the answer: *the level of necessary needs adjusts!* If the price of labour-power is below the value of labour-power for any considerable time, the tendency will be for the customary standard of necessity to contract. Without trade unions, Engels (1881b: 104) had noted, 'the work-people gradually get accustomed to a lower and lower standard of life'. The same process occurs when rising wages allow workers to satisfy more of their socially developed needs:

> as a result of rising wages the demand of the workers for necessary means of subsistence will grow. Their demand for luxury articles will increase to a smaller degree, or else a demand will arise for articles that previously did not enter the area of their consumption (Marx, 1981a: 414).

'Man', Marx (1977: 1068) commented, 'is distinguished from all other animals by the limitless and flexible nature of his needs.' Because human beings alter their conception of necessity, labour-power is a '*peculiar*' commodity – one that is distinguished from all others; its value contains what Marx described as a 'historical or social element': 'This historical or social element, entering into the value of labour, may be expanded or contracted, or altogether extinguished, so that nothing remains but the *physical limit*.'

To the extent that the means of subsistence habitually required by workers can change, then, we cannot say along with Marx that 'as with all other commodities, so with labour, its *market price* will, in the long run, adapt itself to its *value*' (Marx, 1865b: 144–5). Marx's statement is only correct if we assume the standard of necessity is fixed – much like the physical input coefficients for other commodities. Insofar, however, as the necessary requirements for workers are 'themselves products of history', *the value of labour-power has a tendency to adjust to its price – rather than the reverse* (Marx, 1977: 275). Thus, the classical population theory has no role left to play here – the equilibrating mechanism of price and value is severed from its classical framework of shifts in the supply of labour; in its place, 'the definite quantity of means of subsistence' changes.

Still, there is nothing automatic about such a movement from the price of labour-power to value. Capital, for example, will push to make an increase in the price of labour-power only temporary whereas workers struggle to make their increased share of civilization permanent. The condition for a shift in the set of necessaries for workers is a change in the balance of forces in the labour market. By organizing trade unions and 'planned co-operation between the employed and the unemployed', workers can reduce the degree of separation among themselves and prevent unemployment from driving wages down (Marx, 1977: 793). In short, the 'respective power of the combatants' is more than simply a matter of supply and demand (that is, of quantitative ratios); the quality of social relations within the labour market is also critical. As we have seen in the last chapter, the balance of forces in the labour market may be affected in many ways – for example, by political movements to use the State to enforce a class's interests and by the replacement of workers by machinery. Class struggle is at the core of changes in the standard of necessity.

Thus, rather than determined as the wage that maintains a constant labouring population for capital, the value of labour-power is the result of capitalist and worker pressing in opposite directions. In the struggle over distribution, the respective power of the combatants is central to determining what can be *maintained* as the standard of necessity for workers. For example, the growth of monopoly in an economy may lead to rising prices facing workers and, all other things equal, to a fall in real wages. In Volume III of *Capital*, Marx points out that that a monopoly price may simply transfer profit from one capitalist to another – that is, it may generate merely a 'local disturbance in the distribution of surplus-value among the various spheres of production'. But this is only one case:

> If the commodity with the monopoly price is part of the workers' necessary consumption, it increases wages and thereby reduces surplus-value, as long as the workers continue to receive their value of labour-power. It could press wages down below the value of labour-power, but only if they previously stood above the physical

minimum. In this case, the monopoly price is paid by deduction from real wages (Marx, 1981b: 1001).

So, *two* possibilities – workers bear the burden of monopoly if they cannot prevent wages from being driven downward or they succeed in shifting the burden of the monopoly price to other capitalists through increased money-wages. Once we treat the standard of necessity as variable, then the ultimate impact of monopoly depends upon class struggle.

Similarly, consider the case of an increase in taxes upon commodities purchased by workers. In Marx's notes on 'Wages' from his 1847 lectures, Marx identified the growth of taxes as a factor 'bringing about the really lowest level of the minimum' wage. The worker, Marx commented, 'is harmed by the introduction of any new tax so long as the minimum has not yet fallen to its lowest possible expression' (Marx, 1847b: 425). If we assume, indeed, that the standard of necessity is given and fixed (whether it is at its lowest possible level or not), then the burden of any increase in the prices of means of subsistence will necessarily be shifted upward; in the absence of that assumption, however, the precise incidence of a monopoly price or growth of taxes depends upon the respective power of the combatants.

Although the link between class struggle and the value of labour-power appears obvious, it was obscured by Marx's treatment of the value of labour-power in *Capital*. Not until his book on Wage-Labour did Marx intend to remove his assumption of a fixed standard of necessity. As he noted, 'the level of the necessaries of life whose total value constitutes the value of labour-power can itself rise or fall', and analysis of variations in those necessary needs belonged in the theory of wages (Marx, 1977: 1068–9). The central place of class struggle in Marx's wage theory can be seen most clearly in this case where the standard of necessity is treated as variable while productivity is fixed.

Is there any limit, then, to what class struggle by workers in the labour market can achieve under these circumstances? Obviously, the standard of necessity and necessary labour cannot continue to rise without bringing about reduced accumulation of capital and thus a reduced demand for labour-power. Any increases in wages are 'therefore confined within limits that not only leave intact the foundations of the capitalist system, but also secure its reproduction on an increasing scale' (Marx, 1977: 770–1). In particular, for Marx, the critical factor in developed capitalism that ensures that 'the oscillation of wages is confined within limits satisfactory to capitalist exploitation' is the substitution of machinery for workers (Marx, 1977: 935).

IV   Standard of necessity variable; productivity variable

Now we are in a position to treat both productivity and the standard of necessity as variable. In his 1861–3 *Economic Manuscript*, Marx set out the various options much more clearly than in *Capital*. Assuming an increase in productivity, he noted, there were three possible cases. In the first, the worker '*receives the same quantity* of use values as before. In this case there is a fall in the *value* of his labour capacity or his *wage*. For there has been a fall in the *value* of this quantity, which has remained constant.' This, as we know, is the case assumed in *Capital* for the purpose of understanding the capital-relation.

In the second case, 'there is a rise in the amount, the *quantity*, of the means of subsistence, and therefore in the *average wage*, but not in the same proportion as in the worker's productivity.' Accordingly, in this case, necessary labour and the value of labour-power fall: 'Although his *real* wage has risen (relating the real wage to use value), its *value*, and therefore the worker's relative wage – the proportion in which he shares with capital the value of his product – has fallen.' As we will see, this is a case that Marx entertains in *Capital* as a possibility.

'Finally the *third* CASE', where productivity (q) and the standard of necessity (U) rise at the same rate:

> The worker continues to receive the same *value* – or the objectification of the same part of the working day – as before. In this case, because the productivity of labour has risen, the quantity of use values he receives, his real wage, has risen, but its *value* has remained constant, since it continues to represent the same quantity of realised labour time as before. In this case, however, the surplus value too remains unchanged, there is no change in the ratio between the wage and the surplus value, hence the *proportion* [of surplus value] *to the wage* remains unchanged (Marx, 1994: 65–6).

In short, in this case, 'there would be no CHANGE in *surplus* value, although the latter would represent, just as wages would, a greater quantity of use values than before' (Marx, 1994: 66).

In *Capital*, this third case in which both capitalist and worker may obtain more use-values without any change in surplus value is introduced as follows:

> Now, if the productivity of labour were to be doubled without any alteration in the ratio between necessary labour and surplus labour,

there would be no change in the magnitude either of the surplus-value or of the price of labour-power. The only result would be that each of these would represent twice as many use-values as before, and that each use-value would be twice as cheap as it was before (Marx, 1977: 659).

Thus, remove the assumption of fixity in the standard of necessity and the possibility of a quite different story emerges – an increase in productivity with no change in surplus value.

As in Section II above, increased productivity means the value of commodities falls while leaving unchanged the money the worker receives for the sale of her labour-power. Where productivity doubles, the value of the given means of subsistence falls in half. Thus, as above, the price of labour-power now would have 'risen above its value', and workers receive back a portion of their 'own surplus product' in the form of money (Marx, 1977: 659, 769). Yet, since here the worker's consumption bundle is no longer fixed, the quantity of use-values that she can acquire now doubles; and, as the worker becomes accustomed to the new consumption bundle, the value of labour-power tends to adapt to the price of labour-power. *All other things being equal, real wages rise in accordance with productivity increases.*

The basis, in short, for relative surplus value is *not* the growth in productivity. If an increase in social productivity dropped from the sky, then, all other things equal, workers – rather than capital – would be the beneficiaries.[7] Such productivity increases in the production of the workers' shopping basket mean, simply, that workers are able to secure *additional* use-values – a larger bundle which incorporates the same portion of the total social labour. The point is critical and deserves emphasis: *if the balance of class forces is such as to keep the rate of exploitation constant, then the effect of productivity increases will be an increase in real wages and no development of relative surplus value.*[8]

What does this do, then, to Marx's argument in *Capital* with respect to the generation of relative surplus value? *An argument based solely upon increases in social productivity, we see, does not stand up.* Rather, it is essential to understand that the *real* basis for relative surplus value must be located in the labour market. For any result other than this third case to prevail, a change in the labour market is required – one which leads to a reduction in money-wages. Only an increased degree of separation among workers initiated by the introduction of machinery ensures that productivity will rise relative to the real wage.

In the 'competitive regime' that Marx considered, the condition for the real wage to rise at the same rate as productivity is a constant money-wage (or price of labour-power); to the extent, however, that the displacement of workers by machinery intensifies competition among workers and violates this condition, relative surplus value is generated. This was, as Marx noted, 'the great beauty of capitalist production': unemployment generated by introduction of machinery has the tendency to keep wages 'confined within limits satisfactory to capitalist exploitation' (Marx, 1977: 935). When productivity is increasing, the weakening of the relative power of workers is the necessary and sufficient condition for the creation of relative surplus value.[9]

As Marx's second case indicates, though, rising exploitation associated with relative surplus value definitely does not preclude rising real wages. While often acknowledged, the importance of this aspect of Marx's wage theory has been obscured because of the authority of *Capital*'s assumption that 'in a given country at a given period, the average amount of the means of subsistence necessary for the worker is a known *datum*' (Marx, 1977: 275). As we have seen, increasing productivity creates conditions in which real wages can increase, and Marx was well aware of this:

> the presence and growth of relative surplus value by no means require as a condition that the worker's *life situation* should remain *unchanged*, i.e. that his average wage should always provide the same quantitatively and qualitatively determined amount of means of subsistence and no more ... Indeed, relative surplus value might well rise continuously, and the *value of labour capacity*, hence the value of average wages, fall continuously, yet despite this the range of the workers means of subsistence and therefore the pleasures of his life could expand continuously (Marx, 1988: 245).

Marx introduces this same possibility in *Capital*, where – with doubled productivity – he assumes 'a fall in the price of labour-power' (by, for example, one-sixth). 'This lower price', he points out, 'would still represent an increased quantity of means of subsistence' (Marx, 1977: 659). Accordingly, he indicates, 'it is possible, given increasing productivity of labour, for the price of labour-power to fall constantly and for this fall to be accompanied by a constant growth in the mass of the worker's means of subsistence' (Marx, 1977: 659).

It is *possible*, in short, that real wages will rise while the rate of exploitation rises. *Possible* that workers might achieve a 'certain quantitative participation in the general growth of wealth' – although, nevertheless, 'the abyss between the life-situation of the worker and that of the capitalist would keep widening' (Marx, 1971: 312; 1977: 659). As he commented further, increasing productivity is 'accompanied by a higher rate of surplus-value, even when real wages are rising. The latter never rise in proportion to the productivity of labour' (Marx, 1977: 753). *Why* real wages necessarily lag behind productivity growth, though, remained unexplained.[10]

The coexistence of rising real wages and a rising rate of exploitation, however, was more than a theoretical possibility. Marx, indeed, found that frequently in countries where capitalism was more highly developed, real wages were higher but so *also* was the rate of exploitation:

> it will frequently be found that the daily or weekly wage in the first nation [with a more developed capitalist mode of production] is higher than in the second while the relative price of labour, i.e. the price of labour as compared both with surplus-value and with the value of the product, stands higher in the second than in the first.

Interestingly, Marx offers no explanation for this observation about national differences in wages other than to point out that productivity of labour tends to be higher 'in proportion as capitalist production is developed in a country' (Marx, 1977: 702). By itself, however, high productivity explains little: both a higher rate of exploitation with no differences in real wages, at one extreme, and higher real wages with no difference in the rate of exploitation, at the other, are consistent with higher productivity. Without incorporating class struggle into our analysis, we cannot understand the effect of higher productivity. Presumably, the combination of both higher real wages and higher exploitation emerges because, where capitalism is more highly developed, not only productivity but also the forms of cooperation developed among wage-labourers tend to be higher.

V Marx's assumption

In the theory of wages (or 'the doctrine of the wages of labour'), Marx intended to analyse variations in 'the level of the necessaries of life whose total value constitutes the value of labour-power' (Marx, 1977: 1068–9). This was where Marx's assumption of a fixed set of necessaries was to be removed. The purpose of this chapter has been to remove that critical assumption – and to do so in the context of the understanding that workers have their own goals and are engaged in a constant struggle against capital to satisfy their own need for development.

As we have seen, the place of class struggle in the determination of the value of labour-power revolves around the establishment of a specific standard of necessity. Depending upon the balance of class forces, that 'historical or social element, entering into the value of labour, may be expanded or contracted, or altogether extinguished'.[11] This point is critical to recognize. Once the standard of necessity is acknowledged to vary with 'the respective power of the combatants', then many inferences about the value of labour-power and surplus value made based upon the assumption of a definite set of necessaries (such as the effect of productivity changes, monopoly prices, taxes, etc.) lose their foundation.

Consider the implications as well for the modelling of Marxian economics. If workers spend what they get, it is a tautology to define the value of labour-power as equal to the value of 'the necessaries of life'. If we then assume that the standard of necessity is 'definite' and constant, it naturally appears that the direction of causation is from the value of those given necessary needs to the value of labour-power. It is accordingly a simple step to employ Occam's Razor and to represent the value of labour-power (and workers) *only* by the labour necessary to produce that fixed set of necessaries. (We are, of course, left with the production of things by things.) Having reversed the correct direction of causation in the case of this peculiar commodity, a result is presented as a premise. With the removal of Marx's assumption, Marxian models and arguments resting on the technical characteristics of production of that definite set of necessities hang in mid-air.[12]

The problem, though, is not just that people have failed to recognize the significance of Marx's assumption with respect to analytical inferences. There is a further concern: *Marx's assumption was not neutral.* By putting aside changes in the 'definite quantity' of the means of subsistence until the theory of wages, he was free to focus upon capital's inherent tendency to drive down necessary labour and to revolutionize the means of production. And, by freezing the set of use-values in the workers' consumption bundle at the beginning, he could demonstrate the nature of capital 'without confounding everything' – he could show that capital grows by expanding unpaid labour and accumulating its results (Marx, 1973: 817).

Yet, insofar as it posited real wages constant when productivity increases (that is, that money-wages fall at the same rate as money-prices), *Capital* assumed that 'the respective power of the combatants' changes to ensure that workers are prevented from sharing in the fruits of productivity gains.[13] Analytically, the effect is the same as if it were assumed that workers always must receive only the physiological

minimum set of necessaries (much like the requirement for the maintenance and servicing of a piece of machinery). *By freezing the standard of
necessity in the face of increasing productivity, Marx froze the worker's side of
class struggle.*

Had he assumed, in contrast, that the rate of surplus value were given
and fixed (thereby permitting him to focus upon purely objective and
technical factors and to leave questions of class organization and sub-
jectivity aside), the implication would have been quite different: productivity increases would be shown to yield rising real wages. Productivity
increases would be seen as in the interests of workers – as creating the
potential for workers realizing more of their socially-generated needs and
having more time and energy for themselves. The cooperation and combination of labour which produces a growing social productivity would
be understood as consistent with the 'worker's own need for development' (Marx, 1977: 772).

Capital's silence on such matters is not surprising when we recall that
it looks upon workers from the perspective of capital and not as subjects
for themselves. But, what can we say about a wage theory in which
the effect of class struggle on the part of workers is submerged through
this assumption of a 'definite quantity of means of subsistence'? Recall
E.P. Thompson's comment (noted in Chapter 2) that *Capital* is 'a study
of the logic of capital, not of capitalism' and that Marx was led into a
trap, one baited by classical political economy – or, more accurately, that
'he had been sucked into a theoretical whirlpool' (Thompson, 1978: 65,
59). Understanding Marx's assumption as part of the one-sidedness of
Capital is critical. Without determination of the standard of necessity by
class struggle, Marx was led away from a focus on workers as human
beings and in the direction of explanations both naturalistic and functionalist. Like the political economists he criticized in his youth, he
could advance the proposition that the proletarian, same as any horse,
must get as much as will enable him to work' (Marx, 1844c: 241). This
is one aspect of the one-sidedness of *Capital's* concepts and of a one-
sided Marxism that does not go beyond *Capital* – a subject that will be
considered in the next chapter.

7
One-Sided Marxism

> We must now consider some of the phenomena which result from the isolation of Being and Nothing, when one is placed without the sphere of the other, and transition is thus denied.
>
> Hegel (1961: 106–7)

Marx wrote more than *Capital*. Yet, insofar as *Capital* is acknowledged as the pinnacle of Marx's theoretical work, what is outside it invariably is viewed as of lesser theoretical importance – even when it is acknowledged that Marx completed neither *Capital* nor the other works in his Economics that he envisioned. There are real problems in studying *Capital* as if it stands by itself. As noted in Chapter 5, Marx's work outside *Capital* suggests that he retained his early conception of capitalism as a whole – a conception encompassing the sides of both capital and wage-labour and their interactions. The fact, however, that *Capital* does not explore the side of wage-labour and those interactions has meant that the Marxism that uncritically rests upon it shares its one-sidedness.

I One-sided tendencies

What constitutes this one-sidedness? Without exploration of the side of wage-labour for itself, *Capital* is an incomplete epistemological project. How, then, can it present the tendencies of capitalism as a whole? If *Capital* develops only one side of the totality, we find only capital's tendencies and not those of wage-labour, only capital's thrust to increase the rate of surplus value and not wage-labour's thrust to reduce it. Without the worker pressing in the opposite direction to capital, the tendencies presented in *Capital* are necessarily one-sided.

So much flows from this. In the absence of the examination of the part of workers' struggles in shaping the course of the development of capitalism, capital's tendencies are taken as objective, even technical, laws inherent in its own essence. Accordingly, it cannot be considered surprising that inexorably rising organic compositions of capital and a falling rate of profit displace consideration of workers' struggles when the latter are not developed as an essential element within capitalism as a whole. In place of the centrality of class struggle, productive forces march until they march no more.

And, if *Capital* does not focus upon that struggle of workers to satisfy their own need for development, what drives capital forward? The silence as to the opposition from wage-labour has produced the theoretical substitution of the opposition of individual capitals as the explanation for the development of productive forces within capitalism. In contrast to Marx's concern to develop the introduction of machinery 'out of the relation to living labour, without reference to other capitals', what prevails is a focus on how competition drives individual capitalists to innovate (Marx, 1973: 776–7). Thus, a phenomenal, outer explanation similar to that which Marx rejected in the course of (and after) the *Grundrisse* displaces an inner account based upon the opposition of capital and wage-labour; lost is the extent to which workers' struggles impose upon capital the continuing necessity to revolutionize the instruments of production.[1]

Similarly, centralization of capital, that 'expropriation of many capitalists by a few' which is prelude to the expropriation of the expropriators, is seen as the result of the immanent laws of capital itself (Marx, 1977: 929). Rather than emerging out of the opposition of capital and wage-labour, centralization appears as the outcome of the struggle of capital against capital in the battle of competition (Marx, 1977: 777).[2] Thus, the basis not only for its dynamism but also for its senility is discovered in capital alone.

All of this is one aspect of the one-sidedness in the tendencies presented in *Capital*. But, it would be wrong to think that *Capital*'s one-sidedness is limited to the absence of one of the sides of capitalism as a whole. There is more than a failure to understand the wage-labourer within capitalism; we also do not fully understand *capital* within capitalism. Only with the completion of the totality are new sides of capital revealed. Only then do we have capital that faces workers who are struggling for their goals, workers who are more than mere technical inputs to be stretched to emit more labour or to be produced more cheaply. In this respect, *Capital* does *not* present one 'half' of the totality – but is,

rather, merely a *moment* in the development of the totality. *Only when w* *have a completed totality can we grasp properly the distinctions within th* *unity.*

If the goals of workers and their struggles to realize them are no acknowledged explicitly, how can we consider those actions of capita that are undertaken to divide wage-labour against itself, to defeat wage labour? Consider the discussion in Chapter 5. There we saw that, b uniting in combination, workers can secure for themselves the fruits c cooperation in productive activity. Yet, capital captures the bulk of th gains from social production, and it does so by reproducing a separatio and division in social relations among workers. *Indeed, a necessary cond tion for the existence of capital is its ability to divide and separate workers – i order to defeat them.* Rather than a contingent, incidental characteristic c capital, this is an inner tendency of capital. In capitalism as a whole, th two-sided totality, capital does not merely seek the realization of its ow goal, valorization; it also must seek to suspend the realization of th goals of wage-labour. Capital, in short, must defeat workers; it mus negate its negation in order to posit itself.

Once we recognize that workers cannot be viewed as 'lifeless instru ments of labour' (Marx, 1977: 719) but have their own goals, then capi tal's tendencies must be understood to be permeated by its need t divide workers. As we saw in Chapter 6, the standard story of capital drive for relative surplus value collapses once *Capital*'s assumption of fixed standard of necessity is relaxed. Instead of flowing seamlessly fron increased productivity, the necessary condition for a fall in necessar labour is the weakening of the relative power of workers. Of course given that the assumption of a fixed standard of necessity presumes tha capital is the beneficiary of all productivity gains, it naturally appear that capital has an inherent interest in increased productivity and tha workers have none. What *prevents* workers, however, from capturing al the benefits of productivity gains? Drop the assumption of a fixed set o necessities, and we see that capital requires an increase in the degree o separation among workers. The implication is significant.

Failure to understand capital's inner tendency to separate workers ha as a result the treatment of technology and productive forces as 'neutral and abstract in character – rather than as an embodiment of capitalis relations of production. When we grasp this side of capital, not only is i logical that capitalists will be constantly searching for ways to increas the degree of separation of workers but also they cannot be assumed t be indifferent to the effect of any given innovation upon the ability o workers to combine. If a specific innovation were to reduce the socia distance between workers (i.e., reduce their transaction costs in forming coalitions), it would be consistent not with capital's goals but with those of workers.

Once we understand that the degree of separation among workers is a critical variable, we cannot ignore the decentralizing tendency inherent in the benefits to capital from an increase in separation and competition among workers; thus, capital's tendency cannot be viewed simply as one that inexorably yields an increasing scale of productive plant (and which has as its unintended consequence the centralizing, uniting and organizing of the working class). Capital's drive for surplus value may lead to specific alterations in the mode of production that *lower* productivity as such – as long as they are effective in creating divisions among workers. Much of capitalist globalization, indeed, may be driven by the desire to weaken workers – by an attempt to *de*centralize, *dis*unite and *dis*organize workers.

In short, a given innovation may be introduced if it sufficiently suspends the ability of workers to realize their goals, if it divides and separates them – even if it is less efficient (in the narrow technical sense). Rather, for example, than depending upon 'the difference between the labour a machine costs and the labour it saves, in other words, the degree of productivity the machine possesses', the introduction of a machine (or, indeed, any alteration in the mode of production) can have as its *immediate* purpose the defeat of workers in their attempt to realise their own goals (Marx, 1977: 513). Machines, as Marx (1977: 562–3) commented, 'enabled the capitalists to tread underfoot the growing demands of the workers.' They provide capital 'with weapons against working-class revolt.'[3]

Precisely because capital's goal is not the development of productive forces for itself but is valorization, the character of instruments of production and of the organization of the capitalist production process at any given point expresses capital's goals in the context of two-sided class struggle. In short, unless the behaviour of capital is considered in the context of wage-labour for itself rather than just wage-labour in itself, the clear tendency is to think in terms of the autonomous development of productive forces and the neutrality of technology. Both conceptions are characteristic of economism.

Of course, the very same point must be made on the side of wage-labour. Recognition of the immanent tendency of capital to separate workers is critical. It means that divisions among workers must be understood as more than incidental historic presuppositions. They may pre-exist capitalism, but they are developed and shaped anew within that whole. Divisions among workers are produced and reproduced as a condition of existence of capital.[4]

Thus, to look merely at wage-labour for itself and its struggles to achieve its *immediate* goals (higher wages, lower workday, and so on) is not to situate it adequately within the totality – as wage-labour in relation to capital. The necessary struggle of workers to dissolve differences among themselves (to constitute themselves as One) and to divide capital against itself – i.e., the struggle of wage-labour to *defeat* capital, to negate its negation in order to posit itself – would be obscured. And, this, too, is economism.

Once we posit capitalism as a whole as a totality whose essence is class struggle, we recognize it as a one-sided, economistic view not to explore those goals and practices of *both* capital and wage-labour that emerge out of their reciprocal interaction. As we have seen, the failure of *Capital* to complete that totality makes the acceptance of economism as well as of deterministic and automatic objective laws easy. One-sided tendencies are a natural product of *Capital*. As significant, however, are the one-sided concepts embodied in *Capital*.

II   One-sided concepts

A   The reproduction of wage-labour

At the core of the concept of the value of labour-power is the reproduction of wage-labour, which 'remains a necessary condition for the reproduction of capital' (Marx, 1977: 718). What does it cost capital to secure the labour it requires – now and in the future? As we saw in Chapter 6, Marx answered that the value of labour-power is the value of the necessaries 'required to produce, develop, maintain and perpetuate the labouring power' (Marx, 1865b: 130). But, what does this mean? In particular, what does it mean to 'perpetuate the labouring power'?

Marx tells two different stories in *Capital* – both from the perspective of capital. One of those stories, as we noted in Chapter 6, draws upon the texts of classical political economy and is reinforced by Marx's assumption that a 'definite quantity of means of subsistence' underlies the value of labour-power. In the classical story, capital's rising demand for labour leads to increasing wages, increasing labour supply and a wage returning to its natural rate once the desired level of workforce has been achieved.

Despite Marx's description of Malthus' population theory as a '*lampoon on the human race*', however, intimations of workers as natural subjects who, if given a little extra for the feed-bag, provide for capital's future requirements surface in Marx's own discussion (Marx, 1865a: 27). His statement that 'a certain quota of children' is required to replace current workers, his argument that the value of labour-power must include the value of means of subsistence 'necessary for the worker's replacements, i.e. his children, in order that this race of peculiar commodity-owners may perpetuate its presence on the market', and his inference that an increased workday requires an increase in the value of labour-power 'because the forces used up have to be replaced more rapidly' – all these positions reflect a naturalistic perspective, a demographic sensibility (Marx, 1865b: 129; 1977: 275, 377). A definite quantity of means of subsistence is required to produce a definite quantity of labour for capital.

Perpetuating the labouring power in this respect means to ensure that workers receive wages high enough to maintain the existing stock of workers – enough 'to reproduce the muscles, nerves, bones and brains of existing workers, and to bring new workers into existence' (Marx, 1977: 717). Thus, if wages fall below the value of labour-power, the number of workers available to capital in the present and future will shrink – a compelling argument if the value of labour-power is based upon 'the physically indispensable means of subsistence' (Marx, 1977: 277). Reproduction of wage-labour from this perspective, then, revolves around ensuring that capital does not foul its own nest, that its appetite for surplus labour does not bring about the 'coming degradation and final depopulation of the human race' and thus the non-reproduction of capital (Marx, 1977: 381).

While this story is definitely present in *Capital*, it doesn't quite fit with other aspects of *Capital*. Why, for example, does capital require a definite quantity of labour if the technical composition of capital is rising? To the extent that the substitution of machinery for labour can reduce capital's need for workers, the core argument of a downward limit to the wage is weakened; the link between the reproduction of capital and the reproduction of wage-labour, accordingly, becomes rather elastic.

More significant as an immanent critique, however, is the presence of *Capital*'s second story linking the value of labour-power to the reproduction of wage-labour. And, its focus is quite different. Consider the significance of the concluding chapter of Volume I of *Capital*, 'The Modern Theory of Colonization'. In contrast to the classical story, Marx's argument here was that 'perpetuating the labouring power' means to ensure that workers receive wages *low enough* to maintain the existing stock of workers! In the normal situation within capitalism, the worker cannot save to extract herself from the position of wage-labourer. Her wages provide her with the equivalent of the means of subsistence she needs, and her 'constant annihilation of the means of subsistence' compels her 'continued re-appearance on the labour-market' (Marx, 1977: 716, 719). But, in the colonies, the 'new world', something quite different occurred – wage-labourers *escaped*: 'Today's wage-labourer is tomorrow's independent peasant or artisan, working for himself' (Marx, 1977: 936).

What exactly was taking place? In the *Grundrisse*, Marx (1973: 579) described the process as one in which 'the worker appropriates a part of his surplus labour for himself' and thus was able to accumulate sufficiently to extract himself from his relation with capital; similarly, in *Economic Manuscript of 1861–63*, Marx indicated that in colonies, 'the worker receives more than is required for the reproduction of his labour capacity and very soon becomes a peasant farming independently, etc, the original relation is not constantly reproduced' (Marx, 1988a: 116). Wages, in short, were above the value of labour-power, and instead of the latter adjusting, workers in the colonies saved. The result was the tendency for the *non*-reproduction of wage-labour. In this situation, Marx commented, the wage-labourer 'loses, along with the relation of dependence, the feeling of dependence on the abstemious capitalist' (Marx, 1977: 936).

Thus, in Marx's second story, rather than the reproduction of a definite number of people, at issue is the reproduction of a social relation. Critical is not whether the worker receives more or less wages but that 'the worker continues to result merely as labour capacity' – i.e., that 'the worker always leaves the process in the same state as he entered it' – as one who is dependent upon capital (Marx, 1988: 116; 1977: 716). In this respect, other than manna from heaven (which allows for the reproduction of the human being but not the wage-labourer), nothing can be worse for capital than workers' wages rising more rapidly than workers' needs – the situation in the colonies. Capital, it appears, *cannot* always 'safely leave' the maintenance and reproduction of wage-labour 'to the worker's drives for self-preservation and propagation' (Marx, 1977: 718).

In the normal course of things, capital works both sides of the street to prevent such a situation. For one, it substitutes machinery for workers and therefore exerts downward pressure on wage. This, recall, is 'the great beauty of capitalist production' – the production of a relative surplus population of wage-labourers keeps wages within their proper limits and ensures that 'the social dependence of the worker on the capitalist, which is indispensable, is secured' (Marx, 1977: 935). On the other side, however, capital constantly generates new needs for workers. As we saw in Chapter 3, not only is this inherent in the alienating nature of capitalist production but, in its effort to realize surplus value, capital attempts to create new needs for the worker, always seeks to place the worker 'in a new dependence.' Every new need, we noted, is a new link in the chain that binds workers to capital, yet another 'invisible thread' that holds workers down (Marx, 1977: 719). Recognizing capital's need for the reproduction of workers as wage-labourers, we understand how absolutely critical was Marx's comment that the creation of new needs for workers is the side of the relation of capital and wage-labour 'on which the historic justification, but also the contemporary power of capital rests' (Marx, 1973: 287).

Although this second concept of the reproduction of the wage-labourer, in contrast to the classical remnant, goes well beyond demographics to focus on the question of how social dependence is reproduced, its concern remains the problem of how capital can get the labour it requires. But, think about the value of labour-power from the side of the worker. As indicated in Chapter 3, in a given country in a given period, the worker has a set of socially generated needs – the requirements of 'socially developed human beings'. Insofar as these needs, under the existing circumstances, are needs for commodities and are not fully satisfied, the worker accordingly struggles to increase the level of wages. For the worker, the value of labour-power is both the means of satisfying needs normally realized and the barrier to satisfying more – that is, is simultaneously affirmation and denial.

Thus, the value of labour-power looks different from the two sides of the capital/wage-labour relation. Just as for capital it is the cost of an input for the capitalist process of production, for workers it is the cost of inputs for their own process of production. Two different moments of production, two different goals, two different perspectives on the value of labour-power: while for capital, the value of labour-power is a means of satisfying its goal of surplus value (K-VLP-K), for the wage-labourer, it is the means of satisfying the goal of self-development (WL-VLP-WL).

Between these two processes of production, too, there is an essential difference – one obscured by the classical symmetry of things and people, which turns 'men into hats' (Marx, 1847a: 125). Forgotten is the 'peculiarity' of labour-power as a commodity. We have seen the classical proposition that rising wages lead to an increase in population, an increase in quantity – much like every product of capital. Nobody would ever suggest, however, that when the price of hats rises, hats would be produced in a higher *quality*. In contrast to capital (which produces more in response to higher prices), the wage-labourer secures his goals when the price of his commodity rises by satisfying more of his existing social needs – and, thus, by producing himself *better*. Lost through the one-sided concept of the value of labour-power in *Capital* is the centrality of quality from the side of the worker.

Consider the case of a decline in the price of labour-power below its value. By definition, all necessary needs cannot be secured; inputs that previously and customarily entered into the production of the worker are reduced. With what result? In such a case, the *quality* of the product of this second moment of production falls. At its limit, the tendency will be one of 'brutalization' – to 'degrade' the worker 'to the level of the Irish, the level of wage-labour where the most animal minimum of needs and subsistence appears to him as the sole object and purpose of his exchange with capital' (Marx, 1973: 285–7). The historical or social element in the value of labour-power is in this case 'extinguished'. No animal, Marx proposed, is as able as man 'to restrict his needs to the same unbelievable degree and to reduce the conditions of his life to the absolute minimum' (Marx, 1977: 1068).

Production in this case of declining wages *remains* a process of reproduction of the wage-labourer as wage-labourer, but it is one in which the historical or social element in the value of labour-power 'contracts'. In short, this is a process of *contracted reproduction* – one in which the customary standard of necessity declines.

By contrast, as we have seen, when the price of labour-power exceeds its value, this is precisely the time when the worker widens 'the sphere of his pleasures':

> the worker's participation in the higher, even cultural satisfactions, the agitation for his own interests, newspaper subscriptions, attending lectures, educating his children, developing his taste, etc., his only share of civilization which distinguishes him from the slave, is economically only possible by widening the sphere of his pleasures at the time when business is good ... (Marx, 1973: 287).

The additional money at the disposal of the worker is a means of realizing more social needs; it permits the production of the worker as an altered human being, one richer in *quality*, one for whom more historic and social needs are 'posited as *necessary*.' In this case, the historical or social element in the value of labour-power 'expands'. At its limit, there is:

> the cultivation of all the qualities of the social human being, production of the same in a form as rich as possible in needs, because rich in

qualities and relations – production of this being as the most total and universal possible social product … (Marx, 1973: 409).

When workers are able to satisfy more of their social needs, there is *expanded reproduction* of wage-labour.

Finally, we can see that the assumption in *Capital* that necessary needs are constant represents *simple reproduction* of the wage-labourer; again, the quality of the wage-labourer produced is central – in this case, the worker who secures that definite quantity of means of subsistence is assumed able to produce himself 'in his normal state as a working individual' (Marx, 1977: 275). However, whether we are considering contracted, expanded or simple reproduction, reproduced in each case is a working individual who is a wage-labourer, one who annihilates the means of subsistence in that process of production and thus must reappear in the labour market. Thus, we are still describing the 'perpetuation' of wage-labourers as such–' the absolutely necessary condition for capitalist production' (Marx, 1977: 716). We are not yet at the point when we can consider why the worker remains dependent upon capital, why the reproduction of this social relation occurs from the perspective of the worker.

Nevertheless, by considering the side of the worker, the reproduction of the worker can be explored in its own right rather than just noted as a condition for the reproduction of capital. Quite different questions emerge. For one, it is obvious that, from the side of the worker, reproduction is not at all limited to commodity requirements. For capital, all that matters is what capital must *pay* for this productive input; thus, only the workers' commodity requirements count – i.e., only those necessities for which the worker requires money. This narrow conception of the requirements for the reproduction of the wage-labourer flows naturally from *Capital*'s consideration of the value of labour-power from the perspective of capital and not from that of wage-labour – that is, as the cost of an input for capital. Yet, as every worker knows, far more than the ability to purchase commodities is required for the reproduction of wage-labour – a question to be explored further in this chapter and in Chapter 8.

Even remaining for the moment within the realm of commodities, however, considering reproduction from the side of the worker points to an important difference. Although suspended by the assumption of a definite quantity of means of subsistence, expanded reproduction is the goal of the worker – just as it is for capital. The struggle between capitalist and worker, in short, can be seen as a two-sided struggle over expanded reproduction.[5] Yet, there is a critical asymmetry. What the capitalist wants is the growth of value (indeed, the growth of surplus value); what the worker wants, on the other hand, is the growth of use-value. As seen in Chapter 6, with constant productivity, this is a zero-sum game. However, the two expanded reproductions are compatible if productivity increases; accordingly, the capitalist drive to develop productive forces should be viewed in the light of the struggle of workers for expanded reproduction.

B   Wealth

The asymmetry present in the two sides of expanded reproduction reflects an essential difference in the concept of *wealth*. We all know what wealth is for capital. It is value, surplus value, accumulated surplus value – in its general form as money and in its particular form as means of production, the objectified products of workers. Can we say that, for workers, wealth is use-values?

Marx certainly referred repeatedly to use-values as wealth, describing them, for example, as 'the *material of wealth*' (Marx, 1973: 349). In particular, when identifying the *source* of wealth, he was careful to stress that wealth was not simply the result of labour. '*Nature*', he insisted, is just as much the source of use-values (and it is surely of such that material wealth consists!) as labour, which itself is only the manifestation of a force of nature, human labour power' (Marx, 1875: 18). In this respect, Marx followed the lead of William Petty: 'As William Petty says, labour is the father of material wealth, the earth is its mother' (Marx, 1977: 134).[6] Thus, Marx clearly equates use-values with material wealth when he refers to 'the two primary creators of wealth, labour-power and land' and 'the original sources of all wealth – the soil and the worker' (Marx, 1977: 752, 638).

Obviously, the two concepts of wealth may overlap: insofar as use-values are products of capital and take the form of commodities, they are the bearers of wealth for capital. But, just as obviously, they need *not* overlap. The production of commodities outside capitalist relations and, indeed, of *non*-commodities is the production of wealth from the standpoint of the worker to the extent that those use-values enter into the production and reproduction of the worker.[7] Further, such wealth is not limited to the consumption of the results of human activity; it includes 'every kind of consumption which in one way or another produces human beings in some particular aspect' (Marx, 1973: 90–1).

In this respect, Marx's identification of Nature as a source of wealth is critical in identifying a concept of wealth that goes beyond capital's perspective. Insofar as Nature is critical to the production and reproduction of workers, Marx stressed that it was essential to preserve and, indeed, *improve* this basis of human wealth. 'From the standpoint of a higher socio-economic formation,' Marx proposed, private ownership of portions of the earth would appear absurd:

> Even an entire society, a nation, or all simultaneously existing societies taken together, are not the owners of the earth. They are simply its possessors, its beneficiaries, and have to bequeath it in an improved state to succeeding generations, as *boni patres familias* (Marx, 1981b: 911).

Yet, in itself, the identification of wealth and use-values is insufficient. Marx's concept of wealth for workers does not revolve not simply about the accumulation of use-values – such that it grows quantitatively with each additional use-value secured by workers. Rather, each use-value is only 'a moment of wealth by way of its relation to a particular need which it satisfies' (1973: 218). And, that need is the need not of an abstract human being but of a particular human being produced within society:

> Hunger is hunger, but the hunger gratified by cooked meat eaten with a knife and a fork is a different hunger from that which bolts down raw meat with the aid of hand, nail and tooth ... The object of art – like every other product – creates a public which is sensitive to art and enjoys beauty (Marx, 1973: 92).

Wealth, in short, is inseparable from human beings and their qualities in a given country in a given period.

Consider the concept of the expanded reproduction of the worker. In envisioning a rich human being – 'as rich as possible in needs, because rich in qualities and relations', Marx (1973: 409–10) returned in the *Grundrisse* to a conception of human wealth already present in 1844:

> It will be seen how in place of the *wealth* and *poverty* of political economy come the *rich human being* and rich *human need*. The *rich* human being is simultaneously the human being *in need of* a totality of human manifestations of life – the man in whom his own realisation exists as an inner necessity, as *need* (Marx, 1844c: 304).

Once we focus upon the side of the worker rather than upon capital, this alternative concept of wealth comes into view – one in which 'regarded *materially*, wealth consists only in the manifold variety of needs' (Marx, 1973: 527). It follows, then, that the greater the extent to which historical and social needs 'are posited as *necessary*, the higher the level to which real wealth has become developed' (Marx, 1973: 527). Thus, while political economy's conception of wealth has obscured this alternative emphasis upon the growth of wealth as the growth of needs, as the '*development of the human productive forces*', as the 'richest development of the individuals', it is not difficult to grasp Marx's alternative (Marx, 1973: 540–1, 708). As he asked: 'In fact, however, when the limited bourgeois form is stripped away, what is wealth other than the universality of individual needs, capacities, pleasures, productive forces etc., created through universal exchange' (Marx, 1973: 488)?

At the core of Marx's understanding of real wealth is his concept of the 'rich human being'; it is the focus on a human being who has developed his capacities and capabilities to the point where he is able 'to take gratification in a many-sided way' – 'the *rich* man *profoundly endowed with all the senses*' (Marx, 1844c: 302). Thus, look at the side of the worker, and you see that Marx's perspective (like that more recently advanced by Amartya Sen) stresses the human capacities and capabilities that 'constitute the person's freedoms – the real opportunities – to have well-being' (Sen, 1992: 40). It is an emphasis upon what Lucien Sève (1978: 312) defined as 'capacities' – 'the ensemble of "actual potentialities", innate or acquired, to carry out any act whatever and whatever its level.'[8]

For Marx, it is characteristic of capital that it tends to foster the development of the real wealth of workers – that, in its 'ceaseless striving' to grow, capital 'creates the material elements for the development of the rich individuality which is as all-sided in its production as in its consumption' (Marx, 1973: 325). Yet, capital does this in a contradictory way – in a way that prevents the free and full development of human potential, the all-round development of the individual. Thus, while the growth of human wealth is the 'absolute working-out of his creative potentialities', the 'complete working-out of the human content', the 'development of all human powers as such the end in itself', it cannot be realized within capitalism (Marx, 1973: 488, 541, 708).

In contrast to the capitalist conception of wealth, then, we have a rich concept of human wealth, a concept of expanded reproduction which Marx describes as 'the production of *fixed capital*, this fixed capital being man himself' (Marx, 1973: 712). Although Marx did refer to 'the worker's own need for development', you won't find this conception of real wealth in *Capital*. And, why should you? That, after all, was not the point of the book. What Marx did in *Capital* was to identify and analyse the nature of *capitalist* wealth. He revealed that wealth from the standpoint of capital (and thus from that of the political economy of capital) was the result of the exploitation of the wage-labourer. Nevertheless, the subsequent failure of Marx's disciples to articulate the *alternative* conception of wealth is equivalent to subservience to capital's concept. The absence of an alternative class concept of wealth allows the conclusion that wealth emerges only in and through capital. *To permit the unchallenged rule of the one-sided concept of wealth is tantamount to abandonment of the theoretical struggle.*

C Productive labour

This brings us to the last of the one-sided concepts we will consider here – 'productive labour'. The concepts of productive labour (and its opposite, unproductive labour) have been the subject of endless (and singularly unproductive) discussion among Marxists. On its face, however, there would seem to be few less likely candidates for dispute – at least with respect to Marx's own perspective on the question, which was both simple and consistent.

After all, what did Marx do? In the course of his critique of political economy, he subjected the concept of productive labour, part of the theoretical baggage of classical political economy, to a critique. And, the essence of that critique was to demonstrate that at the core of this confused and disputed concept within political economy was a quite simple concept: *productive labour is labour which produces surplus value.*

With this conception (in essence, the concept of the production of surplus value), Marx was able to unravel the various confusions over physical commodities vs services, activity in circulation proper vs production of capital, necessities vs luxuries, production within capitalist relations vs identical activities outside those relations, and so on. In short, the concept with which political economy had been struggling (and of which there were sporadic glimpses – just as there were glimpses of the concept of surplus value) was revealed to be that of labour which produces capital, labour which produces capitalist wealth.

All this is well known, and we do not need to use up any more space for its demonstration.[9] So, the question that necessarily must be confronted is – why all the disputation among Marxists? In part, one must admit that Marxists are not inherently immune to a more widespread inability to read and understand. (How else can one explain occasional outbreaks of the fetishism of physical commodities – which Marx was so eloquent and specific in criticizing?) Yet, underlying the disputes is something more critical – the belief that Marx's specification of productive labour is *wrong and inadequate*.

Precisely because various writers have considered the concept of productive labour as formulated to be inadequate, they have attempted to alter or reinterpret it to be more serviceable in the context of current struggles. What is our understanding of the concept of productive labour in the context of state activity, a sphere that has expanded significantly in scope since Marx's time? Is household labour to be rescued from theoretical invisibility only to be dubbed 'unproductive' (which, regardless of its denotation, always seems somewhat less worthy)? In all this, there is the salutary attempt to make theory correspond to the 'real movement'; nevertheless, the eclecticism inherent in such endeavours is always vulnerable to the fundamentalist refrain, 'That is not what Marx said' (which, indeed, is correct).

At this point in our discussion, the suggestion of inadequacy in Marx's concept of productive labour is not likely to be surprising. But our argument is not that Marx's critique of the concept of productive labour was faulty. Marx was correct in his deduction of the essence of the concept of productive labour in classical political economy – and in his understanding of the centrality of productive labour for capital. Rather, our argument is that, as in the case of the value of labour-power, reproduction and wealth, the concept of productive labour is *one-sided*. What we are presented with is *productive labour for capital*, labour which serves the need and goal of capital – valorization.

The recognition, however, that capitalism as a whole contains a *second* ought, the 'worker's own need for development', points to a separate and distinct concept – *productive labour for the worker*, defined as labour which produces use-values for the worker. The failure to grasp this second concept (which is hidden and latent in Marx's work) underlies both the eclectic trimming and the fundamentalist criticisms in the swamp that we have come to know as the productive labour debate.

Like productive labour for capital, the concept of productive labour for the worker (which corresponds to Ian Gough's concept of 'reproductive' labour) has a specific class bias. It excludes, for example, 'luxuries' (non-'basics') which do not enter into the production of workers; it is not in this sense to be confused with the concept of productive labour *in general* (although it coincides with the latter in a society of associated producers). Thus, productive labour for the worker is consistent with what E.K. Hunt (following Paul Baran) has defined as labour that 'fulfills a real human need that would be important to fulfill even after the triumph of a socialist regime' (Gough, 1979; Hunt, 1979: 324).

There is a cost to the failure to articulate this concept of labour that produces wealth for workers and to distinguish it from labour that produces wealth for capital. Not only is there confusion in discussions of productive labour; there is also the tendency to lose sight of the specific class content of the concept of productive labour introduced in *Capital*. Thus, an important aspect of the one-sidedness of the categories of *Capital* is the extent to which 'productive labour' and 'the productive sector' have been eternalized in particular material forms traditionally subsumed under capital.

For example, activities so obviously oriented to the 'worker's own need for development' as educational and health services – indeed, any activities which nurture the development of human beings – are designated as 'unproductive' labour. From the perspective of capital, it may be true that 'such services as those which train labour-power, maintain or modify it' (for example, 'the schoolmaster's service' or 'the doctor's service') are unproductive; yet, they are obviously *productive* from the standpoint of the worker into whose reproduction they are inputs (Marx, n.d.: 162–3).

Similarly, activities performed by workers and members of their families within the household are a part of the total labour necessary for the reproduction of the worker. Although this labour may be unproductive for capital (in that it does not produce wealth for capital), it is both necessary and productive for the worker. Once we consider the reproduction of the worker as the subject, we cannot ignore this part of the collective labour that produces the worker – even though it is private and invisible from the perspective of capital.

Significantly, the acceptance of capital's concept of productive labour (and of wealth) among workers cannot be attributed to the influence of one-sided Marxism. When the worker in the capitalist sphere is able 'to bargain and to argue with the capitalists, he measures his demands against the capitalists' profit and demands a certain share of the surplus value created by him' (Marx, 1973: 597). The very struggle against capital thus leads workers in the capitalist sector to view themselves as the wealth producers. They accept the legitimacy of capital's conception of wealth in order to assert their claims against their adversary, capital. But, this necessarily suggests that, from this perspective, workers who do *not* produce surplus-value, who do not work for capital, are *not* productive workers – i.e., are not the producers of wealth. As long as capitalist relations prevail and as long as workers continue to look upon capital as the necessary mediator for them in realizing their needs, capital's concepts are spontaneously reproduced on a daily basis.

Thus, it is not one-sided Marxism that produces capital's definition of productive labour and capital's definition of wealth. However, as long as it *accepts* those definitions (and thus fails to recognize the class character of its own concepts), it will not only be found wanting by feminists and others but it also does not challenge capital.

III One-sided Marxism

Insofar as Marxists have mistaken *Capital* for a presentation of the inner nature of capitalism as a whole, the result has been a one-sided Marxism. It is a Marxism whose concept is inadequate to grasp the concrete totality. On offer are objective economic laws, determinism, economism and one-sided concepts that bear little relation to the real movements in society.

But, we can't blame it all on those who followed Marx. We have to acknowledge that Marx brought baggage with him – particularly from classical political economy. Consider a few examples. Recall that 'certain quota of children' that Marx identified. To suggest that the value of labour-power contains provisions for the maintenance of children *because capital needs future recruits* twenty years hence – rather than because workers have struggled to secure such requirements – is a teleological absurdity! However, it is a logical result of the disappearance of wage-labour for itself from *Capital*.

A similar functionalism surfaces in *Capital*'s discussion of the workday. Due to capital's tendency to exhaust its human inputs, Marx proposes that the state had to limit the workday in capital's interest: 'the limiting of factory labour was dictated by the same necessity as forced the manuring of English fields with guano' (Marx, 1977: 348). The limiting of the workday, in short, occurred (was *dictated*) because it corresponded to capital's requirements (just as farmers had to replenish the fertility of the soil). But, how did that happen? Capital, Marx noted, concerns itself as little with the 'coming degradation and final depopulation of the human race, as by the probable fall of the earth into the sun'. Accordingly, since *individual* capitalists are unconcerned about 'the physical and mental degradation, the premature death, the torture of over-work' (that is, they care little about the conditions for 'the maintenance and reproduction of the working class'), they must be *forced* to take these into account (1977: 380–1). We have here the basis for a conception of the capitalist state as representing the ideal interests of capital against all real capitalists. All those struggles by workers over the length of the workday (that victory for the political economy of working class celebrated by Marx) apparently demonstrate that capital works in mysterious ways.

Note the conflicting messages. Having indicated that capital 'takes no account of the health and length of life of the worker unless society forces it to do so', Marx observes:

> But looking at these things as a whole, it is evident that this does not depend on the will, good or bad, of the individual capitalist. Under free competition, the immanent laws of capitalist production confront the individual capitalist as a coercive force external to him (Marx, 1977: 381).

But, what is the 'immanent' law in this case? Not that 'capital's drive towards a limitless draining away of labour-power' must be checked on behalf of capital as a whole – that is, that the state acts as a coercive force in order to ensure the reproduction of the working class for capital (Marx, 1977: 348). Rather, 'the immanent laws of capitalist production manifest themselves in the external movement of the individual capitals, assert themselves as the coercive laws of competition' through the compulsion felt by individual capitalists to extend the workday (whatever their own inclinations) in order to survive (Marx, 1977: 381–2n, 433). What Marx calls 'immanent' here is not 'the immanent laws of capitalist production' but the 'immanent' tendency of *capital*; and, checking that 'limitless draining away of labour-power' is not capital's need to maintain 'the vital force of the nation at its roots' but, rather, the immanent tendency of the working class which flows from the needs of workers (Marx, 1977: 348, 380).

Thus, Marx himself must bear responsibility for some of the absurdities of his disciples. Precisely because the worker as subject is absent from *Capital*, precisely because the only subject is capital – and the only needs and goals those of capital, there is an inherent functionalist cast to the argument that flows from *Capital*. Characteristic of a one-sided Marxism that fails to recognize that *Capital* presents only one side of capitalism is the presumption that what happens occurs because it corresponds to capital's needs (which are the only ones acknowledged).

As a result, in one-sided Marxism, if the workday declines, it is because capital needs workers to rest. If the real wage rises, it is because capital needs to resolve the problem of realization. If a public healthcare system is introduced, it is because capital needs healthy workers and needs to reduce its own costs; if a public school system, capital requires better-educated workers. If sectors of an economy are nationalized, it is because capital needs weak sectors to be operated by the State. Such arguments are inherently one-sided. When the needs of workers are excluded at the outset and only capital's needs are recognized, it cannot be considered surprising that a one-sided Marxism will find in the results of all real struggles a correspondence to capital's needs.

Nowhere is the functionalism that flows from the one-sidedness of *Capital* more apparent than with respect to the Abstract Proletarian, the mere negation of capital. That productive worker for capital within the sphere of production (that is, the wealth producer) and epitomized as the factory worker, that productive instrument with a voice which can gain no victories which allow it to take satisfaction in capitalist society (any apparent victories being in fact those of capital), that not-capital who is united and disciplined as the result of capitalist development – the Abstract Proletarian has no alternative but to overthrow capital.

Alas, the real proletariat has seemed to lag behind its abstract counterpart and does not appear adequate to its concept. Rather, however, than considering real workers with their expressed needs and aspirations, one-sided Marxism in doctrinaire fashion declares, 'Here are the true struggles, kneel here!' It thus seeks to substitute its Abstract Proletariat for the real proletariat; its point of departure is not 'reality, but the theoretical form in which the master had sublimated it'. Certainly, though, it is time to say goodbye to the Abstract Proletarian.

8

The One-Sidedness of Wage-Labour

> Since capital *as such* is indifferent to every particularity of its substance, and exists not only as the totality of the same but also as the abstraction from all its particularities, the labour which confronts it likewise subjectively has the same totality and abstraction in itself.
>
> Marx (1973: 296)

I The abstraction of wage-labour

What is this thing we have called wage-labour, about which we have theorized? Clearly, it is that which stands opposite to capital within capitalism. Wage-labour is the necessary mediator for capital in capital's thrust to grow. The reproduction of capital requires the reproduction of a body of wage-labourers, a mass of human instruments of production who must enter into a relation in which they perform surplus labour for capital. Thus, wage-labour is a necessary moment within the reproduction of capital.

At the same time, however, we have seen that wage-labour is *more*. The wage-labourer enters into this relation with capital for her *own* goals. Considered from the side of the worker, wage-labour is the means by which it is possible to secure use-values necessary for her reproduction (both simple and expanded). In short, wage-labour is more than just 'means'; it is also its own movement. In this respect, capital is a mediator for wage-labour, a necessary moment within the reproduction of wage-labour.

Thus, we have argued that an adequate understanding of capitalism as a whole requires us to recognize explicitly that the capital/wage-labour relation is two-sided and that *Capital* is one-sided insofar as it merely explores the relation from the perspective of capital. Only by considering the struggle over expanded reproduction (that of both capitalist and wage-labourer), the struggle between two 'oughts', do we grasp the basis for the specific laws of motion of capitalism. The development of this second side is necessary to understand properly the mutual interaction of the different moments and the distinctions within capitalism as an organic system.

The conception of capitalism as a whole we have offered, accordingly, is one in which there is both K-WL-K and WL-K-WL. It is one where capital and wage-labour constitute a whole (as represented in Figure 5.1) characterized by inimical mutual opposition, by a two-sided class struggle that drives capitalism along its specific trajectory.

Yet, something rather important is missing from this picture. If this conception of the totality is meant to represent the real concrete totality, then it must be admitted that it *fails* to do so. Many of the questions raised by critics of Marxism and posed in Chapter 2 remain as relevant as ever. About this newly constructed totality in which presumably all presuppositions are results and all results are presuppositions, we can still say:

> *Not only the absence of socialist revolution and the continued hegemony of capital over workers in advanced capitalist countries, but also the theoretical silence (and practical irrelevance) with respect to struggles for emancipation, struggles of women against patriarchy in all its manifestations, struggles over the quality of life and cultural identity – all these point to a theory not entirely successful.*

Even though we have risen above a conception of political economy which considers the worker 'as just as much an appendage of capital as the lifeless instruments of labour are', the totality developed here still appears to exclude from its field of enquiry anything other than the immediate class struggle between capital and wage-labour (Marx, 1977: 719). *Measured by the real concrete totality, the representation of capitalism as a whole is 'defective'.*

The problem, of course, is that our conception of wage-labour is merely an abstraction. It has been a 'rational abstraction' insofar as it has permitted us to consider what is common to all wage-labourers in their relation to capital (Marx, 1973: 85). Yet, there is no such animal – wage-labour as such. Wage-labour exists only insofar as a living human being enters into this relation; its existence presupposes, therefore, human beings who are wage-labourers.

Figure 5.1 Capitalism as a whole

But human beings as such have not been our subject. Just as in Marx's *Capital*, 'the characters who appear on the economic stage' heretofore are considered merely as the bearers and repositories of a particular economic relation. For Marx, this delimitation was explicit: 'individuals are dealt with here only insofar as they are the personifications of economic categories, the bearers of particular class-relations and interests' (Marx, 1977: 179, 92).[1] Thus, despite our passage beyond *Capital*'s treatment of the wage-labourer, we have not *completely* transcended it; rather than as human beings who are wage-labourers, the workers we have considered are *only* wage-labourers. In this respect, our discussion thus far remains infected by Marx's treatment.

Is that really a problem? The Young Marx certainly thought so. 'The political economist,' he noted, 'reduces everything ... to man, i.e., to the individual whom he strips of all determinateness so as to classify him as capitalist or worker' (Marx, 1844c: 317) This was no casual remark. It was a precise charge – that political economy posits as the Ground (or sufficient basis) of the individual only the condition that they are capitalist or worker. Nothing else matters. How, though, can we speak about real, determinate workers as if they only exist in this one particular relationship with capital? As Hegel had argued, any determinate being has a variety of Grounds:

A Something is a concretion of such a manifold of determinations, each of which manifests itself in it in equal permanence and persistence. Each, therefore, as much as any other, can be determined as Ground, that is, as essential, the other consequently in comparison with it being merely posited (Hegel, 1961: II, 92).

Any particular determination, in short, can be selected as the Ground while all others were treated as non-essential. 'Again, an official has a certain aptitude for his office, has certain relationships as an individual, has such and such acquaintances, and a particular character; he could show himself in such and such circumstances and occasions, and so on. Each of these characteristics may be, or be regarded as, the Ground of his holding his office.'

Indeed, every one of those characteristics could be identified as essential to the official 'because he is the determinate individual that he is, by virtue of them' (Hegel, 1961: II, 93). Nevertheless, there is an inherent problem in focussing upon *particular* grounds:

> in their form of essentiality one is as valid as another; it does not contain the whole volume of the thing, and is therefore a one-sided Ground, and each of the other particular sides has again its group of Grounds; but not one exhausts the thing itself, which constitutes their connexion and contains them all. Not one is *sufficient* Ground, that is, the Notion (Hegel, 1961: II, 94).

The Young Marx's criticism of political economy for stripping individuals of all determinateness and presenting them merely as capitalist or worker, thus, was a clear statement that only the human being as a whole, the connection that contains all particular Grounds, is a sufficient basis for study. In this respect, to examine the human being *only* insofar as he is wage-labourer is clearly one-sided. The political economy of capital treats the proletarian 'only as a *worker*' and 'does not consider him when he is not working, as a human being' (Marx, 1844c: 241).

So, did the mature Marx, as E.P. Thompson (1978: 60–3) has argued, really forget all this and fall here into 'the trap baited by "Political Economy" '? Did he forget about the worker as human being? It is difficult to reconcile such a conclusion with the evidence that Marx *continued* to stress the multiple determination of individuals. Not only is the *Grundrisse* filled with comments such as those about the many-sided needs of the social human being but there is as well the quite explicit statement in *Theories of Surplus Value* that 'all circumstances, therefore, which affect man, the *subject* of production, more or less modify all his functions and activities, and therefore too his functions and activities as the creator of material wealth, of commodities.' In short, for Marx (both young and mature), insofar as human beings are the subjects, we necessarily are concerned with '*all* human relations and functions, however and in whatever form they may appear' (Marx, n.d.: 280).

Thus, rather than forgetting about the worker as human being, Marx explicitly did in this case exactly what he had done with respect to the standard of necessity – he *assumed* in *Capital* that the individuals considered were only the bearers of a particular class relation, only the personifications of economic categories.[2] *It no more means that Marx believed that this assumption was sufficient, however, than that he thought the standard of necessity was indeed constant.* As he had noted to Engels in the latter case, 'only by this procedure is it possible to discuss one relation without discussing all the rest'.

The problem, of course, is that Marx did not himself *subsequently* proceed to release this assumption and to consider human beings as subjects. Only when we go beyond *Capital* to interrogate the subject matter of Marx's intended book on wage-labour can we explore all those 'human relations and functions, however and in whatever form they may appear' which produce the determinateness of the worker.

It has always been implicit in our discussion of wage-labour that the person is *more* than merely wage-labourer. Right from our first consideration of the 'second moment' of production, the production of wage-labourers, a side that goes beyond the capital/wage-labour relation was apparent. Further, we have seen glimpses of such a region in the discussion of use-values for workers originating from outside capitalist relations, in the positing of Nature as a source of wealth for workers and in a concept of productive labour for workers that includes activities nurturing the development of human beings.

The very concept of wage-labour, in short, includes within it that which is necessary to wage-labour but which is not exhausted and encompassed within wage-labour as such. Wage-labour contains a distinction; it divides into the wage-labourer as wage-labourer and the wage-labourer insofar as she is *non*-wage-labourer. Thus, rather than the relation shown earlier in Figure 5.1, capitalism as a whole is more appropriately represented as two overlapping sets as in Figure 8.1. This

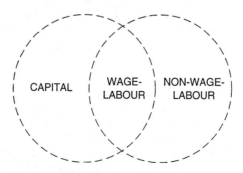

Figure 8.1 Capitalism as a whole (II)

representation corresponds to the overlapping sets implied in the discussion of wealth and productive labour in the preceding chapter.

II The wage-labourer as non-wage-labourer

What can we say about this other side of the wage-labourer (and, thus, the determinateness of the worker) within the framework of Marx's theory? Return to the concept of the production of the worker as a labour process (explored in Chapter 4). Like every other product of human activity, the specific nature of workers produced depends upon both the nature of the inputs and the process by which those inputs are transformed into a final product.

As we have seen, Marx proposed that human beings not only produce themselves by consuming food but also do so through 'every kind of consumption which in some way or another produces human beings in some particular aspect'. It follows, then, that the nature of the product of labour will vary in accordance with the process of production. 'Hunger is hunger, but the hunger gratified by cooked meat eaten with a knife and fork is a different hunger from that which bolts down raw meat with the aid of hand, nail and tooth.' In short, as indicated in Chapter 7, the quality of the human being produced is not independent of the precise character of the inputs consumed: 'The object of art – like every other product – creates a public which is sensitive to art and enjoys beauty' (Marx, 1973: 90, 92).

Of course, the inputs, the use-values that workers consume in the process of producing themselves, correspond to a 'manifold variety of needs'. Not only are they material inputs necessary for physiological reproduction but they also encompass those required for 'the higher, even cultural satisfactions' – the newspaper subscriptions, the lecture attendance, the development of taste that Marx describes. Not only are these use-values *things* (the need for which arises from 'the stomach or from the imagination') but they are also intangibles such as the 'fresh air and sunlight' available from Nature (Marx, 1977: 375–6).

But, how are those use-values secured? Obviously, in the case of the wage-labourer, some are obtained through the purchase of articles of consumption with money resulting from the sale of labour-power. Others may be accessible by virtue of the worker's membership within society – just as the Roman citizen had an 'ideal claim (at least) to the *ager publicus* and a real one to a certain number of *iugera* of land etc' (Marx, 1973: 490). Thus, for example, Marx in the *Critique of the Gotha*

Programme noted the existence in 'present-day society' of '*that which is needed for common satisfaction of needs*, such as schools, health services, etc.'[3] Still other use-values for the worker (such as fresh air and sunlight) may be available as the 'free service' provided by the forces of nature (Marx, 1977: 751, 757).

We cannot assume, however, that these use-values are already in a form appropriate for workers to consume in the process of their own production. Where they are *not*, workers clearly must act upon those use-values to adapt them to their needs. Marx did not ignore such activities; he stressed, however, that they were dependent upon the previous performance of labour for capital. The working class, he noted, 'can only cook meat for itself when it has produced a wage with which to pay for the meat; and it can only keep its furniture and dwellings clean, it can only polish its boots, when it has produced the value of furniture, house rents and boots' (Marx, n.d.: 161). Consistently, Marx described such activity by the worker that satisfied his own needs as 'unproductive' (which, of course, it is – for capital).

Activities that are 'absolutely necessary in order to consume things', Marx classified as 'costs of consumption' (Marx, n.d.: 179). Everyone, he indicated, has a number of functions to fulfil which are not productive and which in part enter into the costs of consumption. 'The real productive labourers have to bear these consumption costs themselves and to perform their unproductive labour themselves' (Marx, n.d.: 288). Insofar as they perform such activities for themselves, it lowers their money requirements. 'The cost of production of the working-class family', Marx recognized, is lowered by the existence of domestic work rather than the 'purchase of ready-made articles'. Conversely, 'diminished expenditure of labour in the house is accompanied by an increased expenditure of money outside' (Marx, 1977: 518n).

Implicit in all this is that there is *more than one* production process outside the sphere of capital – not only the process whereby human beings produce themselves but also the production of various use-values as inputs into the production of human beings. And, that, of course, raises the question of the nature of the relations of production characteristic of the latter production processes.

In the case where free workers perform these 'absolutely necessary' operations themselves, they do so as the owners of their own labour-power and of the use-values that serve as means of production; they thus are also the owners of the product of labour. Of course, while such labour performed is 'absolutely necessary' labour, it is also *private* labour that is outside the capital/wage-labour relation. Thus, this labour (which Marx acknowledged and deemed 'unproductive') is 'invisible' for the capitalist insofar as he does not have to pay for it.[4] On the other hand, to the extent that this labour has products of capital as its presupposition, 'this unproductive labour never enables them to repeat the same unproductive labour a second time unless they have previously laboured productively' (Marx, n.d.: 161).

The treatment of the individual worker as isolated is, however, a special case and serves us mainly as a heuristic device. As Marx and Engels early noted, individuals need 'connections with one another, and since their *needs*, consequently their nature, and the method of satisfying their needs, connected them with one another (relations between the sexes, exchange, division of labour), they *had to* enter into relations with one another' (Marx and Engels, 1846: 437). What is the *nature*, however, of those relations?

There are many possible relations under which the use-values required for the production process of the wage-labourer can be obtained. Equal exchange between two wage-labourers who 'recognize each other as owners of private property' is one such possibility. In this case, each owner of his own labour-power continues to perform this necessary private labour (which remains unproductive for capital) but there is a division of this labour between the two (Marx, 1977: 178).

Another possible division of labour is one in which 'unproductive labour' becomes 'the exclusive function of one section of labourers and productive labour the exclusive function of another section'. Marx described the paid activities of cooks, maids, physicians and private teachers as falling under the heading of this 'unproductive labour' and noted that a considerable portion of services belonged to the 'costs of consumption' (Marx, n.d.: 288, 179, 392–3), Here again, not only does the continuation of this 'unproductive labour' require the continuation of wage-labour but also that labour 'absolutely necessary in order to consume things' does not change its character simply as the result of a division of labour; it remains private and is counted as 'social' only insofar as the wage-labourer succeeds in passing these costs of consumption to the capitalist (Marx, n.d.: 181, 288).

Let us focus (for reasons which will become apparent), however, on one particular relation under which this 'unproductive' labour may be performed. Through the ownership of a *slave*, it is possible for the wage-labourer to secure necessary use-values without either working to produce them or exchanging for them. In this case, the use-values required as inputs for the process of production of labour-power are obtained through a process of exploitation – defined simply as compelling the performance of surplus labour.

In the slave relation, a dependent producer 'belongs to the *individual, particular* owner, and is his labouring machine'. Labour-power here does not 'belong' to the dependent producer, and the disposition of its expenditure (as well as the enjoyment of the fruits of its activity) is the right of the owner (Marx, 1973: 464). All use-values produced by the slave are themselves the property of the master; however, a portion of these must be allocated to his 'labouring machine' in order to preserve the natural conditions of his existence as master. In this case, rather than economic compulsion, it is '*direct compulsion*' which maintains the slave in his position. He works under the spur of fear – although 'not for *his existence* which is *guaranteed* even though it does not belong to him' (Marx, 1977: 1031).

Exploitation means that the slave 'must add to the labour-time necessary for his own maintenance an extra quantity of labour-time in order to produce the means of subsistence for the owner of the means of production' (Marx, 1977: 344). It means that the master benefits by receiving surplus products and/or 'free time' – the reduced requirement to perform that labour 'absolutely necessary in order to consume things.' Free time – how critical! This is time that not only allows restoration of one's energy but also time that permits the development of human capacity. Historically, Marx noted, the free time that non-workers have at their disposal for such things as

> the performance of activities which are not directly productive (as e.g. war, affairs of state) or for the development of human abilities and social potentialities (art, etc., science) which have no directly practical purpose has as its prerequisite the surplus labour of the masses, i.e. the fact that they have to spend more time in material production than is required for the production of their own material life (Marx, 1988: 190–1)

In short, 'the development of the human capacities on the one side is based on the restriction of development on the other side.' Simply, 'free time on one side corresponds to subjugated time on the other side' (Marx, 1988: 191–2).

Of course, in the particular case we are exploring, these are not 'non-workers'. Rather, they are wage-labourers who must re-enter the labour market to sell their labour-power to the capitalist. Thus, they offer up to the capitalist the results of the process of exploitation of their slaves: 'Free time – which is both idle time and time for higher activity – has naturally transformed its possessor into a different subject, and he enters into the direct production process as this different subject' (Marx, 1973: 712). In short, the very benefits of the slave relation to the wage-labourer may be captured by capital in forms such as an increased intensity of the capitalist workday or reduced wage requirements. Yet, the fact that the master may not retain all the fruits of exploitation for himself no more alters the character of slave exploitation than occurs in the case of capitalist exploitation where a capitalist is unable to realise all the surplus value generated in the process of capitalist production.

Insofar as the slave's labour yields surplus products or free time to the slave-owner, it is obviously productive for the slave-owner; the slave produces to this extent both slave and master – that is, contributes to the reproduction of the slave relation. Yet, with respect to capital, the slave's labour remains private and unproductive; only insofar as the wage-labourer is successful in securing the money-requirements for the slave's means of subsistence that take a commodity-form will there be any representation under the heading of 'social' labour. Similarly, the ability of the master to secure these money-requirements through wage-labour will be a condition for the maintenance of the slave relation. However, the value of labour-power would not include provision for the necessities consumed by the slave *because capital wants wage-labourers to have slaves!* (This would be yet another absurdity consistent with the one-sided concept of the value of labour-power described previously.) Rather, the value of labour-power includes such provisions to the extent that the wage-labourer has been successful in struggling for them.

Although it is possible to explore this particular relation and its inherent dynamics further, the obvious question is – *why even raise the spectre of slave-ownership in the context of our discussion of the production of the wage-labourer*? Of course, the answer is that this is precisely the way in which Marx described relations within the family at the time. In the *German Ideology*, he and Engels spoke of the 'latent slavery in the family', where 'wife and children are the slaves of the husband;' the latter in this case had 'the power of disposing of the labour-power of others' (Marx and Engels, 1846: 46). Similarly, in the *Communist Manifesto* (Marx and Engels, 1848: 501–2), they emphasized that the programme of the Communists would do away with both the 'exploitation of children by their parents' and 'the status of women as mere instruments of production'.

Marx explicitly returned to this theme in his notes for *Capital*. 'In private property of every type,' he indicated, 'the *slavery* of the members of the family at least is always implicit since they are made use of and exploited by the head of the family' (Marx, 1977: 1083). As well, Engels

(1962: II, 232) subsequently commented that 'the modern individual family is based on the open or disguised domestic enslavement of the woman.'

In defining the relationship within the family as one of slavery, Marx was clearly stating that 'the family labour necessary for consumption', that 'independent labour at home, within customary limits, for the family itself' (including the exercise of 'economy and judgement in the consumption and preparation of the means of subsistence') occurs in a situation where the producer in the household is exploited within a slave relation (Marx, 1977: 517–18, 518n). *How could it be denied that this is what Marx was arguing?*

Yet, this is a point that Marxists have resisted. As Nancy Folbre comments, there has been a 'reluctance to consider the possibility of exploitation within the realm of reproduction' with the result that such exploitation was 'largely defined out of existence in the domestic labor debates' (Folbre, 1986: 326). Further, the very designation of the relation by Marx and Engels as one of slavery has been described 'as more metaphorical than scientific' – and, indeed, as evoking 'dangerous metaphors' (Vogel, 1983: 61, 130). Yet, not only does this assertion display a curious selectivity in drawing upon Marx but it also ignores the *consistency* in his argument.

Consider what happens to this 'old family relationship' characterized by patriarchal authority ('*patria potestas*') when the degree of immiseration increases – either because of a fall in real wages or because of a growth in social needs (Marx, 1977: 620). One option is an increase in exploitation within the household – that is, an increase in the extra quantity of labour performed by wife and children. An increased expenditure of labour in the house, we know, will be accompanied by a reduced requirement for expenditure of money outside. Referring to the exploitation of children, Marx noted that 'this exploitation always existed to a certain extent among the peasants, and was the more developed, the heavier the yoke pressing on the countryman' (Marx, 1977: 385n).

Yet, there is another possible response when wages are too low to satisfy requirements (one likely to occur when increased domestic labour is inadequate to satisfy needs) – an extension of the labour-time performed directly for capital. Just the individual worker may offer more labour when wages are inadequate (thereby making the supply of labour 'to a certain extent independent of the supply of workers'), so also can we find a backward-sloping supply of labour in the case of the worker's family 'when the quantity of labour provided by the head of the family is augmented by the labour of the members of the family' (Marx, 1977: 793, 687–8, 684). When more money is needed, more labour can be furnished to capital 'by enrolling, under the direct sway of capital, every member of the worker's family, without distinction of age or sex' (Marx, 1977: 517).

In itself, this development does not change the nature of the relation between 'the head of the family' and those whom he exploits – any more than the slave-owner of antiquity ceased to be the owner of the person of others when he rented his slaves out. From slaves within the household, the chattels of the head of the family become income-earning slaves as the result of the need for additional money. And, this is exactly how Marx described this development. Working-class parents, he argued, 'have assumed characteristics that are truly revolting and thoroughly like slave-dealing'. Not only did the male wage-labourer sell his own labour-power. 'Now he sells wife and child. He has become a slave dealer' (Marx, 1977: 519–20, 519n).[5]

Of course, Marx did propose that this very process in which capital assigned 'an important part in socially organized processes of production, outside the sphere of the domestic economy, to women, young persons and children of both sexes, does nevertheless create a new economic foundation for a higher form of the family and of relations between the sexes' (Marx, 1977: 620–1). It is not at all contradictory that something undertaken for short-term benefits may have quite different long-term implications.[6] In any event, it is not difficult to see *why* Marx considered this development to be a basis for the potential alteration of social relations within the household. The seller of labour-power is 'formally posited as a person', as one who has labour-power as her own property (Marx, 1973: 289, 465). Accordingly, with the entry of women into wage-labour, there is the potential for the end of the 'old family relationships':

> With the slave's awareness that he *cannot be the property of another*, with his consciousness of himself as a person, the existence of slavery becomes a merely artificial, vegetative existence, and ceases to be able to prevail as the basis of production (Marx, 1973: 463).

In the same manner, Engels commented that the shift of women from the household to the labour market removed 'all foundation' for male domination in the proletarian home. 'The first premise for the emancipation of women is the reintroduction of the entire female sex into public industry' (Engels, 1962: 231, 233). Of course, that is only the *first* premise, and 'a new economic foundation for a higher form of the family' is not equivalent to the *realization* of that form.

Now, how critical is the precise designation of this relation as one of slavery? Many feminists would be uncomfortable with this term, and certainly not all of the attributes of property in people (such as the right to buy and sell people) were present at the time that Marx wrote. On the other hand, it is well to recall that, as a student of the classics, Marx's primary reference point would have been to slavery in Antiquity (rather than in the New World) and that in the former case slavery displayed a variety of characteristics (including that of individuals entering into that state voluntarily because of the unacceptability of their available options).

Nevertheless, the central issue is not the precise term but the essential characteristic – exploitation. What Marx described is entirely consistent with the argument that, *in addition to capitalist relations*, wage-labourers also can exist within a 'patriarchal mode of production', defined by Nancy Folbre as 'a distinctive set of social relations, including but by no means limited to control over the means of production, that structures the exploitation of women and/or children by men' (Folbre, 1986: 330).

For our purpose here, which is to explore Marx's consideration of the determinateness of the worker, we need say no more. Whatever the potential future implication of the entry of women and children into wage-labour, it is evident that Marx viewed the male wage-labourer *at the time* as existing within two relationships, two class relationships: as wage-labourer in relation to capital and as slave-owner. He is not an abstract wage-labourer at all but is, rather, the *patriarchal* wage-labourer!

Similarly, wife and children, insofar as they became wage-labourers, also existed in two class relations. *In short, to speak of wage-labourers is to describe people who are in no way identical in their relations.* They are identical *only* insofar as they are wage-labourers for capital. As long as our subject is capital, it may be appropriate to consider these human beings only in their characteristic as wage-labourer. Yet, as soon as the subject becomes wage-labour, it is necessary to consider the *other* relations in which people exist.

In positing the existence of male and female wage-labourers who exist within patriarchal relations, we are considering workers with differing goals and differing hierarchies of needs. For the patriarchal wage-labourer, the struggle for higher wages is in part a struggle to permit the reproduction of patriarchy; his increased wages, all other things equal, will allow for an increased expenditure of labour in the house for him by his wife (and children). (The 'family wage' is the condition for reproduction of both relations in which he exists.) For the female wage-labourer, on the other hand, the struggle for higher wages is in part the struggle to *escape* that set of relations in which men control the means of production within the household and exploit women and/or children; it is, indeed, a struggle for her own free time – one rooted in her own need for self-development.

Certainly, there is here the basis for a divergence of interests between wage-labourers of differing age and sex. To the extent that patriarchal wage-labourers have been our subject, it places our discussion in Chapter 5 of the struggles of wage-labourers in a somewhat different light. For example, any individual patriarchal wage-labourer ('head of the family') gains, all other things equal, 'by enrolling under the direct sway of capital, every member of the worker's family, without distinction of age or sex'. Yet, patriarchal wage-labourers *as a whole* lose as the result of the increased competition (and lower wages) that occurs when *all* patriarchal wage-labourers act in this way. In this context, restrictions (through a form 'possessing general, socially coercive force') upon the ability of individual patriarchal wage-labourers to sell their wives and children by voluntary contract to capital appear as the result of the political movement of patriarchal wage-labour as a whole.[7]

The implications of patriarchy, however, go further. Within this patriarchal (or slave) relation, men and women are produced *differently*. Since, as we have noted, 'their *needs*, consequently their nature, and the method of satisfying their needs, connected them with one another (relations between the sexes, exchange, division of labour), they *had to* enter into relations with one another'. Yet, the nature of the people produced is not independent of the precise relations into which they have entered. As Marx and Engels (1846: 437–8) continued:

> since this intercourse, in its turn, determined production and needs, it was, therefore, precisely the personal, individual behaviour of individuals, their behaviour to one another as individuals, that created the existing relations and daily produces them anew...Hence it certainly follows that the development of an individual is determined by the development of all others with whom he is directly or indirectly associated.

Not only do men and women produce themselves differently in the course of the labour 'absolutely necessary to consume things' as it is carried out under patriarchal relations, but they also produce themselves differently *through the consumption of the output of that process*. For, although the specific material use-values produced may be independent of relations of production, the *content* of those use-values is not. Marx touched upon this question in considering the difference between purchasing a coat from a 'jobbing tailor' who performs the work in the buyer's home and having a domestic servant. In both cases, there was a relation of buyers and sellers. But there was a critical difference in these two exchanges. In the case of the domestic servant, he noted:

> But the way in which the use-value is enjoyed in this case *in addition* bears a patriarchal form of relation, a relation of master and servant, *which modifies the relation in its content*, though not in its economic form, and makes it distasteful (Marx, n.d.: 287; emphasis added).

In the course of producing ourselves, in short, we *consume not only specific use-values but also the social relations under which those use-values are produced*. There is a difference between consuming a use-value produced by the independent owner of labour-power and one produced in a patriarchal form of relation. Much like the object of art creates 'a public which is sensitive to art and enjoys beauty', human beings who consume patriarchal relations produce themselves in a particular way. 'The development of an individual is determined by the development of all others with whom he is directly or indirectly associated.'

Thus, from the time of their birth, males and females produce themselves by consuming not only the use-values provided under a gendered division of labour but also the patriarchal relations that determine that division. Implicit in this process, then, is the production of different persons, different personalities, differing natures with respect to domination and nurturance. As Sandra Harding has emphasized, 'the kinds of persons infants become are greatly influenced by the particular social relations the infant experiences as it is transformed, and transforms itself, from a biological infant into a social person' (Harding, 1981: 147).[8]

We are here considering a subject upon which Marxist feminists have made and continue to make major contributions. At this point, therefore, it seems appropriate to comment upon the limitations of Marx's discussion. Despite Marx's description of the existing relationship within the working-class household as slave in nature, there is no consideration of this class relation as one of struggle (now open, now hidden) or of the wives (and children) as subjects and actors.[9] All of this is precluded, of course, by Marx's restricted subject in *Capital*. Yet, it would be naïve to be confident that any of this would have appeared in the missing book on Wage-Labour if Marx had ever written it.

True, Marx hoped for a 'higher form of the family and of relations between the sexes'. And, certainly, he found the existing arrangement personally 'distasteful' and repugnant (as he did slavery in the

New World). Yet, there is little reason to assume that he would have explored these questions in any detail. There is no indication that he was able to go beyond Victorian conventions in a manner similar to his contemporary John Stuart Mill, who specifically criticized the Factory Acts' restriction of women's labour 'in order that they might have time to labour for the husband, in what is called by the advocates of restriction, *his* home' (Pujol, 1992: 25).

In raising these questions, therefore, it is not my goal to present Marx, the historical individual, as having been adequate. That would be rewriting history. *Rather, it is to demonstrate that within the Marxian framework there is the theoretical space to develop these questions.* In short, one does not have to add alien elements onto Marxian theory in an eclectic manner in order to create a 'usable' Marx. It certainly is also not my intention to suggest that the questions raised here constitute an adequate treatment; that is a project that many Marxist feminists continue to explore.[10] So, the issues raised here are not what would have been in *Wage-Labour* but, rather, point to what *belongs* in it.

It may appear as if we have gone somewhat far afield in our discussion of the wage-labourer as non-wage-labourer. Yet, consideration of these issues is essential if we are to explore the determinateness of the wage-labourers who face capital. It similarly underlines the significance of a missing book on wage-labour. For, certainly the specific exploitation of women will always remain peripheral and non-essential for one-sided Marxism so long as the implications of that missing book are not recognized. *Patriarchy is necessarily secondary as long as workers are stripped 'of all determinateness' and regarded only as abstract wage-labourers.*

Of course, the wage-labourers who face capital do not only live in families. They live in neighbourhoods and communities – indeed, are concentrated by capital in particular neighbourhoods and cities, and they live in different nations (Engels, 1845: 344, 394). They are distinguished not only as men and women but also as members of different races, ethnic groups, and so on. Once we acknowledge that 'every kind of consumption ... in one way or another produces human beings in some particular aspect', then it is not a great leap to extend this discussion of differently-produced wage-labourers to differences based on age, race, ethnicity, religion, nationality, historical circumstances and, indeed, on '*all* human relations and functions, however and in whatever form they may appear'.

Marx did not take this step. He limited his comments to the matter immediately at hand – the question of the value of labour-power. Thus, he acknowledged that 'historical tradition and social habitude' played an important part in generating different standards of necessity for different groups of workers (Marx, 1865b: 145).[11] Not only do necessary needs vary over time; they also vary among individuals and groups of workers at any given time. An obvious example was the situation of the Irish worker, for whom 'the most animal minimum of needs and subsistence appears to him as the sole object and purpose of his exchange with capital' (Marx, 1973: 285). Marx argued that their low necessary needs (compared to those of the English male worker) reflected the historical conditions under which Irish workers entered wage-labour, conditions which drove the standard of necessity to which they became accustomed to the level of physiological needs (Marx, 1977: 854–70).

Yet, differences in the value of labour-power reflect *more* than differences in 'the social conditions in which people are placed and reared up'. The latter are merely the 'historical' premises; and, on this basis, we could never explain *changes* in relative wages – for example, the equalization (upward or downward) of the value of labour-power of differing groups of workers. Limited to historical premises as an explanation, 'the more or less favourable conditions' under which various groups of workers 'emerged from the state of serfdom' would appear as original sin (Marx, 1865b: 145).

In short, just as in the case of changes in the standard of necessity over time, differences in that standard for different groups of workers are the result of class struggle – the result of capitalist and worker pressing in opposite directions. The historical premises (insofar as they have affected the level of social needs) may explain why particular workers do not press very *hard* against capital; however, it is what workers accept in the present rather than the historical premises that determines the level of their necessary needs.

The principle, of course, goes beyond the case of Irish and English workers. It encompasses not only workers of differing ethnic and national background but also male and female workers. Unless, for example, we recognize the central place of class struggle in the determination of the value of labour-power, we are left with an explanation of male/female wage differentials that rests upon the assumption of lower subsistence requirements for women. This would be as absurd as to assume that Marx believed that the value of labour-power of Irish workers would *always* be below that of English workers.

Rather than thinking that all workers are identical, Marx's understanding was that every individual is an ensemble of the social relations in which she acts. That has its implications. Given that workers produce themselves as heterogeneous human beings (with differing hierarchies of needs) and that the needs they are normally able to satisfy reflect the results of struggle, it is clear that at any given point there exist differing degrees and dimensions of immiseration.[12] Although the point was not developed in *Capital*, once we begin to explore workers insofar as they are non-wage-labourers, we see that, rather than abstract wage-labourers, the workers in question are human beings in all their determinateness.[13]

III   The production of the worker as a whole

It would be wrong, however, to view the process of production of the worker as occurring *only* outside wage-labour. If we think of the household as *the* site in which the production of the worker takes place, then there remains an implicit view of the process as natural and physical rather than as social. If *every* activity of the worker produces her in some particular aspect, however, then obviously this must include as well the process of capitalist production.

Recall the discussion of capitalist production in Chapter 3. A certain type of human being is produced under the alienating conditions of capitalist production – one with the need to possess alien commodities. And, as noted, those needs are generated not only by production proper but also through capital's sales efforts to expand the sphere of circulation. Those needs are needs that, within capitalist relations, can only be secured by the sale of labour-power. Capital, thus, necessarily appears as the mediator for the wage-labourer.

The worker, accordingly, is produced as one conscious of his dependence upon capital. And, everything about capitalist production contributes not only to the relation of dependence but also to the 'feeling of dependence' (Marx, 1977: 936). The very nature of capital is mystified – 'all the productive forces of social labour appear attributable to it, and not to labour as such, as a power springing forth from its own womb'. Having surrendered the right to his '*creative power*, like Esau his birthright for a mess of pottage', capital, thus, becomes 'a very mystical being' for the worker because it appears as the source of all productivity (Marx, 1981b: 966).

Fixed capital, machinery, technology, science – all necessarily appear only as capital, are known only in their capitalist form: 'The accumulation of knowledge and of skill, of the general productive forces of the social brain, is thus absorbed into capital, as opposed to labour, and hence appears as an attribute of capital' (Marx, 1973: 694).

Thus, as Marx noted, this transposition of 'the social productivity of labour into the material attributes of capital is so firmly entrenched in people's minds that the advantages of machinery, the use of science, invention, etc. are *necessarily* conceived in this *alienated* form, so that all these things are deemed to be the *attributes of capital'* (Marx, 1977: 1058). *In short, wage-labour assigns its own attributes to capital in its mind because the very nature of the capital/wage-labour relation is one in which it has already done so in reality.*

In the normal course of things, thus, capital can rely upon the worker's dependence upon capital. The very process of capitalist production produces and reproduces workers who view the necessity for capital as self-evident:

> The advance of capitalist production develops a working class which by education, tradition and habit looks upon the requirements of that mode of production as self-evident natural laws. The organization of the capitalist process of production, once it is fully developed, breaks down all resistance (Marx, 1977: 899).

Capital, however, does more than simply produce workers for whom the very thought of going beyond capital appears contrary to natural law. *It also produces workers who are separated.* In part, this is the result of the conscious effort of capital to divide and separate workers – both in the labour market and in the process of production. (Both moments of the circuit of capital are characterized by the struggle of capital to divide workers and to equalize their conditions downward versus the struggle of workers to unite and to equalise their conditions upward.) Yet, the separation of workers is produced spontaneously as well by the form of existence of capital as a whole.

Capital exists as 'many capitals'. And, that existence of capital as individual capitals separate and even competing against each other in turn separates workers insofar as they feel dependent not only upon capital as a whole but also on *particular* capitals. In the battle of competition of capitals, there is thus a basis for groups of workers to link their ability to satisfy their needs to the success of the particular capitals that employ them. Thus, there is a classic inversion in competition – rather than the competition among workers being recognized as a form of the competition of capitals and as a condition of capital securing its goals, the competition of capitals spontaneously appears as a form of the competition of workers and as a means for them to satisfy *their* goals. In the real existence of capital as many capitals, there exists a basis for separation between workers in different firms (within and without a country) and for 'concessions' to capital in the battle of competition.[14]

From their earliest writings, Marx and Engels grasped the significance of this division among workers. Engels wrote in 1847:

> This division into farm labourers, day labourers, handicraft, journeymen, factory workers and lumpen proletariat, together with their dispersal over a great, thinly populated expanse of country with few and weak central points, already renders it impossible for them to realise that their interests are common, to reach understanding, to constitute themselves into *one* class. This division and dispersal makes nothing else possible for them but restriction to their immediate, everyday interests, to the wish for a good wage for good work. That is, it restricts the workers to seeing their interest in that of their employers, thus making every single section of workers into an auxiliary army for the class employing them. The farm labourer and day labourer supports the interests of the noble farmer on whose estate he works. The journeyman stands under the intellectual and political sway of his master. The factory worker lets himself be used by the factory owner in the agitation for protective tariffs ... And where two classes of employers have contradictory interests to assert, there exists the same struggle between the classes of workers they employ (Engels, 1847: 83–4).

Thus, even if *outside of wage-labour* workers were produced perfectly homogeneously, there would still be a basis for divisions among them given by the normal workings of capitalist production. As we have seen in Chapter 5, capital's ownership of the products of social labour serves to hide from both mental and manual labourer their unity as differing limbs of the collective worker. Similarly, we noted in Chapter 7 that the very struggle wherein the worker 'measures his demands against the capitalist's profit and demands a certain share of the surplus value created by him' tends to the reproduction of capital's concept of productive labour and to the maintenance of the separation between those who work for capital and those workers who constitute the other limbs of the collective worker. Thus, the unity of workers that is a condition for going beyond capital is precisely what is not produced by capital.

In short, capital tends to produce the working class it needs – that body of wage-labourers which looks upon its requirements 'as self-evident natural laws'. Yet, the breaking-down of resistance to the rule of capital and the separation of workers occur not only because capital itself produces the workers who face it. Capital faces workers who have been produced outside of their relation to capital, and that *also* contributes to the education, tradition and habit which make the requirements of capital appear as self-evident. '*All* human relations and functions', in short, 'influence material production and have a more or less decisive influence on it.' Thus, drawing upon this very point by Marx, Wilhelm Reich stressed the relationship between patriarchy and the acceptance of the rule of the authoritarian state and capital:

> The authoritarian position of the father reflects his political role and discloses the relation of the family to the authoritarian state. Within the family the father holds the same position that his boss holds toward him in the production process. And he reproduces his subservient attitude toward authority in his children, particularly in his sons (Reich, 1976: 49, 14–15).

Capital is strengthened in many ways by the production of workers as non-wage-labourers. We have seen that a condition of existence of capital is its ability to divide and separate workers. Yet, the very process by which workers are produced outside of their relation to capital ensures that they approach capital as heterogeneous human beings – that is, as wage-labourers who are *already divided* by (among other aspects) sex, age, race and nationality. This does more than add to the difficulties in uniting workers – it provides a terrain where capital can *use* those differences.

Consider the case of Irish workers. Their historically-given standard of necessity meant that they were prepared to work for lower wages than those to which English workers were accustomed. The tendency was to drive down the wages of the latter; and, the result, Marx saw, was one that clearly strengthened the rule of capital. There was *far more* to the matter, however, than a general competition among workers which weakened them in relation to capital:

> Every industrial and commercial centre in England now possesses a working class *divided* into two *hostile* camps, English proletarians and Irish proletarians. The ordinary English worker hates the Irish worker as a competitor who lowers his standard of life. In relation to the Irish worker he feels himself a member of the *ruling* nation and so turns himself into a tool of the aristocrats and capitalists of his country *against* Ireland, thus strengthening their domination over *himself.* He cherishes religious, social and national prejudices against the Irish worker…The Irishman pays him back with interest in his own money. He sees in the English worker at once the accomplice and the stupid tool of the *English rule in Ireland.*

Thus, there was not merely the division between competing sellers of labour-power but an '*antagonism*' that drew for its strength upon all those characteristics (for example, religious, social and national) which formed the Irish and English workers as differing human beings. *Difference became, under the normal workings of capitalism, hostility.* In this antagonism, Marx saw 'the *secret of the impotence of the English working class*, despite its organization. It is the secret by which the capitalist class maintains its power. And that class is fully aware of it.'[15]

When one recalls, however, all of the ways in which the hegemony of capital is reinforced, it is uncertain that this particular separation of workers *by itself* can be seen as the single 'secret' by which capital maintains its power. And, that is the question that comes to the fore once we consider workers as the subject and move away from the concept of an abstract wage-labourer. Once we think about how the workers who face capital are produced, about workers in all their determinateness, the question before us is – *why did Marx ever think that workers could go beyond capital?*

9
Beyond Capital?

> For Marx was before all else a revolutionist. His real mission in life was to contribute, in one way or another, to the overthrow of capitalist society and of the state institutions which it had brought into being, to contribute to the liberation of the modern proletariat, which *he* was the first to make conscious of its own position and its needs, conscious of the conditions of its emancipation.
>
> Engels (1883: 682)

I The primacy of needs

There is a familiar tale told by some Marxists – capitalism will come to an end when it no longer permits the development of productive forces. As described by G.A. Cohen in his book, *Karl Marx's Theory of History: a Defence*, the thesis of 'the primacy of productive forces' proposes that the existence of a set of productive relations is explained by the level of development of the productive forces and that a new set of relations of production emerges when the old set 'fetters' the productive forces (Cohen, 1978).

Marx's 'Preface' of 1859 to the *Contribution to the Critique of Political Economy* is the classic source for this thesis:

> At a certain stage of development, the material productive forces of society come into conflict with the existing relations of production … From forms of development of the productive forces these relations turn into their fetters. Then begins an era of social revolution … No social formation is ever destroyed before all the productive forces for which it is sufficient have been developed, and new superior relations

of production never replace older ones before the material conditions for their existence have matured within the framework of the old society (Marx, 1859: 263).

Certainly, this is a clear and powerful statement. *But how could it be denied that this thesis allows for a rather conservative interpretation – a conservative's Marx as envisioned by Schumpeter (1950: 58)?* In this framework, how do we explain the continued existence of capitalism? Cohen reasons that it follows from this thesis that capitalism 'persists because and as long as it is optimal for further development of productive power and... is optimal for further development of productive power' (Cohen, 1978: 175). In short, there is a very simple answer to those 'anomalies' noted in Chapter 2 that 'confront Marxism as its refutation': capitalism is not *yet* at the point where its relations of production are fettering the development of productive forces. We go beyond capital only when it is no longer 'optimal', only when the productive forces have been developed to the point when they have outgrown their capitalist shell.[1] For Marx, Cohen (1978: 150) proposes, the revolution: 'takes place because the expansion of productive power has been blocked, and the revolution will enable it to proceed afresh. The function of the revolutionary social change is to unlock the productive forces.' And, this point would surely come, Cohen offers, because Marx thought 'high technology was *not only necessary but also sufficient* for socialism, and that capitalism would certainly generate that technology' (Cohen, 1978: 206; emphasis added).

What does this Marxism offer to all who would reject capitalism? *Wait.* Wait until capitalism runs out of steam. Indeed, the true revolutionaries would appear to be those who speed the development of the productive forces, the agents who generate that 'high technology'! This 'conservative Marxism', however, differs rather significantly from the Marx and Marxism outlined in this book. Where, for example, is the place in this thesis of the primacy of productive forces for the effect of class struggle upon the course and nature of the development of productive forces within capitalism? As Cohen's associated 'Development Thesis' ('The productive forces tend to develop throughout history') indicates, the suggestion is that productive forces develop *autonomously* (Cohen, 1978: 134). And, how can we talk about capitalism as being optimal for the development of productive forces when we know how central the ability to separate workers is for capital – i.e., that the goal of capital is valorization rather than efficiency as such?

After all, we cannot forget a central premise of Marxism – all development of the productive forces occurs within and through a specific set of social relations.[2] Any suggestion, then, of autonomous development of the productive forces or the neutrality of technology (as noted in Chapter 7) is an economism contrary to the importance that Marx attributed to productive relations. Nevertheless, simply stressing productive relations would not alter the central argument of this thesis of the primacy of productive forces – that at a certain stage specific relations of production become fetters on the productive forces and that this leads to the replacement of the former.[3]

But, what determines that 'certain stage'? Far more problematic than neglect of productive relations in this formulation is another disappearance – the disappearance of human beings as subjects. As Cohen argues in his 'defence' of Marx's theory of history, the course of history from this perspective 'is not subject to human will' (Cohen, 1978: 148). Thus, the fundamental explanation of historical development follows from the march (or failure to march) of productive forces. And human beings? They are mere servants of the 'Development Thesis'. All impulse and dynamic, in short, appears to emerge from abstract categories – confirming Gramsci's observation 'that by trying to be ultra-materialist one falls into a baroque form of abstract idealism' (Gramsci, 1971: 467). *The consistency of the thesis of the primacy of productive forces with the one-sided Marxism that flows from* **Capital's** *neglect of the worker as subject is evident.*

Why does the fettering of productive forces by capitalist relations of production lead to the replacement of the latter? Not because capitalist relations of production sheepishly step aside to let the new era begin. The implicit argument is that people *recognise* the inadequacy of capitalist relations and proceed to do away with them. Yet, inadequate in what respect? Presumably, inadequate with respect to the satisfaction of their needs as socially developed human beings.

Consider, therefore, an alternative thesis – that it is the needs of socially developed human beings (that is, people developed in particular societies) that are central in determining the course of historical change. Definite human beings both develop their productive forces and change their production relations, and they do so in order to satisfy their needs. In this alternative formulation of Marx's theory of history (*the primacy of needs*), social change occurs when the existing structure of society no longer satisfies the needs of people formed within that society; it occurs when the relations of production prevent the development of productive forces *in the way which conforms to the particular needs of definite human beings*. Within capitalism, accordingly, the ought which drives beyond capital is 'the worker's own need for development'.

It seems so obvious. Further, it will be quickly recognized (and readily acknowledged) that this alternative was always implicit in the thesis of the primacy of productive forces. Indeed, the thesis of the primacy of needs is simply the Preface of '59 with a human face. Yet, more is involved in the restoration of human beings to the 'hub' than the addition of a few phrases.

The thesis of the primacy of needs, for example, emphasizes not only capital's tendency to fetter productive forces but also its constant generation of new social needs for commodities, the production of new links in the golden chain which binds workers to capital. Thus, it is not difficult to conceive of two societies with equivalent rates of development of productive forces but which differ significantly with respect to the generation of needs – with the result that growing immiseration in one (but not the other) brings into question the adequacy of its relations of production. The thesis of the primacy of needs, indeed, permits us to ask a question logically outside the bounds of the thesis of the primacy of productive forces: is the particular dilemma of capitalism its inherent tendency to generate new needs for commodities *too much and too rapidly*?[4]

Once the focus is upon human beings and their needs, centre stage is occupied by the concept of immiseration set out in Chapter 3 – the gap between socially developed needs and those normally satisfied. This is the context in which the question of capital's tendency to hold back the development of productivity should be considered. Underlying the worker's struggle for higher wages is a set of needs that exceeds the existing standard of necessity. Yet, there is a 'capitalist limit' to the ability of workers to realize their commodity-needs: real wages cannot be increased to the extent that it would check the ability of capital for self-valorization. 'The rise of wages is therefore confined within limits that not only leave intact the foundations of the capitalist system, but also secure its reproduction on an expanding scale' (Marx, 1977: 771). As indicated in Chapter 6, only increased productivity alters those limits, permitting workers to satisfy more of their needs without reducing the rate of surplus value. Implicit, then, is that capitalism must develop productive forces or face workers who are dissatisfied.

Of course, as we saw in Chapter 1, capitalism 'contains within itself a barrier to the free development of the productive forces' (Marx, 1968: 528). In the very process of developing productive forces and increasing the rate of surplus value, capital itself restricts the possibilities for realization of surplus value (cf. Lebowitz, 1982b, 1976b). Precisely because the consumption of the mass of producers 'does not grow correspondingly with the productivity of labour,' Marx argued that there is a tendency for crises of overproduction (Marx, 1968: 468). He recognized, however, that such crises are not permanent – their effect is to 're-establish the disturbed balance'; these crises, thus, reflect a Barrier (but not a Limit) to the development of productive forces (Marx, 1981b: 357; 1973: 446).[5]

The difficulty of realizing surplus value is not the only such barrier capital faces. Once established on its own foundations, Marx noted, capitalism acquires 'a capacity for sudden extension by leaps and bounds, which comes up against no barriers but those presented by the availability of raw materials and the extent of sales outlets' (Marx, 1977: 579). Capital, thus, is subject not only to barriers inherent in its own nature but also to barriers common to all forms of production. The barrier in this case, Nature, takes a specific capitalist form: given that the production of plant and animal products is 'subject to certain organic laws involving naturally determined periods of time,' in periods of expansion 'the demand for these raw materials grows more rapidly than their supply, and their price therefore rises' (Marx, 1981b: 213–14). All other things equal, this underproduction of raw materials produces a fall in the rate of profit: 'the rate of profit falls or rises in the opposite direction to the price of the raw material' (Marx, 1981b: 201, 206). 'The more capitalist production is developed', Marx observed, the more likely are 'violent fluctuations in price' which 'lead to interruptions, major upsets and even catastrophes in the reproduction process' (Marx, 1981b: 213–14).[6]

Nevertheless, such crises contain within them the means by which capital can transcend its barriers – in this case, by stimulating the expansion of raw materials production (Marx, 1981b: 214). Crises *within* capitalism should not be confused with crises *of* capitalism; the former drive capital forward (as noted in Chapter 1) and are part of the process of capital's development. Still, we should not exclude the possibility that a check to the development of productive forces may be the result of a Limit rather than a Barrier. While Nature is a 'general' barrier for capital (rather than one specific to the essence of capital), capital faces not an Abstract Nature but one already shaped by capital. Insofar as Nature (like the worker) is only a *means* for capital, it faces the same fate as workers at the hands of capital: '*Après moi le deluge!* is the watchword of every capitalist and every capitalist nation. Capital therefore takes no account of the health and the length of life of the worker, unless society forces it to do so' (Marx, 1977: 381).

Capital's tendency to destroy Nature was very clear to Marx. Indeed, he proposed that 'the entire spirit of capitalist production, which is oriented towards the most immediate monetary profit – stands in contradiction to agriculture, which has to concern itself with the whole gamut of permanent conditions of life required by the chain of human generations' (Marx, 1981b: 754n). Rather than 'a conscious and rational treatment of the land as permanent communal property, as the inalienable condition for the existence and reproduction of the chain of human generations, we have the exploitation and the squandering of the powers of the earth' (Marx, 1981b: 949). Accordingly, insofar as Nature is merely a means for the production of surplus value, Marx argued that 'all progress in capitalist agriculture is a progress in the art, not only of robbing the worker, but of robbing the soil; all progress in increasing the fertility of the soil for a given time is a progress towards ruining the more long-lasting sources of that fertility' (Marx, 1977: 638).

We have here a clear statement of what James O'Connor described as capital's inherent tendency not merely to check the growth of productivity but also to *impair* its conditions of production.[7] 'Treated correctly', the earth continuously improves and can be bequeathed in an improved state to succeeding generations; yet, 'a genuinely rational agriculture' and forest management 'in the common interest' are inconsistent with 'the entire spirit of capitalist production' (Marx, 1981b: 916, 911, 754–5n).[8] As Marx concluded, 'capitalist production, therefore, only develops the technique and the degree of combination of the social process of production by simultaneously undermining the original sources of all wealth – the soil and the worker' (Marx, 1977: 638).

Once we acknowledge that Nature is a source of wealth and that workers as human beings have needs for use-values that do *not* take a commodity-form, we can no longer measure immiseration solely along the one-dimensional scale of social and necessary needs for commodities. Thus, any worker whose hierarchy of needs includes use-values (e.g., fresh air and sunlight) that Nature supplies will be immiserated by the destruction of the natural environment. Accordingly, both by restricting production to that which is profitable (a unique characteristic dramatically revealed in crises of overproduction) and also by impairing the natural conditions of production, capital checks the realization of the needs of workers.

The thesis of the primacy of needs proposes that, as the result of the immiseration of workers, there is a point when capital will be recognized as no longer compatible with the worker's ought, the worker's own need for development. In contrast to the thesis of the primacy of productive forces, it recognises the importance of workers' needs (and thus points explicitly to the importance of struggling to satisfy those needs). The greater the immiseration of workers, the greater their dissatisfaction, the greater the likelihood that workers will choose to go beyond capital. The thesis of the primacy of needs would suggest that increased immiseration is sufficient to explain the transcendence of capital as a mediator for workers. *Yet, that is precisely what we cannot accept as Marx's position.*

II Capital's products

After all, it is not abstract human beings who are immiserated. The recognition that capital is not compatible with the worker's own need for development is one that is made by specific subjects, and it is by no means an automatic process.

Consider Marx's argument about crises generated by overproduction. What is unique about such events is that the tendency of capital to restrict production (which is always present but hidden) can be seen in clear view. On those periodic occasions when 'too much wealth is produced in its capitalist, antagonist forms', the barriers to capitalist production 'show themselves'. We can *see* then that the rate of profit 'determines the expansion or contraction of production, instead of the proportion between production and social needs, the needs of socially developed human beings'. Even when production *appears* to be unchecked, it is completely inadequate from the perspective of the needs of human beings. But when the crisis occurs, the barrier 'comes to the surface'. It is possible *then* to see that 'production comes to a standstill not at the point where needs are satisfied, but rather where the production and realization of profit impose this' (Marx, 1981b: 367).

Rather than as the source of a 'breakdown' of capitalism, crises from this perspective represent a point when capital's specific barrier to 'the development of the forces of production, the expansion of needs, the all-sided development of production, and the exploitation and exchange of natural and mental forces' *comes to the surface and allows capital itself to be recognized as the real barrier* (Marx, 1973: 410). Crises – both those which are the result of capital's impairment of natural conditions as well as those reflecting overproduction – merely offer an opportunity to identify the essence of capital. As Gramsci (1971: 184) commented:

It may be ruled out that immediate economic crises of themselves produce fundamental historical events; they can simply create a terrain more favourable to the dissemination of certain modes of thought, and certain ways of posing and resolving questions involving the entire subsequent development of national life.

Thus, the immiseration of wage-labourers (i.e., the fettering of productive forces) by capital *in itself* does not point beyond capital! Immiseration, as we have seen, is an inherent characteristic of capitalism; its existence is not contingent. Nor is there any reason to assume that there is a critical value for the degree of immiseration beyond which an era of social revolution begins.

After all, the recognition that capital is 'the real barrier' is one that must be made by specific subjects – the workers described in Chapter 8. Given their heterogeneity and their consciousness of dependence upon capital, is it likely that these definite human beings will identify capital as the source of immiseration? What, in short, ensures that capitalist barriers to the satisfaction of needs (even when they *do* come to the surface) will be perceived as such and as a reason to go beyond capital?

Here, then, is a central problem with the thesis of the primacy of needs as we have stated it. *Rather than pointing beyond capital, the inability to satisfy their needs in itself leads workers not beyond capital but to class struggle within capitalism.* The immiseration of workers with respect to the commodity requirements which capital creates does not, for example, point to the inadequacy of capitalist relations of production; rather, it immediately generates the demand for higher wages. Every particular level of wages appears as a barrier to the satisfaction of needs, a barrier that must be transcended quantitatively – and, if wage-labour can drive beyond that barrier, it finds itself confronted by a new, higher level of needs (that basis of 'the contemporary power of capital'). In short, the worker can transcend particular barriers to the satisfaction of her needs but not the existence of a barrier as such. The 'real barrier' of wage-labour is wage-labour itself – *but it does not appear as such.*

Similarly, in the struggle over working conditions or over the length of the workday, the immediate impulse of workers is to struggle within capitalism to satisfy their needs. The point may be extended to other issues as well: while recognizing capital's tendency to undermine 'the original sources of all wealth – the soil and the worker' or to turn their sexual, racial or ethnic differences into antagonisms in order to divide them, why should workers not simply see the necessity (as in the case of the limitation of the workday) that capital must be *forced* by 'society' to take account of that which it would not otherwise? Why should they not attempt to use the State as 'their own agency' within capitalism? *In short, why go beyond capital? Why not capitalism with a human face – a capitalism humanized by the struggles of workers?*

Once we recognize capitalism not only as K-WL-K but also as WL-K-WL, then it is clear that within this relation capital appears as the *necessary* mediator for wage-labour. (This understanding flows easily from a consideration of the side of capitalism not developed in *Capital*.) As we have seen, too, this feeling of social dependence upon capital is reproduced spontaneously. So long as the inversion of subject and object by which all the attributes of workers appear to be the attributes of capital continues, there is no basis for the critical leap from wage-labour as a force which struggles against capital (but which can only exist as such *through* capital) – to a wage-labour which recognizes the necessity to abolish capital. Accordingly, no matter how significant the crisis or the immiseration gap, 'the social dependence of the worker on the capitalist, which is indispensable, is secured' (Marx, 1977: 935).

As long as capital appears as productive, the struggles of workers do not occur outside the bounds of the relation. Or, stated more familiarly, capital spontaneously produces 'a trade-union consciousness' – but not a consciousness that reaches beyond the capital/wage-labour relation. This was precisely the argument made by Lenin (1967: 122):

> The history of all countries shows that the working class, exclusively by its own effort, is able to develop only trade union consciousness, i.e., the conviction that it is necessary to combine in unions, fight the employers, and strive to compel the government to pass necessary labour legislation, etc.

That is the necessary result of functioning within the bounds of a relation in which (as noted in Chapter 4):

> *If capital does not go through its circuit, the worker cannot go through his; if the worker does not go through his circuit, capital cannot proceed through its. The reproduction of capital requires the reproduction of wage-labour as such; the reproduction of wage-labour as such requires the reproduction of capital.*

Without an understanding of the nature of capital, then what is specific to capital necessarily appears as a natural condition, independent of any particular relations of production. The degradation of the worker described by Marx, for example, appears as the result of industrial production *as such* rather than as the product of the specifically capitalist mode of production that emerges out of relations in which human beings are mere means for capital. Similarly, when specific barriers of capital come to the surface, they necessarily appear as barriers inherent in production *in general*! Thus, a crisis related to the destruction of the

Acid - Oil - Pollution

environment presents itself as a crisis of the 'economy' – (as perhaps, indeed, the result of 'too much consumption' by workers) rather than as inherent in 'the entire spirit of capitalist production'. When the specific nature of capitalist crisis is not recognized, it suggests the necessity not to go beyond capital but, rather, the need for 'sacrifice' – by all.

For Marx, the Limit that makes capital finite is the working class. This and only this turns a crisis within capitalism into a crisis *of* capitalism. Yet, capital produces the workers it needs, workers who consider the necessity for capital to be self-evident. Once we recognize the significance of the mystification of capital, we cannot accept the proposition that capitalism persists because it is 'optimal'. *This is a total distortion of Marx's understanding of capitalism, however rigorously such a proposition may be presented.* Capitalism may be suboptimal and persist precisely because:

> The advance of capitalist production develops a working class which by education, tradition and habit looks upon the requirements of that mode of production as self-evident natural laws. The organization of the capitalist process of production, once it is fully developed, breaks down all resistance (Marx, 1977: 899).

Indeed, as Marx continued:

> In the ordinary run of things, the worker can be left to the 'natural laws of production', i.e. it is possible to rely on his dependence on capital, which springs from the conditions of production themselves, and is guaranteed in perpetuity by them (Marx, 1977: 899).

Guaranteed *in perpetuity*? Marx here has described capitalism as an organic system, one that produces all its premises – including its working class – in their necessary form: 'While in the completed bourgeois system every economic relation presupposes every other in its bourgeois economic form, and everything posited is thus also a presupposition, this is the case with every organic system' (Marx, 1973: 278).

III   The necessity of theory

Ultimately, what all deterministic theses have in common is that they cannot explain why – if the transcendence of capital is only a matter of 'high technology' or increasing immiseration – Marx considered it necessary to 'sacrifice my health, happiness, and family' in order to complete the first volume of *Capital* (Marx and Engels, 1987b: 366).

As Lukács (1972: 208) noted, 'History is at its least automatic when it is the consciousness of the proletariat that is at issue.' And, that is precisely what is at issue here. As the owner of the products of labour and as mediator between the worker's needs and her labour, capital's power is not the power of this or that capitalist but, rather, is that of capital as a whole. That power, as we have seen in Chapter 5, appears as the powerlessness of the worker in the face of a world with its own laws outside and independent of her.

To challenge the rule of capital, it is necessary to challenge its ownership of the products of labour, which underlies its power as mediator in the labour market and the sphere of production. Since, however, 'the development of the *social* productive forces of labour and the conditions of that development come to appear as the *achievement of capital*', nothing seems more natural than the justice and optimality of capitalist ownership. Given the inherent mystification of capital, *demystification* is therefore a necessary condition for workers to go beyond capital.

For this very reason, Marx considered it essential to reveal the nature of capital, to reveal what cannot be apparent on the surface – that capital itself is the result of exploitation. It is 'an enormous advance in awareness', he proposed, when the proletariat recognizes capital as its own product. That 'recognition of the products as its own, and the judgement that its separation from the conditions of its realization is improper – forcibly imposed', indeed, would be the 'knell' to capital's doom (Marx, 1973: 463).

Theory is necessary because the transcendence of capital requires that capital be understood as the result of exploitation. As Marx noted in the Inaugural Address of the First International, workers may be numerous, but they only can succeed 'if united by combination and led by knowledge' (Marx, 1864: 12). Theory offers that knowledge; it 'becomes a material force as soon as it has gripped the masses' (Marx, 1843: 182). The failure, on the other hand, to combat the mystification of capital means that bourgeois ideas exist as a material force. Thus, despite the degree of maturity in the class struggle and the organisation of trade unions in England, Marx nevertheless argued in 1870 that an important element was missing:

The English have all the *material* necessary for the social revolution. What they lack is *the spirit of generalisation and revolutionary fervour*. Only the General Council [of the First International] can provide them with this, can thus accelerate the truly revolutionary movement here, and in consequence, *everywhere* (Marx, 1870: 402).

Engels made a similar comment in his 1874 Preface to *The Peasant War in Germany* when he compared the 'sense of theory' among German workers to 'the indifference towards all theory which is one of the main reasons why the English working-class movement crawls along so slowly in spite of the splendid organization of the individual unions' (Engels, 1956: 32–3). That sense of theory of German workers, however, gave him hope:

> For the first time since a workers' movement has existed, the struggle is being conducted pursuant to its three sides – the theoretical, the political and the practical-economic (resistance to the capitalists) – in harmony and in its interconnections, and in a systematic way (Engels, 1956: 33).

Thus, Engels stressed the necessity that the leadership of the workers' movement 'gain an ever clearer insight into all theoretical questions' and that this new understanding be spread among the masses of workers (Engels, 1956: 34). It was a position followed by Lenin, who argued that class consciousness could be 'brought to the workers *only from without*, that is, only from outside the economic struggle, from outside the sphere of relations between workers and their employers' (Lenin, 1967: 163). In so arguing, he cited Engels' recognition of '*not two* forms of the great struggle of Social-Democracy (political and economic), as is the fashion among us, *but three, placing the theoretical struggle on a par with the first two*' (Lenin, 1967: 118).

But, what are the characteristics of a theory that will reveal the nature of capital? It is not theory *as such* – but a *particular* theory that is required! To understand the necessary characteristics of that theory, we must grasp precisely the basis of the mystification of capital.

Capital cannot appear as the result of exploitation of the worker because exploitation itself is not apparent in the buying and selling of labour-power. Inherently, 'the worker's wage appears as the price of labour, as a certain quantity of money that is paid for a certain quantity of labour' (Marx, 1977: 675). That is the way it looks to the capitalist who purchases his specific requirements for production, and it is the way it looks to the worker as seller.

Rather than providing that certain quantity of labour (d) and being paid only the equivalent of her necessary labour (w), it appears that the worker is paid for *all* labour performed:

> The wage-form thus extinguishes every trace of the division of labour into necessary labour and surplus labour, into paid labour and unpaid

labour. All labour appears as paid labour ... (T)he money-relation conceals the uncompensated labour of the wage-labourer.

Obviously, if the sale of labour-power, that distinctive characteristic of capitalism, inherently hides exploitation, then capital cannot be recognized in the normal course of things as the result of exploitation. Therefore, insofar as it necessarily appears that the worker has received an equivalent for the labour she performs, there is the basis for the entire mystification of capital:

> All the notions of justice held by both the worker and the capitalist, all the mystifications of the capitalist mode of production, all capitalism's illusions about freedom, all the apologetic tricks of vulgar economics, have as their basis the form of appearance discussed above, which makes the actual relation invisible, and indeed presents to the eye the precise opposite of that relation (Marx, 1977: 680).

Accordingly, that 'actual relation' that is hidden from view must be revealed. 'The forms of appearance are reproduced directly and spontaneously, as current and usual modes of thought; the essential relation must first be discovered by science' (Marx, 1977: 682). And, that meant the necessity to demonstrate that the relation between capitalist and worker was *not* what it appeared to be – a market transaction between two commodity owners.

Although the 'exchange between capital and labour at first presents itself to our perceptions in exactly the same way as the sale and purchase of all other commodities,' Marx argued that this appearance of exchange between capitalist and worker was only an *apparent* exchange, 'a mere semblance belonging only to the process of circulation'. It was, indeed, 'a mere form, which is alien to the content of the transaction itself, and merely mystifies it' (Marx, 1977: 681, 729–30).

Why was it wrong to view the relation of capitalist and worker as one of commodity exchange? In commodity exchange, the focus is upon independent, isolated transactions; each transaction is considered as separate from all others, and presupposed is that 'only the mutually independent buyer and seller face each other in commodity production':

> If, therefore, commodity production, or one of its associated processes, is to be judged according to its own economic laws, we must consider each act of exchange by itself, apart from any connection with the act of exchange preceding it and that following it.

And since sales and purchases are negotiated solely between particular individuals, it is not admissible to look here for relations between whole social classes (Marx, 1977: 733).

Yet, that assumption of the independence of transactions and contracting parties cannot be accepted. *Where does the capital that faces the worker in each individual transaction come from?* Considered in the framework of commodity exchange, this question can *never* be answered; capital necessarily appears in each transaction with each individual worker as an *unexplained premise*. Indeed, the capital faced by any individual worker may be only a premise for that worker – rather than the result of *her own* exploitation.[9]

For this reason, Marx argued that the form of the relation as a commodity relation necessarily mystified its real content, the actual relation between capitalist and worker:

> The constant sale and purchase of labour-power is the form; the content is the constant appropriation by the capitalist, without equivalent, of a portion of the labour of others which has already been objectified, and his repeated exchange of this labour for a greater quantity of the living labour of others (Marx, 1977: 730).

Since the actual relation was veiled by the commodity and money-form, Marx proposed the necessity to look at this relation in a way that was not at all apparent on the surface. Every individual transaction *taken by itself* may appear as just and free of any taint of exploitation. Indeed, each wage-labourer necessarily appears to gain as a result of the transaction – compared to the existing alternative of *no* transaction. (How much better to sell labour-power than not to sell it, how much better to be exploited than not to be at all!) The surface form, Marx stressed, 'merely ensures the perpetuation of the specific relationship of dependency, endowing it with the deceptive *illusion* of a transaction, of a contract between equally free and equally matched *commodity owners*' (Marx, 1977: 1064).

Nevertheless, 'the illusion created by the money-form vanishes immediately if, instead of taking a single capitalist and a single worker, we take the whole capitalist class and the whole working class' (Marx, 1977: 713). We gain a different understanding if we 'contemplate not the single capitalist and the single worker, but the capitalist class and the working class, not an isolated process of production, but capitalist production in full swing, and on its actual social scale' (Marx, 1977: 717).

In short, to understand the nature of capital, Marx adopted a standpoint entirely foreign to commodities – the consideration of capitalism as a totality. Only by considering workers as a whole and capital as a whole was it possible to go beyond the illusions inherent in the transactions of individual capitalists and individual workers. Indeed, the 'matter looks quite different', he stressed:

> if we consider capitalist production in the uninterrupted flow of its renewal, and if, in place of the individual capitalist and the individual worker, we view them in their totality, as the capitalist class and the working class confronting each other. But in so doing we should be applying standards entirely foreign to commodity production (Marx, 1977: 732).

With the concept of reproduction (both simple and expanded) for capital as a whole, it was possible for Marx to demonstrate that the source of the capital that confronts workers in each transaction is the result of the previous exploitation of workers. Capital thus no longer appears as an unexplained premise, independent of the exploitation of workers. Viewed 'as a transaction between the capitalist class and the working class', it doesn't matter which individual workers were originally exploited and which are working with new means of production. 'In every case, the working class creates by the surplus labour of one year the capital destined to employ additional labour in the following year' (Marx, 1977: 728–9).

Without the concept of a system of reproduction, premises hang in mid-air. Means of production appear as isolated premises for separate acts of production. They appear as independent sources of productivity – against which the contribution of the individual worker who works with these means seems relatively insignificant. It is only a short step from here to the inference that those who bring these distinct sources of productivity into combination with workers are entitled to an appropriate return.

Considering capitalism as a totality and workers as a whole, the means of production are recognized as the product of *other* workers, other limbs of the collective worker. If there is increased productivity as the result of the existence of particular means of production, it is thus not an occult power inherent in things but the activity of the workers who *produced* those means of production that is central. *More specifically, that increased productivity results (as discussed in Chapter 5) from the combination and cooperation of social labour.*

Between the political economy of capital and the political economy of the working class, there is thus a world of difference. The very argument that capital captures the fruits of cooperation by virtue of its ability to divide and separate workers already presupposes that we can conceive of workers as a whole which can be divided. The political economy of the working class begins from the concept of the collective worker, a concept that implies an alternative ('counterfactual') society in which capital is no longer the mediator between and above workers. For the political economy of capital, on the other hand, the starting point is separate, individual workers who are 'brought together' by capital; for it, all the achievements of combined labour are those of capital, the necessary mediator.

There is no neutrality in theory and method, as Marx well understood. By considering capitalism as a totality in which all premises are results of the system itself, Marx broke dramatically with a theory that focussed upon commodity exchange, the law of supply and demand and market transactions – the phenomena which provide ' "the free-trader *vulgaris*" with his views, his concepts and the standard by which he judges the society of capital and wage-labour' (Marx, 1977: 280). Thus, when self-proclaimed 'analytical' Marxists rejected Marx's methodological holism for assuming 'that there are supra-individual entities that are prior to individuals in the explanatory order', their assertion of the identity of methodological individualism and good science was merely the embrace of the political economy of capital en route to the complete rejection of a Marxist perspective (Lebowitz, 1988a).

Marx's method of looking at capital and wage-labour as a whole (which has served as a premise for our entire discussion) was precisely what was required to reveal the nature of capital as the result of exploitation. As Lukács (1972: 27) so correctly argued, Marx provided in *Capital* a distinct theory for workers:

> Proletarian science is revolutionary not just by virtue of its revolutionary ideas which it opposes to bourgeois society, but above all because of its method. *The primacy of the category of totality is the bearer of the principle of revolution in science.*

To counter the inherent mystification of capital required the theory of *Capital*. Significantly, however, for this particular purpose only *Capital* – and not the six books (or even the first three) – is required; indeed, only Volume I of *Capital* is required! So, finally, we come to a question implicit since Chapter 3: *If the book on wage-labour is so important for the understanding of capitalism as a whole, why didn't Marx write it?*

The answer is simple – but we first need to be absolutely clear as to why Marx wrote *Capital* (and, indeed, Volume I over and over again). *Capital* was Marx's attempt to make the proletariat 'conscious of the condition of its emancipation', conscious of the need to abolish capital's ownership of the products of labour – i.e., 'to inscribe on their banner the *revolutionary* watchword, *"Abolition of the wages system!"* ' (Marx, 1865b: 149). That was a limited object but, nevertheless, a crucial one given Marx's understanding of capital's inherent tendency to develop a working class which looks upon capital's requirements as 'self-evident natural laws'. If we fail to recognize that limited object, however, we may misunderstand entirely *Capital*'s place and importance. *Capital is not merely a moment in the understanding of the totality, capitalism as a whole; it is also a moment in the revolutionary struggle of workers to go beyond capital.*

In this respect, it is essential to recall Engels' speech at Marx's graveside. Marx was a man of science, he noted; but 'Marx was before all else a revolutionist'. The criticism that Marx simply reproduced the inadequacies of the political economy of capital is misplaced. Marx's *Capital* *is* a study of the logic of capital, and that is what it *needed* to be – given the necessity to explain the nature of capital. For this purpose, too, the abstraction from the heterogeneity of wage-labourers is necessary in order to demonstrate what all wage-labourers have in common. We understand Marx's *Capital* better by understanding what it was *not*. Its purpose was neither to interpret capitalism differently nor to change it; rather, it was to give workers a weapon with which to go beyond it.

So, why didn't Marx get around to writing the book on Wage-Labour? The completion of his epistemological project interested him less than his revolutionary project.

10
From Political Economy to Class Struggle

> The coincidence of the changing of circumstances and of human activity or self-change can be conceived and rationally understood only as *revolutionary practice*.
>
> Marx (1845: 4)

Marx's project to demonstrate that capital is the result of exploitation was essential precisely because of the inherent mystification of capital that is rooted in the buying and selling of labour-power. In the absence of the demystification of capital, there is no going-beyond capital. Crises, stagnation, destruction of the natural environment (indeed, all purely economic movements) do not lead beyond capital because so long as capital appears necessary to workers, they will be dependent upon it. The passivity of workers and its corollary, the durability of capitalism, cannot be considered anomalies for the Marx who understood that capitalism itself produces workers who look upon its requirements 'as self-evident natural laws'. Rather than anomalies, these are the essence of the problem.

Capital, thus, is Marx's 'ruthless criticism of all that exists', his attempt at 'making the world aware of its own consciousness', at awakening the working class to the conditions of its emancipation (Marx and Engels, 1975b: 142, 144). Yet, the 'weapon of criticism', as he well knew, is not in itself sufficient. Theory 'becomes a material force as soon as it has gripped the masses'. But, when can it do so? 'Theory', he (1844a: 182–3) recognized, 'can be realised in a people only insofar as it is the realisation of the needs of that people.' But, how do the theoretical needs of abstract and undifferentiated wage-labourers become the 'immediate practical needs' of workers who are well aware that they are *not* identical to each other? In short, what can make *Capital* a use-value for mystified heterogeneous workers in the grasp of capital?

I Class struggle as production

Consider what capital produces. Not merely commodities or surplus value but 'the capital relation itself; on the one hand the capitalist, on the other the wage labourer' (Marx, 1977: 724). And, that wage-labourer, as we have seen, is one who is socially dependent upon capital. Insofar as capital constantly generates new needs for alien commodities and re-orders the hierarchy of needs of workers, it produces workers with the need to possess and the need for money. This generation of new needs is 'precisely this side of the relation of capital and labour... on which the historic justification, but also the contemporary power of capital rests' (Marx, 1973: 287). In this respect, capital produces the workers it needs. Yet, they are a contradictory product.

Because they are immiserated. This is why workers constantly attempt to satisfy more of their social needs. Struggles against capital as mediator in the labour market and in production – as well as all those in which they struggle politically against capital's mediation within society – are inherent in the very position of the wage-labourer. That is, indeed, the unequivocal position of Marx – *capitalism produces class struggle on the part of workers*.

In themselves these struggles do not transcend the capital/wage-labour relation; indeed, the right to engage in them helps to underline the distinction between slaves and free workers. Thus, daily struggles within capitalism are entirely compatible with the continued hegemony of capital. Nevertheless, a critical *qualitative* development (inherent in the concept of the production of the worker) takes place in the course of such struggles.

Consider the existence of workers as heterogeneous human beings. Given the differences in the specific conditions of their individual production (as well as the separation that capital itself produces), there is a definite material basis for seeing themselves as separate and indeed as competing with each other as wage-labourers – rather than as One in opposition to capital. Understanding the working class as One analytically does not mean that it either sees itself or acts as One (nor does it mean that one assumes that it does).

Nevertheless, the very process of struggle against capital as mediator is a process of *reducing* that separation; it is a process of producing the working class as One. Although they are separate, different and heterogeneous, workers must unite for this struggle in order to realize their needs; they thus recognize their necessary interdependence as a condition of achieving their goals. In this process, Marx observed, 'they acquire a new need – the need for society – and what appears as a means becomes an end' (Marx, 1844c: 313). These separate and distinct human beings *posit themselves* as One when they struggle collectively against capital:

> the proletarians arrive at this unity only through a long process of development in which the appeal to their right also plays a part. Incidentally, this appeal to their right is only a means of making them take shape as 'they', as a revolutionary, united mass (Marx and Engels, 1846: 323).

In short, the working class – understood analytically as a class in itself – becomes a class for itself by struggling for its needs against capital. In the struggle, 'this mass becomes united, and constitutes itself as a class for itself' (Marx, 1847: 211). What Marx was describing is class struggle *as a process of production*.

Indeed, here is the Law for which all else is commentary. Just as every activity of the worker alters her as the subject who enters into all activities, similarly the process in which workers struggle for themselves is also a process of production, a process of purposeful activity in which they produce themselves in an altered way. They develop new needs in struggle, an altered hierarchy of needs. Even though the needs that they attempt to satisfy do not in themselves go beyond capital, the very process of struggle is one of producing new people, of transforming them into people with a new conception of themselves – as subjects capable of altering their world.

Nothing is more central to Marx's entire conception than this coincidence of the changing of circumstances and self-change (i.e., the concept of 'revolutionary practice')! The failure to understand this concept leaves theorists with an irresolvable dilemma: how can the old subjects, the products of capital, go beyond capital? If their struggles are for material needs (and nothing more), how can they ever rationally opt for the uncertain future of a society without capital as the mediator?[1] Marx understood, though, that people are not static, that the struggle for material needs can produce new people with new, 'radical' needs.[2]

Woven into his work from the time of his earliest writings is the red thread of the self-development of the working class through its struggles. This concept explicitly surfaced in his *Theses on Feuerbach*, where he introduced the concept of revolutionary practice; and, he evoked it over a quarter of a century later, following the Paris Commune, when he observed that workers know that 'they will have to pass through long struggles, through a series of historic processes, transforming circumstances and men' (Marx, 1871b: 76).

As Marx recognized, this central idea of the development of human beings through their activities was the rational core of Hegel's concept of the self-development of the Idea/Spirit, which develops and increasingly realizes its nature through the creative destruction of all its successive forms of existence. Hegel's 'outstanding achievement', Marx wrote in 1844, is that he 'conceives the self-creation of man as a process,' that he grasps human beings 'as the outcome of man's *own labour*' – although, to be sure, 'the only labour Hegel knows and recognises is *abstractly mental* labour' (Marx, 1844c: 332–3). In the fluid idealism of Hegel, Marx uncovered the centrality of human activity and practice for human development that was missing from the materialism of his predecessors (Marx, 1845: 3).[3]

Nor did he abandon this essential stress upon practice as the result of some variety of epistemological break marking a chronological separation of teleological humanist from sober scientist. Although the worker is not *Capital*'s subject, this idea of the worker as outcome of his own labour enters into Marx's discussion of the labour process; there, Marx notes, the worker 'acts upon external nature and changes it, and in this way he simultaneously changes his own nature' (Marx, 1977: 283). Similarly, in the *Grundrisse*, this concept of joint products (the changing of circumstances and self-change) is also clear in the process of production, where 'the producers change, too, in that they bring out new qualities in themselves, develop themselves in production, transform themselves, develop new powers and ideas, new modes of intercourse, new needs and new language' (Marx, 1973: 494). In all this, there remains a clear conception of growth and self-development; describing the process of cooperation in production, Marx (1977: 447) commented: When the worker cooperates in a planned way with others, he strips off the fetters of his individuality, and develops the capabilities of his species.

Self-development, however, always involves more than just the process of material production. For Marx, it meant in particular the development of socialist human beings through collective struggle. He consistently argued that the process of struggle produces altered human beings, new subjects. In the *German Ideology*, Marx and Engels (1846: 52–3) proposed that the production of a 'communist consciousness' could take place only in a 'practical movement, a revolution.' This was the only way in which wage-labour could 'succeed in ridding itself of all the muck of ages and become fitted to found society anew.' A few years later, in 1850, Marx described his position as saying to workers: 'You will have to go through 15, 20, 50 years of civil wars and national struggles not only in order to bring about a change in society but also to change yourselves, and prepare yourselves for the exercise of political power' (Marx, 1853: 403).

In the same year, Engels outlined the way in which such struggles transform workers. Although it appeared (at the time) that the Ten Hours' Bill had been defeated, he argued that workers had already gained as the result of their struggles for it:

> The time and exertions spent in agitating so many years for the Ten Hours' Bill is not lost, although its immediate end be defeated. The working classes, in this agitation, found a mighty means to get acquainted with each other, to come to a knowledge of their social position and interests, to organise themselves and to know their strength. The working man, who has passed through such an agitation, is no longer the same as he was before; and the whole working class, after passing through it, is a hundred times stronger, more enlightened, and better organised than it was at the outset. It *was* an agglomeration of mere units, without any knowledge of each other, without any common tie; and now it is a powerful body, conscious of its strength, recognised as 'The Fourth Estate', and which will soon be the *first* (Engels, 1850: 275).

In struggling against capital, accordingly, workers produce themselves differently – here, too, they 'transform themselves, develop new powers and ideas, new modes of intercourse, new needs and new language.' By cooperating with others in a planned way in the struggle against capital, the worker 'strips off the fetters of his individuality, and develops the capabilities of his species.' Ridding themselves in this way of 'the muck of ages', in short, they produce themselves no longer as results of capital but as presuppositions of a new society.

In contrast, consider Marx's comments on workers *not* actively in struggle, not in motion against capital. 'I am convinced', he indicated in 1853, that 'the continual conflicts between masters and men ... are ... the indispensable means of holding up the spirit of the labouring classes ... and of preventing them from becoming apathetic, thoughtless, more or less well-fed instruments of production.' Indeed, without strikes and constant struggle, the working classes 'would be a heart-broken, a weak-minded, a worn-out, unresisting mass'.[4] His position was the same in 1865 when responding to Citizen Weston's argument against the effectiveness of the wage struggle. Should workers renounce the struggle against capital's tendency to lower wages? 'If they did, they would be degraded to one level mass of broken wretches past salvation.' Workers who gave way in daily struggles 'would certainly disqualify themselves for the initiating of any larger movement' (Marx, 1865b: 148).

Effectively, such workers are the products of capital; and, as such, they are conditions of existence of capital reproduced by capital itself: 'In the ordinary run of things, the worker can be left to the "natural laws of production", i.e. it is possible to rely on his dependence on capital, which springs from the conditions of production themselves, and is guaranteed in perpetuity by them' (Marx, 1977: 899).

The failure to understand the centrality of 'the coincidence of the changing of circumstances' and of self-change – that coincidence that can only be understood as *revolutionary practice* – is the failure to understand the dynamic element without which there can be no transcendence of capital! 'Apathetic, thoughtless, more or less well-fed instruments of production' can never go beyond capital 'to found society anew'; and they can have no practical need for a theory which demonstrates the necessity for workers to end capital's ownership of the products of labour. Although Marx wrote *Capital* to explain to workers what they were struggling against, 'it is not enough for thought to strive for realisation, reality must itself strive towards thought'. Marx's political economy of the working class, in short, presupposes workers who are struggling against capital (Marx, 1843: 183, 144).

Precisely because he understood class struggle as this critical production process, Marx was uncompromising in his criticism of all those who would 'dilute' class struggle, who would demobilize workers and put an end to 'proletarian snap'. Writing in 1879 against the 'three Zurichers', he (Marx, 1879: 553–5) declared:

> For almost forty years we have stressed the class struggle as the immediate driving power of history and in particular the class struggle between bourgeoisie and proletariat as the great lever of the modern social revolution; it is, therefore, impossible for us to co-operate with people who wish to expunge this class struggle from the movement.

History, in short, was never so automatic for Marx that he abstained from his activities in the First International or from class struggle on the theoretical level. In the absence of the products of class struggle, immediate economic crises (although creating 'a terrain more favourable to the dissemination of certain modes of thought') will not be a threat to capital. The critical question (as Lukács noted) is whether workers experience the crisis 'as object or as the subject of decision'. The 'immaturity of the proletariat' and its subordination to capital's laws means that the specific nature of capital remains hidden:

> This gives rise to the delusion that the 'laws' of economics can lead the way out of a crisis just as they lead into it. Whereas what happened in reality was that – because of the passivity of the proletariat – the capitalist class was in a position to break the deadlock and start the machine going again. (Lukács, 1972: 244)

In short, as Gramsci observed, since the revolutionary process 'has as its actors men and their will and capability – the situation is not taken advantage of, and contradictory outcomes are possible'. Contrary to the thesis of the primacy of productive forces, far more is involved in the transcendence of capital than the social forces linked to the economic structure, which are 'objective, independent of human will, and which can be measured with the systems of the exact or physical systems'. There are also the moments of 'political forces' – involving 'the degree of homogeneity, self-awareness, and organisation attained by the various social classes' – as well as actual 'politico-military' forces (Gramsci, 1971: 180–5). In identifying such factors as important, we are rather far from the proposition that capitalism 'persists because and as long as it is optimal for further development of productive power'.[5]

II Dimensions of class struggle

As we've seen, capital's power rests in large part upon its continued ability to divide and separate workers – its ability to put workers into competition with each other, to turn difference into antagonism. Accordingly, an essential part of class struggle by workers involves the effort to combine and to reduce the degree of separation among them. One aspect of this, as discussed in Chapter 5, is the creation of trade unions, those vital 'centres of organisation of the working class' (Marx, 1866: 348).

The workplace, however, was not the only place for organization. In 1850, Marx and Engels identified the local community as one site in which workers should combine. Workers, they proposed, must 'make each community the central point and nucleus of workers' associations in which the attitude and interests of the proletariat will be discussed independently of bourgeois influences'. Writing at a time of revolutionary energy, they proposed that workers 'immediately establish their own revolutionary workers' governments, whether in the form of municipal committees and municipal councils or in the form of workers' clubs or workers' committees' (Marx and Engels, 1850: 282–3). Echoes of this focus upon the community and self-government of the producers reappear in Marx's conception of the workers' state.

This process of uniting workers, however, can't be limited to the spaces of their communities and immediate workplaces. Writing in 1868 about the struggles of workers in New York over the eight-hour day, Marx observed:

> This fact proves that even under the most favourable political conditions all serious success of the proletariat depends upon an organisation that unites and concentrates its forces; and even its national organisation is still exposed to split on the disorganisation of the working classes in other countries, which one and all compete in the market of the world, acting and reacting the one on the other. Nothing but an international bond of the working classes can ever ensure their definitive triumph (Marx, 1868: 329).

Precisely because he grasped the significance of disunity among workers, Marx did not limit himself to his theoretical work on the nature of capital; he made as a priority his political activity in the Working Men's International Association, an organization that attempted to foster international unity for workers through mutual support and analysis. As we have seen, Marx was especially concerned with the antagonism between Irish and English workers that, he argued, 'makes any honest and serious co-operation between the working classes of the two countries impossible' (Marx and Engels, n.d.: 334–5). The result of such divisions, he saw, was that 'the capitalist class maintains its power'. As Marx (1864: 12) had indicated in the Inaugural Address of the International, workers may be numerous, but they can succeed only 'if united by combination and led by knowledge'.

Yet, class struggle by workers has more dimensions. No theory is necessary to identify as class struggle those activities that occur within the first two moments of the circuit of capital (M-Lp, P). But, capital's real power, we understand from Chapter 5, resides in its ownership of the products of labour – in its ability to turn the workers' own products and power against workers. As the owner of articles of consumption and means of production, capital is in the position to determine which needs within society shall be satisfied. Thus, as mediator between producers within capitalism, it is responsible for all the unsatisfied needs of producers – insofar as the failure to satisfy those needs is inherent in the nature of capital rather than the result of technological considerations. Although this observation may appear extreme, it does so only because of the mystification characteristic of capitalist commodity production: where a state bureaucracy serves as mediator between producers in a society with the common ownership of the means of production, we would not hesitate to blame that bureaucracy for the failure to satisfy needs – insofar as that failure is inherent in its nature.

Thus, the struggles of workers to satisfy their many-sided needs – whether they are struggles, for example, to develop '*that which is needed for the common satisfaction of needs*, such as schools, health services, etc.' or to preserve Nature as a source of their wealth or to secure use-values in a commodity-form – are struggles against capital as mediator within society (Marx, 1875: 22). They are class struggles – struggles of those who are compelled to sell their labour-power to satisfy needs; and, they are struggles against the results of capital's ownership of the products of labour (which derives from its purchase of labour-power). Rather than directed only against *particular* capitals, they are struggles against the power of capital as a whole and against the ruling principle of valorization (*M-C-M'*).

To move from consideration of the political struggle of workers insofar as they are wage-labourers to that of the working class in its other sides, accordingly, is a major leap only if we begin from a stereotyped conception of the worker and her needs in the first place. A strategy calling for 'alliances' between workers and new social actors takes as its starting point the theoretical reduction of workers to one-dimensional products of capital. As stressed in Chapter 8, however, real workers have many determinations and exist simultaneously in many different social relations. Rather than an inherent opposition between 'new social movements' and the struggle of workers as a class against capital, the former should be seen as expressing *other* needs of workers and as the development of *new* organizing centres of the working class, functioning 'in the broad interest of its *complete emancipation*'.[6] And, insofar as they are directed against capital's position as the owner of the products of social labour, such struggles have the potential of *unifying* (rather than maintaining the separation) of all those who have nothing to sell but their labour-power.

Indeed, different movements (and organizing centres) may reinforce each other and strengthen the struggle against capital. Marx wrote from England in 1869, for example, that abolition of the landed aristocracy in

Ireland would 'be infinitely easier than here, because in Ireland it is not merely a simple economic question but at the same time a *national* question ...' (Marx and Engels, n.d.: 328). Again, in the following year, he commented that the struggle in Ireland would be easier because '*the land question* has hitherto been the *exclusive form* of the social question, because it is a question of existence, of *life and death*, for the immense majority of the Irish people, and because it is at the same time inseparable from the *national* question' (Marx and Engels, n.d.: 333). In short, the social question does not only come in one form; combined with the national question (in this case, anti-imperialism), the struggle may be 'infinitely easier'.

Of course, understanding these other struggles as class activity is not such a simple matter. Not all of the new social movements appear to be an attack on capital's position as mediator. In particular, as we have argued, the struggle against patriarchy is a struggle against a particular class exploitation in which men (rather than capital as such) are the exploiters. Are such struggles (as well as those against racism or which assert national or ethnic identities in the context of oppression), then, a digression from (and even a hindrance to) the 'real' struggle against capital?

Viewed superficially, any activity that may immediately widen divisions among workers (thereby reducing their unity against capital) appears to hinder the struggle against capital (which requires and enhances such divisions). Yet such a perspective departs entirely from Marx's materialist focus on the human being as subject. Marxists who regard struggles other than those directly against capital as 'secondary' have forgotten (or never learned) what Marx never forgot – who the subjects of change are. They have forgotten Marx's conception of human beings as beings of 'praxis' and thus have not gone beyond political economy as such. As Gajo Petrovic (1967: 112) explained:

> To rise above the level of political economy means to understand that man in the full sense of the word is not an economic animal, but a practical, hence free, universal, creative and self-creative social being. What distinguishes him from every other being is his special way of Being – praxis.

Why is it relevant to remember here that human beings are subjects of praxis? We need to go back to that concept of the simultaneous changing of circumstances and self-change. People who engage in such agitation, as Engels understood, are 'no longer the same' as they were before. In struggle, they develop new capacities that embody the potential for further acts. 'Every developed personality', proposed Lucien Sève, 'appears to us straight away as *an enormous accumulation of the most varied acts through time'* (Sève, 1978: 304). We have here, on one hand, the concept of capacities as *'fixed capital,* this fixed capital being man himself' (Marx, 1973: 712); and, on the other, that of an accumulation which occurs as the result of the 'numerous dialectical relations [that] exist between an individual's acts and capacities' (Sève, 1978: 313).

In short, every struggle to change circumstances is a process of self-change; it alters the people who engage in it – *and they enter into all their other relations as these altered human beings.* Insofar as those struggles (to be successful) must be collective, they produce people for whom unity becomes an end rather than mere means. It is not that the end to patriarchy or racism as such is incompatible with the continuation of capitalism but, rather, that the people who have struggled to end patriarchy and racism may be. Indeed, the 'initiating of any larger movement' depends upon the development of human beings who understand the importance of collective struggle for the satisfaction of their needs.[7]

Certainly, it is clear what *cannot* be a basis for going-beyond capital – the absence of people in motion. Who benefits from people who are not self-developing through their own activity? In this respect, as we have seen, central to the process which preserves capitalism as an organic system is the reproduction of everyday life – where people produce themselves daily as people with needs for commodities and dependent upon capital. Even some struggles conducted against capital, however, may help to sustain capitalist relations. It is not, for example, the existence as such of powerful trade unions but, rather, the manner in which they conduct themselves that determines whether workers produce themselves as revolutionary subjects. Insofar as workers' struggles are institutionalized and become clever elite manoeuvres in the backrooms, then the products are not workers with a new sense of themselves but 'apathetic, thoughtless, more or less well-fed instruments of production'. To paraphrase Rosa Luxemburg: historically, the errors committed by the working class in motion are infinitely more fruitful than the infallibility of the cleverest trade union leadership (Luxemburg, 1962: 108).

Luxemburg's description of trade unions in her time seems appropriate to call attention to here:

> In place of the direction by colleagues through local committees, with their admitted inadequacy, there appears the business-like direction of the trade union officials. The initiative and the power of making decisions thereby devolve upon trade union specialists, so to

speak, and the more passive virtue of discipline upon the mass of members … But here the technical specializing of wage struggles as, for example, the conclusion of intricate tariff agreements and the like frequently means that the mass of organised workers are prohibited from taking a 'survey of the whole industrial life,' and their incapacity for taking decisions is thereby established (Luxemburg, 1964: 73).

Those who usurp the initiative of their underlying populations become convinced of the weakness of the latter and therefore conduct themselves accordingly.[8]

In this respect, one significant difference at present between the new social movements and the traditional trade union movement (the original and still critical organizing centre of the working class) is not the result of a qualitative difference between such movements. Rather, this is a distinction between new and old, between new movements in which people are in motion (and self-changing) and old structures in which generals conduct a war of position. That same distinction (and the perceptible difference in those engaged in the struggles) does not hold, however, in the case of *new* trade union organizing nor in particular cases of 'fight-back' against capitalist rollbacks in existing contracts; nor, is there any reason to assume that the current state of established trade unions is permanent.

In short, the 'revolutionary practice' which produces people able to go beyond capital and 'to found society anew' is not limited to struggles in the labour market and the sphere of capitalist production. Once we recognize that the subjects of this process are human beings and that 'revolutionary practice' is essential for building human capacities, then a central question to pose with respect to all struggles becomes – *does this help in the self-development of the working class?*

III The workers' state

As we will see, this question is especially important for discussions of the state. Struggles over the state are, of course, a dimension of class struggle. As we saw in Chapter 5, within capitalism, there is an inherent logic to the struggle of workers to make the state serve their interests, to 'transform that power, now used against them, into their own agency' (Marx, 1866: 344–5). Insofar as capital's power as owner of the products of labour is the power of capital as a whole, workers need to develop a '*political* movement, that is to say, a movement of the *class*, with the object of enforcing its interests in a general form, in a form possessing general, socially coercive force' (Marx and Engels, 1965: 270–1).

On matters such as restrictions on the length of the workday, the legalization and fostering of trade unions, the orientation to full employment and the provision of use-values to permit the common satisfaction of needs, capital and wage-labour push the state in opposite directions.[9] The fixation of the actual practices of the state – whether it will be a mediator for capital or whether it will be a mediator for wage-labour – thus 'resolves itself into a question of the respective powers of the combatants'. Between two conceptions of right, force decides.

Can a state within capitalism act on behalf of workers? Obviously. That was Marx's point about the Ten Hours' Bill. Indeed, use of the state by workers is *necessary* because 'in its merely economic action capital is the stronger side' (1865b: 146). Yet, within capitalism, restrictions upon capital are just barriers to its growth; they may control the more flagrant abuses, but capital finds ways to go beyond those barriers in order to posit growth again (as it did by intensifying labour when the length of the workday was restricted). Indeed, all other things equal, the balance of forces that permits the state to act on behalf of workers will tend to be undermined by capital's responses to state measures that reduce the rate of surplus value: reduced accumulation, migration of capital and substitution of machinery for direct labour will increase unemployment and the degree of separation among workers.

Nevertheless, all other things are *not* equal if workers have 'conquered political power' and are determined to use that political supremacy to realize their own need for self-development. This is precisely the content of Marx's term, 'dictatorship of the proletariat' – political rule by workers, the workers' state.[10] As they continued to stress in editions of the *Communist Manifesto*, 'the first step in the revolution by the working class is to raise the proletariat to the position of ruling class, to win the battle of democracy' (Marx and Engels, 1848: 504). 'The class struggle', Marx explained to his friend Joseph Weydemeyer, 'necessarily leads to the *dictatorship of the proletariat*' (Marx and Engels, 1983a: 62–5). Engels made the same point in his draft of the *Manifesto*, his 'Principles of Communism': the first thing the proletariat will do is 'inaugurate a *democratic constitution* and, thereby, directly or indirectly, the political rule of the proletariat' (Marx and Engels, 1976b: 350). This workers' state would then proceed to create the conditions for going beyond capital:

> The proletariat will use its political supremacy to wrest, by degrees, all capital from the bourgeoisie, to centralise all instruments of production in the hands of the State, *i.e.*, of the proletariat organized as the

ruling class; and to increase the total of productive forces as rapidly as possible (Marx and Engels, 1848: 504).

The critical premise for the successful execution of such a programme, however, is that workers no longer view themselves as dependent upon capital. Until workers break with the idea that capital is necessary, a state in which workers have political supremacy will act to facilitate conditions for the expanded reproduction of capital (Lebowitz, 1995). The state, accordingly, remains entirely within the bounds of the capitalist relation and is its guarantor so long as workers look upon capital's requirements as 'self-evident natural laws'.[11] Nevertheless, the *Communist Manifesto* did *not* have as its premise the complete break with the feeling of dependence upon capital. It did not, after all, call for the *immediate* seizure of 'all capital from the bourgeoisie'. Rather, it called upon the workers' state to proceed *by degrees*.

It is essential to grasp that the *Manifesto* describes a *process*, one in which the workers' state proceeds to create the foundations for a communist society. It proposes measures, indeed, 'which appear economically insufficient and untenable, but which, in the course of the movement, outstrip themselves, necessitate further inroads upon the old social order' (Marx and Engels, 1848: 504). Thus, while including abolition of property in land, a heavy progressive income tax, abolition of the right of inheritance and banking and transport centralized in the state, the *Communist Manifesto* did not call for the abolition of capitalist industry; all that was said about factories was that state industry and means of production should be expanded.

What Marx and Engels advocated in the *Manifesto*, thus, was not the dissolution of capitalist property but, rather, 'despotic inroads on the rights of property'. Engels' earlier drafts make this quite clear. In his 'Draft of a Communist Confession of Faith', Engels responded to the question *'Do you intend to replace the existing social order by community of property at one stroke?'* by insisting 'We have no such intention. The development of the masses cannot be ordered by decree. It is determined by the development of the conditions in which these masses live, and therefore proceeds gradually' (Marx and Engels, 1976b: 102). Several months later, in his 'Principles of Communism', Engels returned to the subject. To the question, 'Will it be possible to abolish private property at one stroke?' he responded that this would be no more possible than it is to increase productive forces to the necessary level at one stroke. The proletarian revolution 'will transform existing society only gradually' (Marx and Engels, 1976b: 350).

Those 'despotic inroads', however, set in motion a process – one in which the possibility for the reproduction of capitalist property relations is increasingly restricted at the same time as the emergence of state-owned property is fostered.[12] And, the clear sense is that the process will be self-reinforcing. One measure will always lead on to the next, and 'the proletariat will see itself compelled to go always further' (Marx and Engels, 1976b: 351). But *why*? What is that movement in which initial measures 'which appear economically insufficient and untenable ... outstrip themselves, necessitate further inroads upon the old social order'?

Very simply, the continuation of class struggle. One should not assume that capital is indifferent to 'despotic inroads on the rights of property' or that Marx and Engels thought it would be. As Oskar Lange astutely observed (Lange, 1964: 121–9), if capitalists know in advance that the plan of the workers' state is to 'wrest, by degrees, all capital from the bourgeoisie', then their reaction will be predictable – no investment. The result will be crisis. Capital's response to 'despotic inroads' is to go on strike, and when it does, the workers' state has two choices – give in or move in. Thus, Lange (1964: 129) commented that, for an economist called upon to advise a government that wants to do more than administer a capitalist economy, 'there exists only one economic policy which he can commend to a socialist government as likely to lead to success. This is a policy of *revolutionary courage.*'

There can be little doubt that this was the process that Marx and Engels envisioned. The *Manifesto* and its drafts stress the importance of the growth of state industry, which was essential for displacing capital as the mediator for workers. '*What will be your first measure once you have established democracy?*' Engels posed in his 'Confessions' and answered – 'guaranteeing the subsistence of the proletariat'. And, this was an explicit point as well in his 'Principles'. The rapid development of productive forces under state ownership would deprive capital of its greatest weapon – the dependence of wage-labourers upon it for employment and for the ability to satisfy their requirements. By thus breaking the 'silent seal of economic compulsion', the workers' state would be an essential weapon for carrying out the struggle against capital. As Marx commented on the Paris Commune, this working-class government does not do away with class struggle. Rather, 'it affords the rational medium in which that class struggle can run through its different phases in the most rational and humane way.' This, however, did not preclude 'violent reactions and violent revolutions'. Its work would be 'again and again relented and impeded by the resistance of vested interests and class egotisms'. Indeed, once established, it might face violent attempts by capital to reverse the process:

> the catastrophes it might still have to undergo would be sporadic slaveholders' insurrections, which, while for a moment interrupting the work of peaceful progress, would only accelerate the movement, by putting the sword into the hand of the Social Revolution (Marx, 1871a: 156–7).

Thus, the workers' state would be an essential part of the process of revolutionary practice, the process whereby workers change themselves in the course of struggles and 'become fitted to found society anew'. Yet, as Marx and Engels learned from the actions of workers in the Paris Commune, this process required a special kind of state. 'The working class', Marx (1871b: 68) commented, 'cannot simply lay hold of the ready-made state machinery, and wield it for its own purposes.' Although Marx and Engels argued in their 1872 Preface to the *Manifesto* that its 'general principles were, on the whole, as correct today as ever', the Commune had 'proved' something not in the programme – the need for a new kind of state for workers (Marx and Engels, 1971: 270). The Commune was 'the political form at last discovered under which to work out the economical emancipation of Labour' (Marx, 1871b: 75). *At last discovered!*

Do you want to know what the dictatorship of the proletariat looks like, asked Engels on the twentieth anniversary of the Commune? 'Look at the Paris Commune. That was the Dictatorship of the Proletariat' (Marx and Engels, 1971: 34). He made the same point elsewhere that year (1891), when he commented that 'our Party and the working class can only come to power under the form of a democratic republic. This is even the specific form for the dictatorship of the proletariat, as the Great French revolution has already shown' (Engels, 1891). But, Engels' point was not new – Marx clearly grasped at the time that the Commune was the dictatorship of the proletariat: its role was 'to serve as a lever for uprooting the economical foundations upon which rests the existence of classes, and therefore of class-rule' (Marx, 1871b: 75). Although this would involve 'a long process of development of new conditions', Marx noted, workers 'know at the same time that great strides may be [made] at once through the Communal form of political organisation ...' (Marx, 1871a: 157).

Before examining the specific form of the workers' state, we need to understand why it was *necessary* – that is, why Marx was so insistent that the working class could not use 'the ready-made state machinery ... for its own purposes'. The working class, Marx argued, could not use the existing type of state because it was *infected* – its very institutions involve a 'systematic and hierarchic division of labour', and it assumes the character of 'a public force organized for social enslavement, of an engine of class despotism' (Marx, 1871b: 68–9). How could the working class use such a state for its own purposes – a state whose very nature was hierarchy and power over all from above? Where is the possibility for the self-development of the working class through its activities in such a state?

Rather than being controlled *by* workers, that 'ready-made state machinery' would ensure the control *of* workers, retaining the character of a 'public force organised for social enslavement'. That is why Marx stressed that the Commune was a 'Revolution against the *State* itself, of this supernaturalist abortion of society, a resumption by the people for the people of its own social life'. It was 'the reabsorption of the state power by society as its own living forces instead of as forces controlling and subduing it, by the popular masses themselves, forming their own force instead of the organised force of their suppression – the political form of their social emancipation ...' (Marx, 1871a: 152–3).

In short, as Marx concluded, we cannot be indifferent to the *form* of the state as an agency of workers. Only insofar as state functions are 'wrested from an authority usurping pre-eminence over society itself, and restored to the responsible agents of society' can the state be 'the political form ... under which to work out the economical emancipation of Labour' (Marx, 1871b: 72–3). The state, thus, must be converted 'from an organ standing above society into one completely subordinate to it' (Marx, 1875: 30).

What, then, was the particular form of rule at last discovered? Firstly, the Commune was a decentralized government composed of councillors elected by universal suffrage in every ward within towns, representatives who were recallable and bound by the instructions of their constituents. In the proposals for a national organization, an assembly of delegates would administer common affairs in every district, and these assemblies would select deputies to constitute a central government (Marx, 1871b: 72–3). 'All France', Marx commented, 'would have been organized into self-working and self-governing communes' (Marx, 1871a: 155–6). This was the destruction of state power insofar as that state stood above society. The old centralized government would give way to the 'self-government of the producers'; in its place, a communal constitution linking the individual localities (Marx, 1871b: 72–3). And, yes, Marx responded to Bakunin's doubts about the workers' state, all members of society *would* really be members of government 'because the thing starts with self-government of the township' (Marx, 1874–5: 544–5).

The character of the Commune, though, is to be found in more than just its immediate form of governance – its essence is the thorough rejection of hierarchy. In addition to those 'self-working and self-governing communes', this workers' state meant:

> the standing army replaced by the popular militias, the army of state parasites removed, the clerical hierarchy displaced by the school masters, the state judge transformed into Communal organs, the suffrage for national representation not a matter of sleight of hand for an all-powerful government, but the deliberate expression of the organized communes, the state functions reduced to a few functions for general national purposes.
>
> Such is the *Commune – the political form of the social emancipation…* (Marx, 1871a: 155–6).

In place of the mystification of capital, then, there would not be mystification of the state. In the Commune, 'the whole sham of state mysteries and state pretensions was done away [with]'; now, 'public functions became *real workmen's functions*, instead of the hidden attributes of a trained caste' (155):

> [Gone is] the delusion as if administration and political governing were mysteries, transcendent functions only to be trusted to the hands of a trained caste – state parasites, richly paid sycophants and sinecurists, in the higher posts, absorbing the intelligence of the masses and turning them against themselves in the lower places of the hierarchy (154).

In the dictatorship of the proletariat, the state's absorption of the power of the producers was not to be substituted for capital's absorption of that power. Rather, the state would be the workers' own power, 'forming their own force instead of the organised force of their suppression'.

There should be no surprise that Marx grasped that what the workers of Paris had spontaneously discovered was the political form 'under which to work out the economical emancipation of Labour'. Once we begin from human beings as the subjects and understand that people produce themselves through their activity, it follows that only where the state as mediator for (and power over) workers gives way to the 'self-government of the producers' is there a continuous process whereby workers can change both circumstances and themselves. What is the 'self-government' of the commune? 'It is the people acting for itself by itself' (Marx, 1871a: 130). Thus, the form and the content of the workers' state are inseparable. Only insofar as the state is converted 'from an organ standing above society into one completely subordinate to it' can the working class 'succeed in ridding itself of all the muck of ages and become fitted to found society anew'.

The development of the workers' state produces a new side in the social relationship among workers. That relation emerges in the course of struggles against capital, developing initially as workers organize in trade unions. The growing recognition, however, that 'in its merely economic action capital is the stronger side' propels workers into political action. With the creation of the workers' state, that 'self-government of the producers', workers are linked as self-governing citizens in the project of acting in the interests of producers as a whole. The workers' state brings the producers together in their 'self-working and self-governing' assemblies and councils and calls upon them to drive beyond every barrier that capital puts up to their own self-development. This, for Marx, was the context in which 'the class struggle has to be fought out to a conclusion'(Marx, 1875: 33).

11
From Capital to the Collective Worker

> Feuerbach's great achievement is: ... (3) His opposing to the negation of the negation, which claims to be the absolute positive, the self-supporting positive, positively based on itself.
>
> (Marx, 1844c: 328)

I Theoretical struggle

'Capitalist production', Marx (1977: 929) declared, 'begets with the inexorability of a natural process, its own negation'. Unfortunately (in view of the amount of suffering that capitalism produces), this is not true.

Indeed, how could it be possible – given that capitalist production 'develops a working class which by education, tradition and habit looks upon the requirements of that mode of production as self-evident natural laws'? How, when it 'breaks down all resistance', when it can 'rely on his [the worker's] dependence on capital, which springs from the conditions of production themselves, *and is guaranteed in perpetuity by them'* (Marx, 1977: 899; emphasis added)!

As stressed in Chapter 9, it is precisely because of the inherent mystification of capital that Marx's *Capital* was necessary. Where else can you find the theoretical demonstration that capital is the result of the exploitation of workers, that it is their own product turned against them? *Capital* accomplishes what no other criticism of capitalism does – it reveals the essence of capital.

There are many criticisms of capital because of its tendency to usurp the lives of producers by driving the length and intensity of the workday up to a maximum and to driving down living standards to a physiological minimum. Or, because of the instability, crises, destruction of the environment, the obvious inequality that capital tends to produce. Those who stress these characteristics, this injustice, argue the necessity to *check* capital's tendencies by organizing workers in trade unions or by using the state to force capital to do what it would not otherwise do.

But, these are not Marx's criticisms – although, of course, he demonstrates that such tendencies are not accidents but are inherent in the nature of capital. What distinguishes Marx's analysis is that his is a critique not merely of absolute surplus value but of relative surplus value as well, not merely of absolute or relative wages but of wages themselves. Even when workers succeed in pushing in the opposite direction to capital and thereby lowering the workday and raising real wages, Marx's criticism of capitalism is no less powerful. Every atom of surplus value and capital, for Marx, is the result of *theft*. The issue is slavery – not the level of slave rations. In short, reform of capitalism is not the answer. Marx was unequivocal: capitalism must be ended.

Because these particular insights, however, do not flow spontaneously from the process of struggle, the analysis developed in Marx's *Capital* is essential for going-beyond capital. Without it, there is the unchallenged appearance that the worker sells 'a certain quantity of labour'; accordingly, exploitation presents itself as the result of not receiving a fair return in this transaction – not receiving 'a fair day's pay for a fair day's work'. Marx's analysis of capital provides workers with a critical weapon – the reason to negate and abolish capitalism rather than to attempt merely to change it in order to make it fair.

Yet, understanding the nature of capital is not sufficient to lead workers to go beyond it. Required as well is that they grasp that capital as such is not *necessary*. Workers in motion against capital may become subjects capable of altering their world, but if they do not believe the world of capital *can* be transcended in accordance with their needs, their struggles occur in the context of their dependence upon capital. Add to that the failures of social democratic governments (which have demobilized and disarmed workers' movements and surrendered to capital) and 'Actually Existing Socialism' (that model for crash industrialization marked by hierarchy and proclaimed to be socialist by those at the top). Small wonder that the declaration of TINA ('there is no alternative') has resonated so deeply.

Even though there is no inexorable natural process by which capitalist production begets its own negation, nevertheless there is the *possibility* of negating capitalism. That is why, as Engels (1956: 34) and Lenin (1967: 163) stressed, *'placing the theoretical struggle on a par'* with political and

really ?

economic struggles is essential.[1] In emphasizing the importance of this point, we simply acknowledge the integral link between theory and practice that Marx understood as a condition for the transcendence of capital (and to which he dedicated his life and his work):

> As philosophy finds its *material* weapons in the proletariat, so the proletariat finds its *spiritual* weapons in philosophy ... Philosophy cannot be made a reality without the abolition of the proletariat, the proletariat cannot be abolished without philosophy being made a reality (Marx, 1844a: 187).

Precisely because of the importance of theory to practice, the further development of Marx's political economy of the working class is particularly critical. I have argued here that the absence of *Wage-Labour* left Marx's 'disciples' with a one-sided theory, one that is not adequate to understand capitalism as a whole. The inherent one-sidedness of tendencies and concepts presented in *Capital*, problems flowing from Marx's assumption about the standard of necessity, the significance of the degree of separation among workers as well as the focus on the other sides of wage-labourers and the centrality of the worker as a subject who develops through her struggles – these questions (among many others discussed in the book) would remain undeveloped if we accepted *Capital* as adequate.[2] Couldn't it be said, though, that these are just minor elaborations of *Capital*? How pressing is the need to go beyond *Capital*?

In the absence of a specific exploration of the side of wage-labour, the very concept of the political economy of the working class would remain just an interesting (and aberrant) phrase. This silence, however, takes its toll. Not only does it limit the ability of Marxism to demonstrate to workers that it is *their* products and *their* power that are turned against them, but it also restricts the possibility of revealing that *there is an alternative* to capitalism – one intimately linked to the political economy of the working class.

II The collective worker

Marx envisioned a clear alternative – a society of associated producers, one in which social wealth, rather than accruing to the purchasers of labour-power, is employed by freely associated individuals who produce in accordance with 'communal purposes and communal needs' (Marx, 1973: 158–9, 171–2). Consider the two propositions introduced in

Chapter 5 as part of the political economy of the working class as well as a third from Marx's Inaugural Address for the International:

1. Any cooperation and combination of labour in production generates a combined, social productivity of labour that exceeds the sum of individual, isolated productivities.
2. In any society, separation and division in social relations among producers allow those who *mediate* among the producers to capture the fruits of cooperation in production.
3. 'Social production controlled by social foresight... forms the political economy of the working class' (Marx, 1864: 11).

When we talk here about producers working together within a particular workplace or producing differing use-values corresponding to social requirements (the division of labour within society), we are describing the collective worker within society.[3] This collective or aggregate worker is composed of many different limbs and organs: 'some work better with their hands, others with their heads, one as a manager, engineer, technologist, etc., the other as overseer, the third as manager or even drudge' (Marx, 1977: 1040). The collective worker is not, however, simply the sum of these parts – it is the articulation of them into a productive organism. The cooperation of these parts of the productive organism results in 'the creation of a new productive power, which is intrinsically a collective one' (Marx, 1977: 443).

As we have seen, in capitalism, this 'association of the workers – the cooperation and division of labour as fundamental conditions of the productivity of labour – appears as the *productive power of capital*. The collective power of labour, its character as social labour, is therefore the *collective power* of capital' (Marx, 1973: 585). Within capitalism, capital as such articulates various parts of the collective worker (although never all of it) and mediates among those parts. Accordingly, capital is able to capture the benefits arising from cooperation in the form of surplus value; and it does so, as we've seen, as the result (and to the extent) of its ability to divide and separate workers.

Within capitalism, the association of the producers who comprise the collective worker is wholly external, mediated by their particular connections to capital. 'The worker actually treats the social character of his work, its combination with the work of others for a common goal, as a power that is alien to him; the conditions in which this combination is realized are for him the property of another' (Marx, 1981b: 178). In contrast, with the removal of capital as the mediator and the development of the collective worker *for itself*, that producer composed of differing limbs and organs expends its 'many different forms of labour-power in full self-awareness as one single social labour force' (Marx, 1977: 171).

What kind of society is implied by the political economy of the working class? In contrast to the political economy of capital, the political economy of the working class encompasses more than just the labour mediated by capital – just as the workday for workers is longer than the capitalist workday. This political economy includes the labour where the mediator among workers is the state (which provides 'that which is needed for the common satisfaction of needs, such as schools, health services, etc'), and it includes the labour 'absolutely necessary in order to consume things' – that is, that labour unproductive for capital that Marx included under the costs of consumption. All this is part of the collective worker – even if the particular cooperation is not mediated by capital. From the perspective of the political economy of the working class, the divisions within the collective worker that strengthen capital can be seen as artificial constructs of a society in which capital rules (and of its corresponding political economy). Recognition of the interdependence of all limbs of the collective worker (as well as the interdependence of the wealth of human beings and Nature) is at the core of the political economy of the working class.

In this political economy, all products and activities are acknowledged as mere moments in a process of producing human beings; this is what the productive organism comprised of the collective worker yields as its real result:

> When we consider bourgeois society in the long view and as a whole, then the final result of the process of social production always appears as the society itself, i.e., the human being itself in its social relations. Everything that has a fixed form, such as the product, etc appears as merely a moment, a vanishing moment, in this movement (Marx, 1973: 712).

For combating mystification within capitalism, these theoretical insights – recognition of the necessary interdependence of producers and the understanding that human beings in their social relations are the premise and result of all activity – are critical. *In the society of the collective worker for itself, however, that which is apparent to the analyst becomes 'self-evident natural law' for all members of the society.*

Human beings in their social relations are the explicit goal of production in this society of free and associated producers. Understood as a connected whole, the various limbs and organs of the collective worker combine 'in full self-awareness' to produce that collective worker. Accordingly, in this 'association, in which the free development of each is the condition for the free development of all', the human community is presupposed as the basis of production (Marx and Engels, 1976b: 506). Characteristic of the social relation among the producers in this structure is that they recognize their unity as members of the human family and act upon this basis to ensure the well-being of others within this family. Solidarity, in short, is at the very core of the social relation. In the cooperative society based upon common ownership of the means of production that Marx envisioned, the productive activity of people flows from a unity and solidarity based upon recognition of their differences.

The critique of the political economy of capital is completed only by the realization of the political economy of the working class – a communist society. As long as producers are not their own mediator, the mystification of everyday life and the alienation of human beings from their own powers continue:

> The veil is not removed from the countenance of the social life-process, i.e. the process of material production, until it becomes production by freely associated men, and stands under their conscious and planned control (Marx, 1977: 173).

In this society of associated producers, the cooperation of the collective worker and the absence of an alien mediator demonstrate that 'to bear fruit, the means of labour need not be monopolised as a means of dominion over, and of extortion against, the labouring man himself' (Marx, 1864: 11).[4] Rather, the worker now 'treats the social character of his work, its combination with the work of others for a common goal', as *his* power. This is the creation of *a social form that corresponds to social production* – social production subordinated to the association of free and equal producers. 'Social production controlled by social foresight ... forms the political economy of the working class.'

III The worker's own need for development

But what was the point? Why was the realization of such a society important? There always was a vision that moved Marx and Engels – the idea of a society that would permit the full development of human potential. 'What is the aim of the Communists?' asked Engels in his early version of the *Communist Manifesto*, and he answered, 'To organise society in such a way that every member of it can develop and use all his capabilities and powers in complete freedom and without thereby infringing the basic conditions of this society' (Marx and Engels, 1976b: 96).[5] In the final version of the Manifesto (written by Marx), this goal was represented as the 'association, in which the free development of each is the condition for the free development of all'.

To remove all fetters to the full development of human beings was at the heart of Marx's conception of the society of free and associated producers. As we saw in Chapter 7, this was the essence of Marx's concept of human wealth. Given his hope for that 'development of the rich individuality which is as all-sided in its production as in its consumption' (Marx, 1973: 325), Marx had to reject capitalism. As he pointed out in *Capital* (1977: 772), in that system the worker exists to satisfy the capitalist's need to increase the value of his capital 'as opposed to the inverse situation in which objective wealth is there to satisfy the worker's own need for development'.

The society of associated producers is that 'inverse situation'. This is 'a society of free individuality, based on the universal development of individuals and on their subordination of their communal, social productivity as their social wealth' (Marx, 1973: 158). Here, rather than enhance the power dominating workers, their productivity ensures both the satisfaction of existing needs and also the creation of new capacities by releasing workers from the realm of necessity. Social productivity here means free time – which 'corresponds to the artistic, scientific, etc development of the individuals in the time set free, and with the means created, for all of them' (Marx, 1977: 667; 1973: 706).

In short, unlike earlier periods when 'the development of human abilities and social potentialities (art, etc., science)' had as its premise the surplus labour of the masses, when 'free time on one side corresponds to subjugated time on the other side', this would be free time for *all*. No longer would 'the development of the human capacities on the one side [be] based on the restriction of development on the other side' (Marx and Engels, 1988b: 190–2). Now, for all, there would be 'time for the full development of the individual, which in turn reacts back on the productive power of labour itself as itself the greatest productive power' (Marx, 1973: 711). We now would see that 'development of the rich individuality which is as all-sided in its production as in its consumption': 'Free time – which is both idle time and time for higher activity – has naturally transformed its possessor into a different subject, and he enters into the direct production process as this different subject' (Marx, 1973: 325, 712).

Accordingly, the products of this society of freely associated producers would be human beings able to develop their full potential in a human society: the productive forces would have 'increased with the all-round development of the individual, and all the springs of co-operative wealth flow more abundantly' (Marx, 1875: 24). This link between the collective worker for itself and the flowering of human potential is set out clearly by Lucien Sève:

> The deepest essence of communism consists *in that it realises and even necessitates 'the full and free development of every individual'*, i.e. it frees the expanded reproduction of personalities themselves, at the same time as the expanded reproduction of the productive forces and culture, from every *antagonistic* social contradiction (Sève, 1978: 330).[6]

A beautiful picture. But, not one that drops from the sky; rather, it flows from all the struggles of workers within capitalism, those struggles driven by their own need for development:

> the present 'spontaneous action of the natural laws of capital and landed property' can only be superseded by 'the spontaneous action of the laws of the social economy of free and associated labour' in a long process of development of new conditions, as was the 'spontaneous action of the economic laws of slavery' and the 'spontaneous action of the economic laws of serfdom' (Marx, 1871a: 157).

Workers, we have seen, are constantly driven by their needs – not needs that are innate but needs that are generated within the particular structure of capitalist relations of production. As indicated in Chapter 3, Marx was consistent in stressing the alienating nature of capitalist production and the resulting growth of workers' needs. Central to the situation of the worker in capitalist production is that he impoverishes himself in production 'because the creative power of his labour establishes itself as the power of capital, as an *alien power* confronting him' (Marx, 1973: 307). His need and dependence grow – that source of the contemporary power of capital. Thus, workers are engaged in constant struggle against capital – struggles to reabsorb those alien and independent products of their activity, struggles to find time and energy for themselves, struggles propelled by their own need for development.

The workers' 'ought', the drive of workers for expanded reproduction, constantly comes up against barriers created by capital, barriers erected to support the continuation of exploitation. Workers struggle to get beyond these barriers and, in the process, transform both circumstances and themselves. We find in Marx, then, this essential story of the struggle of workers and their creativity in finding means for their self-development (as when the necessary form of the workers' state was 'at last discovered' by workers).

But, this is not the same story with which we began this book. In Chapter 1, it is *capital* that has the impulse to grow and that constantly comes up against barriers to that growth; capital succeeds in going beyond those barriers but always comes up against new barriers – until ultimately it faces a Limit in the form of the working class. That story, we concluded, is one-sided; among other things, it explains neither why workers struggle to go beyond capital nor, significantly, why they *accept* capital. Capitalism as a whole, we proposed, incorporates *two* 'oughts' – the worker's own need for development as well as capital's impulse to grow.

Is it sufficient, though, to present these two stories as opposites and to see the two sides in struggle, one in which each attempts to reduce the other to a mere barrier?

IV Beyond the negation of the negation

For some people, the Young Marx was a romantic, a pre-Marxist, whereas *Capital* represents science, the highest development of Marx's thought. For others, *Capital* means the unfortunate displacement of the Young Marx's focus on human beings by the logic of capital and objective laws. The absence of Marx's intended book on wage-labour has made it easy to set up such a divide between young and mature Marx (although study of the *Grundrisse* really should be sufficient to dispel this notion). The fact that the seemingly self-contained theory of *Capital* permits such a conception of 'two Marx's' is one particular reason why this book was written (*and why the critical arguments are drawn from the mature Marx*). Understanding the necessary contents of *Wage-Labour* demonstrates the inappropriateness of that division between the Young Marx and the mature Marx; it reveals that there is no gap between the humanist/class struggle theorist and the scientist. To go beyond *Capital* is to acknowledge the 'two Marx's' as one.

Marx's continuity is especially clear with respect to his understanding of what, within the structure that is capitalism, drives beyond capitalism. In their early collaboration, *The Holy Family*, Marx and Engels declared:

> Proletariat and wealth are opposites; as such they form a single whole. They are both creations of the world of private property.

The question is exactly what place each occupies in the antithesis. It is not sufficient to declare them two sides of a single whole.

Recognizing the two sides as part of a single whole, sides that presuppose each other, reciprocally foster and develop each other as two sides of the same relation is critical. So too, however, is grasping *which side represents the reproduction of the system and which represents non-reproduction*. The worker, Marx and Engels argued, is 'the *negative* side of the antithesis, its restlessness within its very self'. In contrast to the 'propertied class', which is at ease and strengthened within this relation, the worker sees in it his 'own powerlessness and the reality of an inhuman existence'. Accordingly, within this relation, the propertied class is the conservative side of the antithesis and 'the proletarian the *destructive* side. From the former arises the action of preserving the antithesis, from the latter the action of annihilating it' (Marx and Engels, 1845: 35–6).

All of Marx's subsequent analysis of the side of capital did not change his understanding of the place each side occupies in the antithesis. Capital, we see, tends to reproduce its necessary premises in their capitalist economic form. In particular, capital acts to produce a working class that looks upon capital's requirements as common sense (Marx, 1977: 899). It tends, in short, to reproduce capitalism as an organic system (Marx, 1973: 278). In contrast, workers transform themselves through their struggles into *other than capital's products* and thus into the historic presuppositions of a new state of society.[7] They do so not because of an abstract class mission assigned to the proletariat (recall Gorz's charge from Chapter 2) but, rather, because of their inherent situation within capitalism.

In the draft for *Capital* known as 'Results of the Immediate Process of Production', Marx argued that capitalist production yields 'the rule of things over man, of dead labour over the living, of the product over the producer'. Thus, at the level of 'the life process in the realm of the social – for that is what the process of production is – we find the *same* situation that we find in *religion* at the ideological level, namely the inversion of subject into object and *vice versa*' (Marx, 1977: 990). As the result of this '*alienation* [*Entfremdung*] of man from his own labour', the worker here again represents the negative side of the relation:

> To that extent the worker stands on a higher plane than the capitalist from the outset, since the latter has his roots in the process of alienation and finds absolute satisfaction in it whereas right from the start the worker is a victim who confronts it as a rebel and experiences it as a process of enslavement (Marx, 1977: 990).

Given the worker's own need for development, inherent in the situation of wage-labour is dissatisfaction with self, the inability to satisfy the needs generated within capitalism. As rebel, as restlessness, the worker struggles against capital and in the process transforms herself. At its core, the thrust of the worker to go beyond capital results from the 'indignation to which it is necessarily driven by the contradiction between its human *nature* and its condition of life' (Marx and Engels, 1845: 36).

Ultimately, then, both for the Young Marx and the mature Marx (the 'scientist'), it is because workers are not *merely* wage-labourers but are human beings that there is a tendency to drive beyond wage-labour. Underlying the struggle against capital is that the worker 'strives not to remain something he has become, but is in the absolute movement of his becoming' (Marx, 1973: 488). *In the end, we understand the contradiction of capital and wage-labour as that of wage-labour and the human being.*

Accordingly, it is not sufficient to identify the contradiction that drives beyond capital as the opposition between capital and wage-labour. While that formulation is a real advance over an implicit conception of capital's self-destruction as the result of its own successes, it (like Hegel's 'bad infinity') is inadequate because wage-labour as such does not transcend capital but is bounded inherently by capital (Hegel, 1961: I, 150–63).[8] Thus, we proceed to the concept of the human being (depicted in Figure 11.1), which contains within it the human being as wage-labourer and the human being as non-wage-labourer, both the inhuman existence as well as the ought that goes beyond.

In this opposition, we understand that what underlies the struggle against capital and drives beyond capital is the contradiction between the worker's self and her conditions of life. (The opposition of capital and wage-labour remains – because insofar as wage-labour is only wage-labour,

WAGE-LABOUR | HUMAN BEING

Figure 11.1 The worker in capitalism

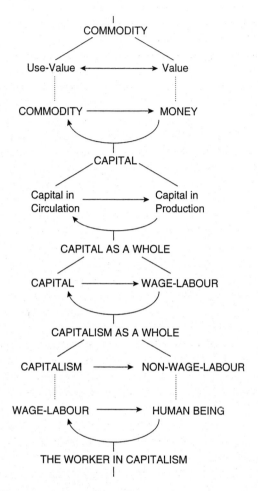

Figure 11.2   The contradiction of capitalism

it is identical with capital.) Thus, as can be seen in Figure 11.2, the
exploration that began with the commodity concludes with the contradiction *within the human being* that is already latent within the
commodity as use-value and value.

Our study of the side of capitalism which was not developed in *Capital*
thus brings us back to Marx's starting point – socially developed human
beings and their struggle against relations which do not correspond
to their requirements. Rather than the determinism and economism
that flow from one-sided Marxism, the Marx who emerges here is

a revolutionary whose optimism was based on the assumption that human beings *will* struggle against inhuman conditions. That struggle against an inhuman existence is what for Marx drove beyond capital.

Should we not, then, take as the real beginning the collective worker – that aggregate worker (some of whom 'work better with their hands, others with their heads, one as a manager, engineer, technologist, etc.') whose cooperation and combination of labour is the fundamental condition of social productivity? In a society organized to allow for the full development of human potential, that collective worker would produce for communal needs and purposes, driven by the worker's need for self-development.

From the vantage point of the concept of the collective worker, we can see that capitalism inverts everything. The 'actual process' whereby the collective worker uses means of production to produce things of use for human beings 'looks quite different in the valorization process. Here it is not the worker who makes use of means of production, but the means of production that make use of the worker' (Marx, 1977: 988). Subjects become objects, means become ends in 'this inversion, indeed this distortion, which is peculiar to and characteristic of capitalist production, of the relation between dead labour and living labour, between value and the force that creates value' (Marx, 1977: 425).[9]

Starting from the concept of the collective worker and of the society of the collective worker for itself, what emerges as logical discovery in *Capital* now can be seen as *self-evident*: the power of capital is, in fact, the power of the collective worker. The transparency of this point demonstrates that underlying *Capital* all along is the implicit perspective of a 'counterfactual' alternative – the 'society of free individuality, based on the universal development of individuals and on their subordination of their communal, social productivity as their social wealth' (Marx, 1973: 158). Where, after all, does that concept of 'the inverse situation in which objective wealth is there to satisfy the worker's own need for development' *come from*? It doesn't come from anything in *Capital*. Rather, it is *Capital*'s premise![10]

The 'silence' that E.P. Thompson identified in *Capital* is indeed in *Capital*. But, it is not limited to the 'missing term' of human experience.[11] Marx's vision of an alternative to capitalism is also missing – even though the society that the collective worker will construct for itself was his premise, his 'self-supporting positive, positively based on itself' (Marx, 1844c: 328).[12] There was a reason for this.

When Marx wrote *Capital*, he wrote at a time when utopian visions were commonplace. Given his belief that workers would develop the elements of the new society in the course of their struggles, Marx was reluctant to write recipes for future cooks (Marx, 1977: 99). Yet, after the experience of the last century with 'Actually Existing Socialism', it is essential to resurrect the vision of a new society, the society of associated producers. But, not for the cooks of the future. Today's cooks need that vision because the recognition that their social productivity can be their own social wealth rather than 'the wealth of an alien subject indifferently and independently standing over against labour capacity' is critical for going beyond capitalism:

> The recognition [*Erkennung*] of the products as its own, and the judgement that its separation from the conditions of its realization is improper – forcibly imposed – is an enormous [advance in] awareness [*Bewusstsein*], itself the product of the mode of production resting on capital, and as much the knell to its doom as, with the slave's awareness that he *cannot be the property of another*, with his consciousness of himself as a person, the existence of slavery becomes a merely artificial, vegetative existence, and ceases to be able to prevail as the basis of production (Marx, 1973: 462–3).

Today, we understand so much more clearly that capitalism does *not* beget 'with the inexorability of a natural process, its own negation' (Marx, 1977: 929). The elements that concerned Marx are there even more strongly than before – in particular, the overwhelming mystification of the nature of capital and the separation and competition of workers internationally. If there is no inevitability, however, there is always possibility – inherent in capital is that it regularly produces a terrain in which the struggle against capital can be pursued.

The continuation of Marx's project means much more than writing the missing books. Marx's project was to do whatever he could to help to bring about that 'inverse situation' – that 'association, in which the free development of each is the condition for the free development of all'. As can be seen in his work, there are many sides to that project. Revealing capital as the workers' own product turned against them, working for unity in struggle, stressing the centrality of revolutionary practice for the self-development of the collective worker and setting out the vision of a feasible alternative – all these now are essential ingredients to the demonstration that A Better World is Possible. Build it Now.

Notes

1 Why Marx? A Story of Capital

1. If workers are separated from the means of production, there are two ways of recombining them: (1) workers sell their ability to perform labour to the owners of means of production or (2) workers rent means of production from their owners. Marx considered the latter case to be *pre-capitalist*. Money-lending capital, although exploitative, 'in which capital does not seize possession of production, hence is capital only formally, presupposes the predominance of pre-bourgeois forms of production'. Marx similarly observed that 'capital arises only where trade has seized possession of production itself, and where the merchant becomes producer, or the producer mere merchant' (Marx, 1973: 853, 859).

2. Marx's analysis of value is an important part of his work but is peripheral to our concerns here.

3. Since the workday (d) is measured in hours of labour of a given intensity, an increase in intensity (or speed-up) represents an increase in labour performed rather than an increase in productivity (which is measured as output per hour of labour of a given intensity).

4. There is a third way in which capital can increase the rate of exploitation – by driving down the worker's standard of living (U), thereby lowering necessary labour (w); however, *Capital* sets aside this option, treating this standard as given: 'in a given country at a given period, the average amount of the means of subsistence necessary for the worker is a known *datum*' (275). As we will see in Chapter 6, however, this assumption introduces unanticipated problems in Marx's account.

5. Recall that this decline in necessary labour does not represent a fall in absolute standards of consumption but simply reflects reduced labour requirements to produce the fixed bundle as the result of productivity increase.

6. 'Contradiction is the root of all movement and life, and it is only insofar as it contains a Contradiction that anything moves and has impulse and activity' (Hegel, 1961, II: 67).

7. This distinction between Barrier and Limit in Marx is introduced in Lebowitz (1976b).

8. Although Hegel's philosophical writings were a very strong influence upon Marx in his youth (and some would say, throughout his life), at the very time of working on his 1857–8 manuscripts which are known as the *Grundrisse* (Marx, 1973), Marx re-read Hegel's *Science of Logic* (Marx and Engels, 1965: 100).

9. 'Its perishing is not merely contingent, so that it could be without perishing. It is rather the very being of finite things, that they contain the seeds of perishing as their own Being-in-Self and the hour of their birth is the hour of their death' (Hegel, 1961, I: 142).

10. Some stories about 'the falling rate of profit' seem to suggest this but offer little reason to see this as a limit rather than a barrier. Cf. Lebowitz (1976b, 1982b).

2   Why Beyond *Capital*?

1. That these 'anomalies' are identified as separate is itself interesting.
2. Marx to Engels, 24 August 1867 in Marx and Engels, 1987b: 407–8.
3. See a similar rejection of labour-power as a commodity in Bowles and Gintis, 1981.
4. As long as Marxists function primarily as 'disciples', however, only the old map (Marx's original) will do. From the perspective of the disciple, those who want to go 'beyond *Capital*' have left Marx's continent to explore elsewhere (and will probably fall off the edge of the earth).

3   The Missing Book on Wage-Labour

1. Marx to Engels, 31 July 1865 (Marx and Engels, 1987b: 173).
2. The alternatives are those posed by Henryk Grossmann, as cited by Maximilien Rubel in O'Malley and Algozin (1981).
3. Marx to Lasalle, 22 February 1858; Marx to Engels, 2 April 1858. See also Marx to Joseph Weydemeyer, 1 February 1859 (Marx and Engels, 1983b: 268–71, 296–304, 374–8).
4. A useful guide to the development of Marx's conception of his work may be found in Oakley (1983).
5. That little was said about the remaining three books (other than to note that their connection was self-evident) may reflect Marx's view (expressed to Lasalle) that 'the actual nub of the economic argument' was to be found in the first three and that only broad outlines would be required for the last three. Marx to Lasalle, 11 March 1858 (Marx and Engels, 1983b: 287).
6. See, for example, O'Malley and Algozin (1981: 151–2), Oakley (1983: 107–8, 130), Marx and Engels (1986: xvi), Meek (1973: viii–x), Mandel (1977: 29).
7. Marx to Engels, 2 August 1862 in Marx and Engels (1965: 128–9). Note, however, Marx's comment (1981b: 752) that he was only concerned in *Capital* with landed property insofar as landowners received a portion of surplus value and that 'the analysis of landed property in its various historical forms lies outside the scope of the present work'.
8. Marx (1844c: 242) also cited Schulz's statement that 'In France it has been calculated that at the present stage in the development of production an average working period of five hours a day by every person capable of work could suffice for the satisfaction of all the material interests of society.'
9. The comment certainly was not entirely fair with respect to Smith and Ricardo, the leading figures in classical political economy; both recognized the role of habit and custom – rather than just physiological requirements – in determining subsistence levels. Smith (1937: 822) included among necessaries 'those things which the established rules of decency have rendered necessary'; and Ricardo (1969: 52–3) viewed the subsistence wage as incorporating 'those comforts which custom renders absolute necessaries'.
10. Note Hegel's comment (1975: 269): 'the need for greater comfort does not exactly arise within you directly; it is suggested to you by those who hope to make a profit from its creation'.

11. In his simple reproduction model, Marx assumes that capitalists spend three-fifths of their income on necessities and the remainder on luxuries (Marx, 1981a: 479–80).

12. This relationship may be expressed by considering capitalist consumption either as a constant function of surplus value or as a constant function of capital. The latter seems more appropriate, since in this case capitalist consumption is presupposed to surplus value in any particular year and thus is anticipatory in nature.

13. Note that Hegel (1975: 128) had emphasized the importance of 'the demand for equality of satisfaction with others. The need for this equality and for emulation, which is the equalizing of oneself with others, as well as the other need also present here, the need of the particular to asset itself in some distinctive way, become themselves a fruitful source of the multiplication of needs and their expansion.'

14. Heller's problem is that she reduces the capitalist structure of need to the need of workers to 'possess' and thus ignores the place of the needs of capital in that structure. The result is to obscure the specific characteristics of capitalism (Heller, 1976; Lebowitz, 1979: 353).

15. Marx also discussed the increase in the consumption of necessary means of subsistence as the result of price declines of a long duration (Marx, 1981b: 796).

16. One may note with respect to this figure that to use the 'origin' (O) or a physiological minimum as the reference point (to which curves are convex) – rather than the bliss point (Y) – corresponds simply to a view which considers the wage from the perspective of the cost of an input rather than in relation to the social needs to be satisfied. In short, necessary needs are considered from the side of the buyer of labour-power and not the seller.

17. The reference to the fixed value of labour-power, as is clear in the context of the succeeding discussion, is to 'a sum of definite use-values' rather than to their value.

18. Unfortunately, these manuscripts were not available to me at the time of writing the first edition of this book; it is very reassuring, however, to see the confirmation of the argument that I first articulated in Lebowitz (1977–8).

4   The One-Sidedness of *Capital*

1. 'When I have cast off the burden of political economy, I shall write a "Dialectic". The true laws of dialectics are already contained in Hegel, though in a mystical form. What is needed is to strip away this form' Marx to Joseph Dietzgen, 9 May 1868 in Marx and Engels (1988: 31).

2. My appreciation of Hegel and of Lenin's *Philosophical Notebooks* (Lenin, 1961) was initially stimulated by reading Raya Dunayevskaya. See, for example, Dunayevskaya (1964).

3. Here we pose a question of epistemology in contrast to the ontological question about the state of the world. For Marx, these were separate questions. 'Marx consistently and sharply separated two complexes: social being, which exists independent of whether it is more or less correctly understood, and the method most suitable to comprehend it in thought' (Lukács, 1978: 26).

4. Henri Lefebvre (1968: 31) defined the 'dialectical moment' as 'that expedient of the mind which finds itself obliged to move from a position it had hoped was definitive and to take account of something further...'. Similarly, in his account of the 'systematic dialectic' of Hegel and Marx, Chris Arthur (1998: 450) comments that 'the basis of the advance is generally that each category is *deficient* in determinacy with respect to the next and the impulse for the transition is precisely the requirement that such deficiency must be overcome'.

5. 'The presentation ends when all the conditions of existence needing to be addressed are comprehended by the entire system of categories developed' (Arthur, 1998: 451).

6. When we grasp the place played by dialectical derivation in *Capital*, it is easy to understand why Marxism is not advanced by grafting on to it alien elements. For Marx, no elements in an argument can drop from the sky.

7. While working through his development of the concept of capital in his 1857–8 notebooks, Marx asks at a particular point: 'Should not demand and supply, in so far as they are abstract categories and do not yet express any particular relations, perhaps be examined already together with simple circulation or production?' Given that the subject is not pursued, presumably the answer was negative (Marx, 1973: 407n).

8. Lukács described this as Marx's 'methodologically decisive criticism of Hegel' for whom the 'the succession of historical epochs and the patterns within them ... correspond by methodological necessity to the derivation of logical categories' (Lukács, 1978: 108–9). In contrast to Marx's break with Hegel, for Engels (who did not have access to Marx's clear argument in the *Grundrisse*), the logical method 'is nothing else but the historical method, only divested of its historical form and disturbing fortuities. The chain of thought must begin with the same thing with which this history begins'. Thus, it follows that beginning *Capital* with the commodity is appropriate not because of its logical priority but, rather, because 'we proceed from the first and simplest relation that historically and in fact confronts us' (Engels, 1859: I, 373–4). Lukács (1978: 110) described this as 'Engels' retreat to Hegel'.

9. Note that, rather than considering household labour, the focus here is on the self-production of the wage-labourer. The question of household labour (properly situated once we have considered the production of wage-labour as such) is introduced in Chapter 7.

10. Marx intended to develop the subject of the relation of the worker to her labour capacity as property in Wage-Labour (Marx, 1973: 465).

11. This same point is made by Negri (1991: 132).

5   The Political Economy of Wage-Labour

1. As Marx (Marx and Engels, 1983b: 270) had indicated to Lassalle while working on the *Grundrisse*, 'the thing is proceeding very slowly because no sooner does one set about finally disposing of subjects to which one has devoted years of study than they start revealing new aspects and demand to be thought out further'.

2. In his *1861–63 Economic Manuscript*, Marx (1988: 277) cites Potter's objection to the concept of the division of labour 'since the fundamental idea is that of

concert and *cooperation*, not of *division* ... It is thus a *combination of labourers* effected through a *subdivision of processes.*' See Beamish (1992) for an excellent study of the development of Marx's thought on the division of labour.

3. See the two articles from 1851 on 'co-operation' by Ernest Jones, included in Marx and Engels (1979a), which the editors of the collection propose were co-authored by Marx (xxv, 687). Whether this suggestion is accurate is unclear, given Marx's own comments in his letter to Engels on 5 May 1851 about Jones' 'truly splendid lecture' on the co-operative movement (Marx and Engels, 1982: 346); however, it is certain that Marx did re-read the 1851 articles in 1864 and that the position in those articles is the same as that held by Marx in 1864 (Marx and Engels, 1979a: 686).

4. Engels' (1891) comment in his critique of the Erfurt Programme was: 'The organisation of the workers, their constantly increasing resistance, will most probably act as a certain barrier against the increase of poverty.'

5. See, for example, the discussion in Gordon, Edwards and Reich (1982).

6. But, what about the effect of machines on productivity and thus the value of the worker's consumption bundle? See a further discussion in the next chapter.

7. Marx to F. Bolte, 23 November 1871, in Marx and Engels (1965: 270–1).

6 Wages

1. Since our purpose here is to explore Marx's theory of wages, we focus (as did Marx) on what may be called a 'competitive regime' in which prices for commodities are flexible – where increases in productivity bring with them declines in value and price, and where prices of commodities tend to oscillate around values. Although nothing in essence changes in a 'monopolistic regime' where money-prices do not fall with productivity increases, the mechanisms of adjustment differ.

2. For the remainder of the chapter, we explicitly assume the workday constant.

3. Characteristically, Kenneth Lapides (2002: 261, 261n) cites the phrase used here, 'subjection to the premises of political economy' and another, 'subservience to capital's concept' (used in Chapter 7 in relation to the concept of wealth) from the first edition of this book as evidence that I question Marx's view of the 'historical necessity' of trade unions. Although it may be difficult sometimes for journal editors to recognize the distortions involved in taking quotations out of context (this example being only one of many), it should be obvious from the last chapter that Lapides' assertion is absurd.

4. Marx (1977: 790–2) also criticized the economists for confusing the 'local oscillations of the labour-market' for particular capitals with those appropriate to the working class as a whole and the 'total social capital'.

5. For a further discussion of the value of labour-power, see Chapter 7, section IIA.

6. Were the workday not assumed to be given and fixed, the level of output could not be said to be given with constant productivity.

7. Of course, the capitalist (like the worker) would receive more use-values – but no more value.

8. Rising real wages are an obvious result in a 'competitive regime' where money-wages are constant in the face of falling money-prices. Yet, they also hold in a 'monopolistic regime' in which productivity increases do not generate falling

prices: if we assume the balance of forces in the labour market is given and fixed, then the ratio of surplus and necessary labour would be constant and real wages would rise in accordance with productivity through the success of workers in securing increases in money-wages.

9. Define X as the degree of separation among workers. Given the argument that the rate of exploitation (s/w) is determined by the balance of class forces, let us propose that the higher the degree of separation, the lower the level of necessary labour:

$$w = \beta/X \tag{6.1},$$

where β is a constant. Then, with equation (1.1), we can represent the real wage (U) with reference to productivity and the degree of separation:

$$U/q = \beta/X.$$
$$U = \beta q/X \tag{6.2}.$$

Accordingly, when productivity is given, real wages are determined only by the respective power of the combatants, and they rise with productivity increases if the degree of separation is constant. Relative surplus value emerges if (and *only* if) a growth in X accompanies increased productivity.

10. Although Marx's statement about rising real wages lagging behind productivity gains is consistent with the proposition that relative surplus value accompanies rising productivity insofar as the machinery that permits the latter also displaces workers, his argument here appears to be tainted by its roots in *Capital*'s assumption that productivity increases *in themselves* lower necessary labour: 'the increasing productivity of labour is accompanied by a cheapening of the worker, as we have seen' (Marx, 1977: 753).

11. Having considered this general proposition, the implications for differing workers will be explored in Chapter 8.

12. In particular, all the learned commentaries on the flaws in Marx's logical transformation from the realm of values to the realm of prices *insofar as they reduce the value of labour-power to the value of a fixed set of necessaries* can be seen to have no foundation.

13. From equation (6.2), we can see that the necessary condition for Marx's assumption is that X increases at the same rate as productivity.

7   One-Sided Marxism

1. Harry Cleaver (1986) identifies the problem perfectly when he criticizes the perspective in which the 'driving force ... is competition among capitalists. Within this framework, workers appear as outside factors capable of resisting the logic of capital, and even, in principle, of overthrowing it, but their struggles are reactive and only have the effect of throwing up barriers to capital's self-propelled development.'

2. For an extended discussion of centralization that also fails to situate the subject adequately within the context of the opposition of capital and wage-labour, see Lebowitz (1985b).

3. With comments such as this, Marx demonstrates that he was clearly aware of both the side of workers struggling for themselves and the response of

capital. In the absence of the development of a systematic logic for the side of workers that *grounds* such scattered observations, however, passages like this hang in mid-air in *Capital*; further, other elements which belong to that same logical structure appear either isolated and indifferent or remain hidden.

4. This question is explored further in Chapter 8.
5. There is a sense in which expanded reproduction can be viewed as involving other than a struggle between capitalist and worker – where the capitalist relation expands relative to other productive relations. In this case, it is appropriate to view the expanded reproduction of wage-labourers in a quantitative sense; however, it is important to distinguish between what happens within the capitalist relation as a whole and the distribution of the working population over different productive relations. Cf. Marx (1977: 790–2).
6. Marx's reference to labour that produces use-values here is to 'concrete useful labour' in contrast to the abstract labour represented by value (Marx, 1977: 137).
7. 'It is in fact capitalist production alone whose surface presents the commodity as the elementary form of wealth' (Marx, 1988: 69).
8. Paul Burkett's position closely corresponds to the one in this book. In Burkett (2001: 352), he comments, 'Given labour's use-value orientation, this means that wage-labourers must look beyond the circuit of capital, so to speak to realise themselves in human-developmental terms … Insofar as labour goes beyond wage-labour in its autonomous human developmental practices, my conception of class is not a static one. Instead, it expands to encompass all forms of human activity that promote human development as an end in itself'. See also Burkett (1999).
9. The idea that labour involved merely in altering the form of value (for example, from commodity-form to money-form) does not create added value and thus is 'unproductive' by definition certainly seems self-evident.

8 The One-Sidedness of Wage-Labour

1. See Marx (1977: 739–40) for a departure from the view of the capitalist as pure personification of an economic category.
2. For example, in discussing the time the capitalist himself spends on the circulation of commodities, Marx says in the *Grundrisse* (1973: 634–5):

   The time a capitalist loses during exchange is as such not a deduction from labour time. He is a capitalist – i.e. representative of capital, personified capital … Circulation time – to the extent that it takes up the time of the capitalist as such – concerns us here exactly as much as the time he spends with his mistress … The capitalist absolutely does not concern us here except as capital.

3. He also referred there to 'funds for those unable to work, etc., in short, for what is included under so-called official poor relief today' (Marx, 1875: 22).
4. The workday from the perspective of the worker by definition exceeds the workday from the perspective of capital. One interesting result is that the rate of surplus value can be seen as an inadequate form of the rate of exploitation (the ratio of surplus labour to necessary labour); the latter is lower insofar as the worker performs necessary labour for himself (i.e., privately). See Lebowitz (1976a).

5. In this context, Marx includes 'the premium that the exploitation of the workers' children sets on their production' as a reason for high population growth among the industrial proletariat (Marx, 1977: 795). Quite consistently, Nancy Folbre has stressed the relation between child labour laws and the decline in average family size within capitalism. See, for example, Ferguson and Folbre (1981: 323).

6. Consider, for example, the long-term effects of the release by manorial lords of peasants from labour-service requirements in return for money-payments.

7. This does not, of course, mean that such state legislation as child labour laws and restrictions on the workday for women and children were not in the interests of workers as a whole.

8. The path-breaking work on the relationship between patriarchy and the social construction of gender personality is Chodorow (1978).

9. Vogel (1983: 61) points out that, in all Marx's comments about slavery, women and children are portrayed 'as passive victims rather than historical actors'.

10. In particular, it is important to stress that concerns over patriarchy go far beyond consideration of its underlying basis and must properly include exploration of matters which cannot be addressed here such as the place and significance of rape. I have not attempted here to incorporate new scholarship by Marxist feminists, but useful recent reviews may be found in Camfield (2002) and Vosko (2002).

11. Marx (1977: 701) also noted the role of differences in the 'extent of the prime necessities of life in their natural and historical development' in explaining national differences in wages.

12. Differing hierarchies of needs – even with identical 'necessary needs' (considered broadly) – will yield differing degrees of immiseration. Alternatively, since the particular needs normally satisfied by workers will differ depending on their success in struggles (and their individual ranking of needs), there will be different degrees of immiseration even if hierarchies of need are identical. The two cases are analogous in a two-commodity indifference map (such as Figure 3.1) to the cases of differing 'bliss points' and differing real wages, respectively.

13. For introduction of additional issues not explored here relevant to wage differentials, see Fine (1998), especially Chapter 7. See also Saad-Filho (2002: ch. 4).

14. Insofar as workers in competing firms cannot co-operate, they are placed in a 'Prisoners' Dilemma' (Lebowitz, 1988b).

15. Marx to S. Meyer and A. Vogt, 9 April 1870 (Marx and Engels, n.d.: 334). In turn, as Marx had noted during the US Civil War, 'The Irishman sees the Negro as a dangerous competitor' (Marx and Engels, 1984: 264).

9 Beyond Capital?

1. The primacy of productive forces thesis also can yield the conservative inference that the rejection of 'actually existing socialism' in the last century is proof that socialism by its very nature fetters the development of productive forces. However, see Lebowitz (1991).

2. 'Needless to say, man is not free to choose *his productive forces* – upon which his whole history is based – for every productive force is an acquired force, the product of previous activity. Thus the productive forces are the result of man's practical energy, but that energy is in turn circumscribed by the conditions in which man is placed by the productive forces already acquired, by the form of society which exists before him, which he does not create, which is the product of the preceding generation.' Marx to P. V. Annenkov, 28 December 1846 (Marx and Engels, 1982: 96).

3. Cohen (1978: 165) is willing to accept the conditioning influence of the relations of production as a 'qualification' of his primacy thesis.

4. In this respect, the thesis of the primacy of needs is a better fit for Cohen's proposal elsewhere that a 'Distinctive Contradiction of Advanced Capitalism' is 'that even if or when it becomes possible and desirable to reduce or transform unwanted activity, capitalism continues to promote consumption instead, and therefore functions irrationally, in the sense that the structure of the economy militates against optimal use of its productive capacity' (Cohen, 1978: 302, 310).

5. Recall the discussion in Chapter 1 of Barriers and Limits.

6. For a discussion of the distinction between the specific barrier of capital and general barriers – as well as for an argument that the underlying basis for Marx's 'falling rate of profit' discussion is relatively lagging productivity in the production of means of production (and ultimately can be traced to Nature), see Lebowitz (1982b).

7. See James O'Connor's important exploration of the concept of 'ecological Marxism' (O'Connor, 1988).

8. See John Bellamy Foster's excellent discussion of Marx's sensitivity to the metabolic relation between human beings and the earth in Foster (2000: 141–77).

9. This inherent mystification – given that workers exist as many – is especially significant in the context of global capitalism.

10 From Political Economy to Class Struggle

1. See such musings, for example, in Przeworski (1986).

2. Heller (1976: 77) defines 'radical needs' as those whose realization implies the transcendence of capital but she detaches these from a concept of struggle. See Lebowitz (1979).

3. Any doubts about the roots of this argument in Hegel will be dispelled by reading its 'rediscovery' in Lenin (1961). On this same theme, see James (1947).

4. Marx, *New York Daily Tribune*, 14 July 1853 in Marx and Engels (1979b: 169).

5. Nevertheless, Cohen seems to find room for every contingent factor in his thesis of the primacy of productive forces: 'There is no economically legislated final breakdown, but what is *de facto* the last depression occurs when there is a downturn in the cycle *and* the forces are ready to accept a socialist structure *and* the proletariat is sufficiently class conscious and organized' (Cohen, 1978: 204).

6. If 'goodbyes' are in order, they should be addressed not to the working class but, once again, to a one-sided conception of the working class.

7. Nevertheless, only the struggle of workers as wage-labourers directly poses the alternative of workers as their own mediator and provides workers with a sense of themselves as the producers of social wealth. In this respect, the new social movements do not in themselves contain the basis for a new form of social production subordinated to the association of free and associated producers. See the discussion in Chapter 11.

8. The effects are predictable – as in the similar case where a social-democratic government (elected as an agency of workers) proceeds to act in an orderly fashion *in place of* the movements that gave birth to its election and to foster 'the demobilization of workers.

9. See Lebowitz (1995) for a discussion of the logic of the capitalist state from the side of workers.

10. As Hal Draper carefully details in his exhaustive examination, the meaning of 'dictatorship' in the mid-nineteenth century is not to be confused with 'despotism'. See, for example, his discussion of the concept of the 'dictatorship of the Democracy' and 'the rule of the proletariat' in Marx (Draper, 1986: 58–67, 112–19).

11. Here, in a nutshell, is the sorry history of social democracy, which never ceases to reinforce the capital relation.

12. As part of the process of encirclement of capitalist industry, Engels' 'Principles' explicitly describes the 'gradual expropriation' of factory owners – a process to be achieved 'partly through competition on the part of state industry and partly directly through compensation in assignations [bonds]'. To the pressure of competition with state industry was added 'compelling the factory owners, as long as they still exist, to pay the same increased wages as the State' (Marx and Engels, 1976b: 350).

11   From Capital to the Collective Worker

1. Agreement with Lenin's recognition of the need for theoretical struggle is not to make the argument for the classical Leninist party. The focus on 'revolutionary practice' here is more consistent with Rosa Luxemburg's famous injunction that 'historically, the errors committed by a truly revolutionary movement are infinitely more fruitful than the infallibility of the cleverest Central Committee'. The point is clear: 'The working class demands the right to make its mistakes and learn in the dialectic of history' (Luxemburg, 1962: 108). For some possible implications of reliance upon that Central Committee, see Lebowitz (2000a).

2. Although there are many glimpses from isolated phrases that indicate that Marx's thinking went beyond *Capital*, it would be wrong to assume that he had indeed developed his thoughts adequately on the subject matter of *Wage-Labour*. Marx did not hesitate to offer a few hints in advance of his theoretical presentation when it came to matters such as the competition or centralization of capitals. For example, see Marx (1977: 433–6, 578–80, 777–9).

3. Marx introduces the concept of the collective worker as 'the living mechanism of manufacture' and as composed of one-sidedly specialized workers who are part of a particular productive organism (Marx, 1977: 458, 481). The concept here is extended to the living mechanism of the productive organism within society.

4. This concept of an alternative in which workers are their own mediator was not advanced by the nature of the Stalinist model forged in the struggle against backwardness. The experience of 'actually existing socialism' is explored in a work in progress, *Studies in the Development of Communism: the Socialist Economy and the Vanguard Mode of Production*. For some aspects of that work, see Lebowitz (1985a, 1986, 1987a, 1991, 2000a).

5. 'Bear in mind', Engels had argued a few years earlier about creation of a communist society, 'that what is involved is to create for *all people* such a condition that everyone can freely develop his human nature and live in a human relationship with his neighbours' (Marx and Engels, 1975c: 263). This focus on the development of human potential was characteristic of the socialist thought of the period. The goal, as Henri Saint-Simon argued, is 'to afford to all members of society the greatest possible opportunity for the development of their faculties' (Manuel, 1962: 126). Similarly, real freedom, Louis Blanc proposed, involves not only the rights achieved but also 'the POWER given men to develop and exercise their faculties' (Fried and Sanders, 1964: 235).

6. Sève explores the question of human development on the individual level, referring to 'the most important problem in the whole of the psychology of personality, from the point of view of Marxist humanism, i.e., that of expanded reproduction, in short, of the *maximum flowering* of every person-ality' (Sève, 1978: 358).

7. Similar themes are raised by Shortall (1994), but see Lebowitz (1998, 2000b).

8. While capital may appear to be the destructive side of capitalism, may appear to drive towards its own dissolution, for Marx and Engels, capital drives to its end 'only insomuch as it produces the proletariat *as* proletariat, poverty which is conscious of its spiritual and physical poverty, dehumanisation which is conscious of its dehumanisation, and therefore self-abolishing. The proletariat executes the sentence that private property pronounces on itself by producing the proletariat' (Marx and Engels, 1845: 36).

9. This inversion, of course, is 'not a merely *supposed one* existing merely in the imagination of the workers and the capitalists' (Marx, 1973: 831). Rather, it is a *real* inversion – one that flows from the surrender of the creative power of workers for a mess of pottage, that 'deceptive *illusion* of a transaction' (Marx, 1977: 730, 1064).

10. Understanding the importance of Marx's premises suggests that, before read-ing *Capital*, one should begin with his discussions of human wealth from the *Grundrisse*, etc. Having firmly grasped Marx's conception of real wealth, the implication of the opening sentence of *Capital* is inescapable.

11. See the discussion in Chapter 2.

12. One of Negri's important insights (in Negri, 1991) is the significance that the concept of communism has in Marx's analysis of capitalism. As noted in Lebowitz (2000b), however, I have serious problems with much of his argu-ment, including his assertion that *Capital* serves 'to subject the subversive capacity of the proletariat to the reorganizing and repressive intelligence of capitalist power' (Negri, 1991: 18–19).

Bibliography

Albelda, Randy, Gunn, Christopher, and Waller, William (eds) (1986) *Alternatives to Economic Orthodoxy: a Reader in Political Economy* (Armonk: M. E. Sharpe).

Arthur, Chris (1998) 'Systematic Dialectic', *Science & Society*, Vol. 62, No. 3.

Beamish, Rob (1992) *Marx, Method and the Division of Labor* (Urbana: University of Illinois Press).

Bowles, Samuel and Gintis, Herbert (1981) 'Structure and Practice in the Labor Theory of Value', *Review of Radical Political Economics*, Vol. 12, No. 4 (Winter).

Bowles, Samuel and Gintis, Herbert (1986) *Democracy and Capitalism: Property, Community and the Contradictions of Modern Social Thought* (New York: Basic Books, Inc.).

Burawoy, Michael (1989) 'Marxism Without Micro-Foundations', *Socialist Review*, Vol. 19, No. 2 (April–June).

Burkett, Paul (1999) *Marx and Nature: a Red and Green Perspective* (New York: St Martin's Press).

Burkett, Paul (2001) 'Marxism and Natural Limits', *Historical Materialism*, No. 8 (Summer).

Camfield, David (2002) 'Beyond Adding on Gender and Class: Revisiting Feminism and Marxism', *Studies in Political Economy*, No. 68 (Summer).

Carver, Terrell (ed.) (1975) *Karl Marx: Texts on Method* (Oxford: Basil Blackwell).

Castoriadis, Cornelius (1975) 'An Interview', *Telos*, No. 23 (Spring).

Castoriadis, Cornelius (1976–7) 'On the History of the Workers' Movement', *Telos*, No. 30 (Winter).

Chodorow, Nancy (1978) *The Reproduction of Mothering: Psychoanalysis and the Sociology of Gender* (Berkeley: University of California Press).

Cleaver, Harry (1986) 'Karl Marx: Economist or Revolutionary?', in Suzanne W. Helburn and David F. Bramhall (eds), *Marx, Schumpeter and Keynes: a Centenary Celebration of Dissent* (Armonk: M. E. Sharpe, Inc).

Cohen, G.A. (1978) *Karl Marx's Theory of History: a Defence* (Princeton, NJ: Princeton University Press).

Cohen, Jean L. (1982) *Class and Civil Society: the Limits of Marxian Critical Theory* (Amherst: University of Massachusetts Press).

Draper, Hal (1986) *Karl Marx's Theory of Revolution, Vol. III: The 'Dictatorship of the Proletariat'* (New York: Monthly Review Press).

Dunayevskaya, Raya (1964) *Marxism and Freedom: From 1776 until Today* (New York: Twayne Publishers).

Elster, Jon (1985) *Making Sense of Marx* (Cambridge: Cambridge University Press).

Engels, Frederick (1845) *The Condition of the Working-Class in England*, in Marx and Engels (1975c).

Engels, Frederick (1847) 'The Constitutional Question in Germany', in Marx and Engels (1976b).

Engels, Frederick (1850) 'The Ten Hours' Question', in Marx and Engels (1978).

Engels, Frederick (1859) 'Karl Marx, A Contribution to the Critique of Political Economy', in Marx and Engels (1962).

Engels, Frederick (1881a) 'The Wages System', *The Labour Standard*, 21 May 1881, in Henderson (1967).

Engels, Frederick (1881b) 'Trades Unions I', *The Labour Standard*, 28 May 1881, in Henderson (1967).

Engels, Frederick (1883) 'Speech at the Graveside of Karl Marx', in Tucker (1972).

Engels, Frederick (1891) 'Critique of the Draft Social-Democratic Programme (1891)', in *Marxism Today* (February 1970).

Engels, Frederick (1956) *The Peasant War in Germany* (Moscow: Foreign Languages Publishing House).

Engels, Frederick (1962) *The Origin of the Family, Private Property and the State*, in Marx and Engels (1962).

Ferguson, Ann and Folbre, Nancy (1981) 'The Unhappy Marriage of Patriarchy and Capitalism', in Sargent (1981).

Fine, Ben (1998) *Labour Market Theory: a Constructive Reassessment* (London: Routledge).

Folbre, Nancy R. (1986) 'A Patriarchal Mode of Production', in Albelda, Gunn and Waller (1986).

Foster, John Bellamy (2000) *Marx's Ecology: Materialism and Nature* (New York: Monthly Review Press).

Fried, Albert and Sanders, Ronald (1964) *Socialist Thought: a Documentary History* (Garden City, New York: Anchor Books).

Gordon, David M., Edwards, Richard and Reich, Michael (1982) *Segmented Work, Divided Workers: the Historical Transformation of Labor in the United States* (Cambridge: Cambridge University Press).

Gorz, Andre (1982) *Farewell to the Working Class: an Essay on PostIndustrial Socialism*, translated by Michael Sonenscher (London: Pluto Press).

Gough, Ian (1979) *The Political Economy of the Welfare State* (London: Macmillan).

Gramsci, Antonio (1971) *Selections from the Prison Notebooks*, edited and translated by Quinton Hoare and Geoffrey Nowell Smith (New York: International Publishers).

Harding, Sandra (1981) 'What is the Real Material Base of Patriarchy and Capital?', in Sargent (1981).

Hegel, G.W.F. (1929) *Hegel's Science of Logic*, translated by W. H. Johnston and L. G. Struthers, two volumes (London: Allen & Unwin).

Hegel, G.W.F. (1967) *The Phenomenology of Mind*, translated by J.B. Baillie (New York: Harper Torchbooks).

Hegel, G.W.F. (1975) *Hegel's Philosophy of Right*, translated by T.M. Knox (New York: Oxford University Press).

Heller, Agnes (1976) *The Theory of Need in Marx* (New York: St Martin's Press).

Henderson, W.O. (ed.) (1967) *Engels: Selected Writings* (London: Penguin).

Hunt, E.K. (1979) 'The Categories of Productive and Unproductive Labor in Marxist Economic Theory', *Science & Society*, Vol. XLIII, No. 3 (Fall).

Jacoby, Russell (1975) 'The Politics of the Crisis Theory: Towards the Critique of Automatic Marxism II', *Telos*, No. 23 (Spring).

James, C.L.R. (1947) 'Dialectical Materialism and the Fate of Humanity', in Anna Grimshaw, *The C.L.R. James Reader* (Oxford: Blackwell, 1992).

Lange, Oskar (1964) *On the Economic Theory of Socialism*, edited by Benjamin E. Lippincott (New York: McGraw-Hill).

Lapides, Kenneth (2002) 'Marx's Doctrine of Wage Labor,' *Science & Society*, Vol. 666, No. 2 (Summer).

Lebowitz, Michael A. (1973–4) 'The Current Crisis in Economic Theory', *Science & Society*, Vol. XXXVII, No. 4 (Winter).

Lebowitz, Michael A. (1976a) 'The Political Economy of Housework: a Comment', *Bulletin of the Conference of Socialist Economists*, Vol. VI (March).

Lebowitz, Michael A. (1976b) 'Marx's Falling Rate of Profit: a Dialectical View', *Canadian Journal Of Economics*, Vol. IX, No. 2 (May).

Lebowitz, Michael A. (1977–8) 'Capital and the Production of Needs', *Science & Society*, Vol. XLI, No. 4 (Winter).

Lebowitz, Michael A. (1979) 'Heller on Marx's Concept of Needs', *Science & Society*, Vol. XLIII, No. 3 (Fall).

Lebowitz, Michael A. (1982a) 'The One-Sidedness of Capital', *Review of Radical Political Economics*, Vol. 14, No. 4 (Winter).

Lebowitz, Michael A. (1982b) 'The General and the Specific in Marx's Theory of Crisis', *Studies in Political Economy*, No. 7 (Winter).

Lebowitz, Michael A. (1982c) 'Marx After Wage-Labour', *Economic Forum*, Vol. XIII, No. 2 (Fall).

Lebowitz, Michael A. (1985a) 'Kornai and Socialist Laws of Motion', *Studies in Political Economy*, No. 18 (Autumn).

Lebowitz, Michael A. (1985b) 'The Theoretical Status of Monopoly Capital', in Resnick and Wolff (1985).

Lebowitz, Michael A. (1986) 'Transcending the Crisis of Socialist Economy', *Socialism in the World*, No. 54.

Lebowitz, Michael A. (1987a) 'Contradictions in the "Lower Phase" of Communist Society', *Socialism in the World*, No. 59.

Lebowitz, Michael A. (1987b) 'The Political Economy of Wage-Labor', *Science & Society*, Vol. 51, No. 3 (Fall).

Lebowitz, Michael A. (1988a) 'Is "Analytical Marxism" Marxism?', *Science & Society*, Vol. 52, No. 2 (Summer).

Lebowitz, Michael A. (1988b) 'Trade and Class: Labour Strategies in a World of Strong Capital', *Studies in Political Economy*, No. 27 (Autumn).

Lebowitz, Michael A. (1991) 'The Socialist Fetter: a Cautionary Tale', in Ralph Miliband and Leo Panitch (eds), *Socialist Register 1991* (London: Merlin).

Lebowitz, Michael A. (1992) 'Capitalism: How Many Contradictions?', *Capitalism, Nature, Socialism*, Vol. 3, No. 3 (September).

Lebowitz, Michael A. (1994) 'Analytical Marxism and the Marxian Theory of Crisis', *Cambridge Journal of Economics* (May).

Lebowitz, Michael A. (1995) 'Situating the Capitalist State', in Antonio Callari et al., *Marxism in the Post-Modern Age: Confronting the New World Order* (New York: Guilford Publishers).

Lebowitz, Michael A. (1998) Review of Felton Shortall, *The Incomplete Marx* in *Historical Materialism*, No. 3 (Winter).

Lebowitz, Michael A. (2000a) 'Kornai and the Vanguard Mode of Production', in *Cambridge Journal of Economics*, Vol. 24, No. 3 (May).

Lebowitz, Michael A. (2000b) 'Answering Shortall', in *Historical Materialism*, No. 6 (Summer).

Lefebvre, Henri (1968) *Dialectical Materialism* (London: Jonathan Cape).

Lenin, V.I. (1961) *Collected Works*, Vol. 38: 'Philosophical Notebooks' (Moscow: Foreign Languages Publishing House).

Lenin, V.I. (1967) 'What is to be Done?', in V.I. Lenin, *Selected Works (in Three Volumes)* (Moscow: Progress Publishers).

Levins, Richard and Lewontin, Richard (1985) *The Dialectical Biologist* (Cambridge: Harvard University Press).

Lukács, Georg (1972) *History and Class Consciousness: Studies in Marxist Dialectics*, translated by Rodney Livingstone (Cambridge: MIT Press).

Lukács, Georg (1978) *Marx's Basic Ontological Principles* (London: Merlin).

Luxemburg, Rosa (1962) 'Marxism vs. Leninism', in Rosa Luxemburg, *The Russian Revolution and Leninism or Marxism?* (Ann Arbor: University of Michigan Press).

Luxemburg, Rosa (1964) *The Mass Strike, The Political Party and the Trade Unions* [1906], translated by Patrick Lavin (Ceylon: Young Socialist Publication).

Mandel, Ernest (1977) 'Introduction' to Marx (1977).

Manuel, Frank E. (1962) *The Prophets of Paris* (New York: Harper Torchbooks).

Marx, Karl (1841) 'Doctoral Dissertation', in Marx and Engels (1975a), *Collected Works*, Vol. 1.

Marx, Karl (1843) *Contribution to the Critique of Hegel's Philosophy of Law*, in Marx and Engels (1975b), *Collected Works*, Vol. 3.

Marx, Karl (1844a) 'Contribution to the Critique of Hegel's Philosophy of Law: Introduction', in Marx and Engels (1975b), *Collected Works*, Vol. 3.

Marx, Karl (1844b) 'Comments on James Mill', in Marx and Engels (1975b), *Collected Works*, Vol. 3.

Marx, Karl (1844c) *Economic and Philosophic Manuscripts of 1844*, in Marx and Engels (1975b), *Collected Works*, Vol. 3.

Marx, Karl (1845) 'Theses on Feuerbach', in Marx and Engels (1976), *Collected Works*, Vol. 5.

Marx, Karl (1847a) *The Poverty of Philosophy*, in Marx and Engels (1976), *Collected Works*, Vol. 6.

Marx, Karl (1847b) 'Wages', in Marx and Engels (1976), *Collected Works*, Vol. 6.

Marx, Karl (1849) *Wage Labour and Capital*, in Marx and Engels (1977), *Collected Works*, Vol. 9.

Marx, Karl (1853) *Revelations Concerning the Communist Trial in Cologne*, in Marx and Engels (1979a), *Collected Works*, Vol. 11.

Marx, Karl (1859) *A Contribution to the Critique of Political Economy*, in Marx and Engels (1987), *Collected Works*, Vol. 29.

Marx, Karl (1864) 'Inaugural Address of the Working Men's International Association', in Marx and Engels (1985), *Collected Works*, Vol. 20.

Marx, Karl (1865a) 'On Proudhon', in Marx and Engels (1985), *Collected Works*, Vol. 20.

Marx, Karl (1865b) *Value, Price and Profit*, in Marx and Engels (1985), *Collected Works*, Vol. 20.

Marx, Karl (1866) 'Instructions for the Delegates of the Provisional General Council. The Different Questions', in *Minutes of the General Council of the First International, 1864–66* (Moscow: Foreign Languages Publishing House, n.d.).

Marx, Karl (1867) 'Address of the General Council of the International Working Men's Association to the Members and Affiliated Societies', 9 July 1867, *Minutes of the General Council of the First International, 1866–8* (Moscow: Progress Publishers, n.d.).

Marx, Karl (1868) 'Fourth Annual Report of the General Council of International Working Men's Association', 9 September 1868, *Minutes of the General Council of the First International, 1866–8* (Moscow: Progress Publishers, n.d.).

Marx, Karl (1870) 'The General Council to the Federal Council of Romance Switzerland', *The General Council of the First International, 1868–70* (Moscow: Progress Publishers, n.d.).

Marx, Karl (1871a) 'First Outline of *The Civil War in France*', in Marx and Engels (1971), *On the Paris Commune.*

Marx, Karl (1871b) *The Civil War in France*, in Marx and Engels (1971), *On the Paris Commune.*

Marx, Karl (1874–5) 'After the Revolution: Marx Debates Bakunin', in Tucker (1978).

Marx, Karl (1875) *Critique of the Gotha Programme*, in Marx and Engels (1962), *Selected Works*, Vol. II.

Marx, Karl (1879) 'Circular Letter to Bebel, Liebknecht, Bracke, and Others', 17–18 September 1879, in Tucker (1978).

Marx, Karl (1879–80) 'Notes on Adolph Wagner', in Carver (1975).

Marx, Karl (1968) *Theories of Surplus Value*, Vol. II (Moscow: Progress Publishers).

Marx, Karl (1971) *Theories of Surplus Value*, Vol. III (Moscow: Progress Publishers).

Marx, Karl (1973) *Grundrisse* (New York: Vintage Books).

Marx, Karl (1977) *Capital*, Vol. I (New York: Vintage Books).

Marx, Karl (1981a) *Capital*, Vol. II (New York: Vintage Books).

Marx, Karl (1981b) *Capital*, Vol. III (New York: Vintage Books).

Marx, Karl (1988) *Economic Manuscript of 1861–63*, in Marx and Engels (1988b).

Marx, Karl (1994) *Economic Manuscript of 1861–63 (Conclusion)*, in Marx and Engels (1994).

Marx, Karl (n.d.) *Theories of Surplus Value*, Vol. I (Moscow: Foreign Languages Publishing House).

Marx, Karl and Engels, Frederick (1845) *The Holy Family*, in Marx and Engels (1975c), *Collected Works*, Vol. 4.

Marx, Karl and Engels, Frederick (1846) *The German Ideology*, in Marx and Engels (1976a), *Collected Works*, Vol. 5.

Marx, Karl and Engels, Frederick (1848) *Communist Manifesto*, in Marx and Engels (1976b), *Collected Works*, Vol. 6.

Marx, Karl and Engels, Frederick (1850) 'Address of the Central Authority to the League', in Marx and Engels (1978) *Collected Works*, Vol. 10.

Marx, Karl and Engels, Frederick (1962) *Selected Works*, two volumes (Moscow: Foreign Languages Publishing House).

Marx, Karl and Engels, Frederick (1965) *Selected Correspondence* (Moscow: Progress Publishers).

Marx, Karl and Engels, Frederick (1971) *On the Paris Commune* (Moscow: Progress Publishers).

Marx, Karl and Engels, Frederick (1975a) *Collected Works*, Vol. 1 (New York: International Publishers).

Marx, Karl and Engels, Frederick (1975b) *Collected Works*, Vol. 3 (New York: International Publishers).

Marx, Karl and Engels, Frederick (1975c) *Collected Works*, Vol. 4 (New York: International Publishers).

Marx, Karl and Engels, Frederick (1976a) *Collected Works*, Vol. 5 (New York: International Publishers).

Marx, Karl and Engels, Frederick (1976b) *Collected Works*, Vol. 6 (New York: International Publishers).

Marx, Karl and Engels, Frederick (1977) *Collected Works*, Vol. 9 (New York: International Publishers).

Marx, Karl and Engels, Frederick (1978) *Collected Works*, Vol. 10 (New York: International Publishers).

Marx, Karl and Engels, Frederick (1979a) *Collected Works*, Vol. 11 (New York: International Publishers).

Marx, Karl and Engels, Frederick (1979b) *Collected Works*, Vol. 12 (New York: International Publishers).

Marx, Karl and Engels, Frederick (1982) *Collected Works*, Vol. 38 (New York: International Publishers).

Marx, Karl and Engels, Frederick (1983a) *Collected Works*, Vol. 39 (New York: International Publishers).

Marx, Karl and Engels, Frederick (1983b) *Collected Works*, Vol. 40 (New York: International Publishers).

Marx, Karl and Engels, Frederick (1984) *Collected Works*, Vol. 19 (New York: International Publishers).

Marx, Karl and Engels, Frederick (1985) *Collected Works*, Vol. 20 (New York: International Publishers).

Marx, Karl and Engels, Frederick (1986) *Collected Works*, Vol. 28 (New York: International Publishers).

Marx, Karl and Engels, Frederick (1987a) *Collected Works*, Vol. 29 (New York: International Publishers).

Marx, Karl and Engels, Frederick (1987b) *Collected Works*, Vol. 42 (New York: International Publishers).

Marx, Karl and Engels, Frederick (1988a) *Collected Works*, Vol. 23 (New York: International Publishers).

Marx, Karl and Engels, Frederick (1988b) *Collected Works*, Vol. 30 (New York: International Publishers).

Marx, Karl and Engels, Frederick (1994) *Collected Works*, Vol. 34 (New York: International Publishers).

Marx, Karl and Engels, Frederick (n.d.) *On Colonialism* (Moscow: Foreign Languages Publishing House).

Meek, Ronald (1973) *Studies in the Labour Theory of Value* (London: Lawrence & Wishart).

Mouffe, Chantal (1983) 'Working Class Hegemony and the Struggle for Socialism', *Studies in Political Economy*, No. 12 (Fall).

Negri, Antonio (1991) *Marx Beyond Marx: Lessons on the Grundrisse* (Brooklyn: Autonomedia).

O'Connor, James (1988) 'Capitalism, Nature, Socialism: a Theoretical Introduction', *Capitalism, Nature, Socialism*, No. 1 (Fall).

O'Malley, Joseph and Algozin, Keith (eds) (1981) *Rubel on Karl Marx: Five Essays* (Cambridge: Cambridge University Press).

Oakley, Allen (1983) *The Making of Marx's Critical Theory: a Bibliographical Analysis* (London: Routledge & Kegan Paul).

Offe, Claus (1985) 'New Social Movements: Challenging the Boundaries of Institutional Politics', *Social Research*, Vol. 52, No. 4 (Winter).

Petrovic, Gajo (1967) *Marx in the Mid-Twentieth Century* (Garden City, New York: Anchor Books).

Przeworski, Adam (1986) 'Material Interests, Class Compromise, and the Transition to Socialism', in Roemer (1986).

Pujol, Michèle A. (1992) *Feminism and Anti-Feminism in Early Economic Thought* (Aldershot: Edward Elgar Publishing).

Reich, Wilhelm (1976) *The Mass Psychology of Fascism* (New York: Pocket Book).

Resnick, Stephen and Wolff, Richard (1985) *Rethinking Marxism: Essays for Harry Magdoff & Paul Sweezy* (New York: Autonomedia).

Ricardo, David (1969) *The Principles of Political Economy and Taxation* (London: Dutton).

Robinson, Joan (1957) *An Essay on Marxian Economics* (London: Macmillan).

Roemer, John E. (1986) *Analytical Marxism* (Cambridge: Cambridge University Press).

Rosdolsky, Roman (1977) *The Making of Marx's 'Capital'* (London: Pluto Press).

Rowthorn, Bob (1980) *Capitalism, Conflict and Inflation* (London: Lawrence & Wishart).

Saad-Filho, Alfredo (2002) *The Value of Marx: Political Economy for Contemporary Capitalism* (London: Routledge).

Samuelson, Paul (1972) 'The Economics of Marx: an Ecumenical Reply', *Journal of Economic Literature* (March).

Sargent, Lydia (ed.) (1981) *Women and Revolution: a Discussion of the Unhappy Marriage of Marxism and Feminism* (Montreal: Black Rose Books).

Schumpeter, Joseph A. (1950) *Capitalism, Socialism and Democracy* (New York: Harper Torchbooks).

Sen, Amartya (1992) *Inequality Reexamined* (Cambridge: Harvard University Press).

Sève, Lucien (1978) *Man in Marxist Theory and the Psychology of Personality* (Sussex: The Harvester Press).

Shanin, Teodor (ed.) (1983) *Late Marx and the Russian Road: Marx and the 'Peripheries of Capitalism'* (New York: Monthly Review Press).

Shortall, Felton C. (1994) *The Incomplete Marx* (Aldershot: Avebury).

Smith, Adam (1937) *Wealth of Nations* (New York: Modern Library).

Thompson, E.P. (1978) *The Poverty of Theory* (New York: Monthly Review Press).

Tucker, Robert C. (1978) *The Marx–Engels Reader*, Second Edition (New York: W.W. Norton).

Vogel, Lise (1983) *Marxism and the Oppression of Women: Toward a Unitary Theory* (New Brunswick, NJ: Rutgers University Press).

Vosko, Leah F. (2002) 'The Pasts (and Futures) of Feminist Political Economy in Canada: Reviving the Debate', *Studies in Political Economy*, No. 68 (Summer).

Name Index

Subject Index